Accelerating Literacy for Diverse Learners

Strategies for the Common Core Classroom, K–8

SOCORRO G. HERRERA

DELLA R. PEREZ

SHABINA K. KAVIMANDAN

STEPHANIE WESSELS

Foreword by
Ester J. de Jong

TEACHERS
COLLEGE
PRESS

Teachers College, Columbia University
New York and London

Templates, rubrics, and checklists as noted below are available for free download from the Teachers College Press website: www.tcpress.com

- Picture This, template, page 29
- Pictures and Words, template, student academic behavior checklist, pages 37, 178
- Mind Map, student assessment rubric, page 179
- Tri-Fold, template, page 52
- Listen Sketch Label, template, student academic behavior checklist, pages 61, 180
- DOTS Chart, template, student academic behavior checklist, pages 80, 181
- Tic-Tac-Tell, template, student assessment rubric, pages 95, 182
- Vocabulary Quilt, template, student academic behavior checklist, pages 103, 183
- Thumb Challenge, student academic behavior checklist, page 184
- U-C-ME, template, student assessment rubric, pages 133, 185
- Extension Wheel, template, student assessment rubric, pages 140, 186
- Hearts Activity, templates, pages 148, 149
- Active Bookmarks, template, student academic behavior checklist, pages 156, 187
- Word Drop, template, page 170

Video clips illustrating teachers' implementation of the strategies listed below are provided on the DVD included with this book and are available for viewing online at www.tcpress.com/ AcceleratingLiteracyVideos.html

- Linking Language
- Mind Map
- Listen Sketch Label
- Vocabulary Quilt
- U-C-ME

Published by Teachers College Press, 1234 Amsterdam Avenue, New York, NY 10027

Text Design: Lynne Frost

Library of Congress Cataloging-in-Publication Data

Herrera, Socorro Guadalupe.
  Accelerating literacy for diverse learners : strategies for the common core classroom, K–8 / Socorro G. Herrera, Della R. Perez, Shabina K. Kavimandan, Stephanie Wessels.
    pages   cm
  Includes bibliographical references and index.
  ISBN 978-0-8077-5450-4 (pbk. : alk. paper)
    1. Language arts (Elementary)—Curricula—United States.   2. Language arts (Middle School)—Curricula—United States.   3. Children with social disabilities—Education—United States.   4. Minorities—Education—United States. I. Title.
  LB1576.H3396 2013
  372.6—dc23   2013003742

ISBN 978-0-8077-5450-4 (paper)

Printed on acid-free paper
Manufactured in the United States of America

20 19 18 17 16 15 14 13   8 7 6 5 4 3 2 1

For Dawn, Kevin, Jesse, and Isamari. May you continue to explore the world and dream throughout your lifetime!

—Socorro Herrera

For my daughter, Ruth, who inspires me every day through her love of reading and life, and for my husband, Miguel, who has supported me on this journey.

—Della R. Perez

For my kids, Ayan Farhan and Anya Suresh, who teach me so much about language and literacy every single day.

—Shabina Kavimandan

To my family for all of their love and support.

—Stephanie Wessels

Together, we also dedicate this book to all of the outstanding educators we have had the pleasure to work with and who have shared their insights and expertise to make this book a reality.

Contents

Foreword, *by Ester J. de Jong*   vii

Preface   ix

PART I   Foundations and Framework   1

Why It's Important   1
Creating Proficient, Lifelong Readers and Learners   2
Making It Happen   2
A Closer Look at the CLD Student Biography   2
Meeting of the Minds: Students and Teachers as Equal Partners   5
A Framework for Linguistic and Academic Development   7
Conclusion   9

PART II   Vocabulary Development Strategies   11

1   Images as Catalysts for Predictions and Connections   13

Linking Language   15
Picture This   22
Pictures and Words   30
Mind Map   38
Tri-Fold   45
Listen Sketch Label   53
Story Bag   62

2   Words and More Words   69

DOTS Chart   72
Vocabulary Foldable   81
Tic-Tac-Tell   88
Vocabulary Quilt   96
Thumb Challenge   104
Magic Book   110
IDEA   118

3 From Word Knowledge to Comprehension 125

U-C-ME 127

Extension Wheel 134

Hearts Activity 141

Active Bookmarks 150

Mini Novela 157

Word Drop 164

PART III On the Path to Standards-Driven Outcomes and Student Success 171

The Framework 171

Standards-Driven Outcomes 172

Making BDI Strategies Your Own 174

Final Reflections 176

Appendix: Strategy Rubrics and Checklists 177

1 Images as Catalysts for Predictions and Connections

Pictures and Words: Student Academic Behavior Checklist 178

Mind Map: Student Assessment Rubric 179

Listen Sketch Label: Student Academic Behavior Checklist 180

2 Words and More Words

DOTS Chart: Student Academic Behavior Checklist 181

Tic-Tac-Tell: Student Assessment Rubric 182

Vocabulary Quilt: Student Academic Behavior Checklist 183

Thumb Challenge: Student Academic Behavior Checklist 184

3 From Word Knowledge to Comprehension

U-C-ME: Student Assessment Rubric 185

Extension Wheel: Student Assessment Rubric 186

Active Bookmarks: Student Academic Behavior Checklist 187

References 188

Index 192

About the Authors 198

Foreword

THE TERM *advocacy* is often applied to organized action aimed at influencing formal legislative initiatives. This definition, however, excludes the daily decision-making of educators as they make linguistic, pedagogical, and curricular choices in order to ensure equitable opportunities for their students (Dubetz & de Jong, 2011). For example, teachers establish informal norms in their classrooms with respect to their own language use and the language(s) their students are encouraged or permitted to use and when they use them. They also decide on whether and how to use materials in languages other than English (e.g., bilingual books for daily lessons or books in students' native languages for classroom libraries). Teachers also construct classroom participation structures by defining how their students are expected to take part in classroom activities and what constitutes appropriate interaction among students and between the teacher and the student. They establish linguistic and cultural classroom norms that reflect who has the authority to initiate a topic of discussion or to change topics and who decides who is allowed to speak. Such norms can position students as passive receivers or active constructors of knowledge and learning. These multiple *acts of advocacy* by teachers are particularly important for students who come from linguistically and culturally diverse backgrounds.

The presence of culturally and linguistically diverse (CLD) students is more common than ever in today's classrooms and will become even more so in the future. Mainstream teachers, English as a second language teachers, and bilingual teachers work with students who come to the classroom with diverse language, literacy, and cultural experiences. Helping teachers develop the knowledge and skills that will allow them to advocate for CLD students and create effective and equitable learning environments for them has been recognized as a national challenge and an imperative (de Jong & Harper, 2005). While there are many books that aim to help teachers teach English language learners (ELLs), this book is unique in that it places the bilingual student front and center and then extends and integrates theoretical principles and practices from this core.

This book presents as nonnegotiable that which we know to be one of the most important learning principles: Always connect new learning (concepts, vocabulary, language, and literacy) with students' personal, community-based, and school-based knowledge and learning. Making this basic understanding the central starting point of teaching has significant implications for how instruction is organized and, at times, challenges what have developed as commonsense approaches to working with ELLs. For example, while general strategies for comprehensible input (pictures, visuals, hands-on activities, cooperative learning, familiar vocabulary) are important, Herrera argues in the introductory chapter that such strategies are generally "insufficient for helping CLD students connect with the academic vocabulary and concepts on a personal level." Rather, she argues, the "links to a student's sociocultural, linguistic, cognitive, and academic biography . . . are essential to a student's full understanding and ownership of the material." This book presents a varied set of strategies that actively engage students in communicating, displaying, sharing, analyzing, reflecting on, and using their own existing understandings to develop new understandings and gain access to a high-quality curriculum.

In short, this book offers teachers a strategy set that allows them to engage in acts of advocacy that effectively support high-quality, equitable learning environments for CLD students. It thus meets the national mandate for establishment of coherent and systematic approaches to professional development for teachers working with CLD students. And it does so in a manner that links theory with practice and provides research-based, practice-oriented, and meaningful strategies for teachers at different grade levels.

—Ester J. de Jong, EdD
Associate Professor, ESOL/Bilingual Education
College of Education, University of Florida

Preface

IN RECENT YEARS, the growth in the numbers of culturally and linguistically diverse (CLD) students in schools, as well as increasing diversity of all kinds among students in classrooms, has raised awareness of the need to differentiate both classroom instruction and instructional strategies for varying student populations. In our prior texts, especially *Biography-Driven Culturally Responsive Teaching* (Herrera, 2010), we have argued that an explicit focus on instructional strategies is needed in today's complex classrooms. The foundation of the strategies described in this book is the teacher's efforts to discover, explore, and build upon the unique biographies of students, with particular attention to the assets that students bring to learning. Such attention to the CLD student's biography reduces both inaccurate assumptions about what students know (and do not know) and redundancies in teaching.

Early, extensive, and ongoing attention to the dimensions of students' biographies—the sociocultural, the cognitive, the linguistic, and the academic dimensions—encourages student–teacher partnerships in the attainment of rich learning and literacy development objectives. The first of these dimensions often tends to determine what students find meaningful in classroom strategies for differentiated instruction. The Common Core State Standards (National Governors Association Center for Best Practices & Council of Chief State School Officers, 2010) especially stress the importance of *meaningful learning* to the student's success in the classroom and beyond.

This text, like our earlier resource for secondary educators (Herrera, Kavimandan, & Holmes, 2011), offers K–8 teachers strategies for academic learning and literacy development that are grounded in, and build upon, the four dimensions of the student biography. Each of the strategies is intentionally designed to *explore students' hearts and minds* as a means of creating a learning experience that is both meaningful and authentic. Each strategy has been *classroom tested with CLD students* in grade-level and ESL classrooms. A systematic, classroom-observation-based study of 239 teachers in 41 different schools in one Midwestern state suggests that when teachers deliberately incorporate such strategies into their lessons, those teachers demonstrate higher-quality instruction (Herrera, Perez, Kavimandan, Holmes, & Miller, 2011). Specifically, teachers using a biography-driven strategy showed significantly higher levels of meeting universal standards of effective pedagogy (Tharp & Dalton, 2007). These standards are emphasized throughout the book and include instructional practices such as

- Referencing students' prior knowledge and background experiences related to language and literacy development
- Leveraging student assets to facilitate a community of learners in which individuals' personal connections with the content are shared and respected
- Providing clear standards and expectations for challenging activities while also monitoring students' individual affective responses to such challenges
- Prompting students to articulate their thoughts and revoicing student connections in ways that promote elaboration

The text offers both teachers and teacher educators a valuable resource and reference for their ongoing efforts to enhance their teaching and professional capacities for delivering highly differentiated classroom instruction that maximizes biography-driven strategies. In addition to detailed descriptions of the research-based rationale and methods for enacting each strategy, printed and online resources are provided. For many strategies, templates for use in the classroom, as well as rubrics and checklists to assist the teacher in assessing student progress, appear in the book and are available for free download from the Teachers College Press website: www.tcpress.com. Real-world implementation of some of these biography-driven strategies with diverse learners in grade-level classrooms is illustrated in video clips on a DVD included with each copy of the book. These clips are also available for viewing online at www.tcpress.com/AcceleratingLiteracyVideos.html.

Acknowledgments

The Center for Intercultural and Multilingual Advocacy (CIMA) is filled with colleagues, graduate students, and undergraduates who all, in one way or another, shared a part of their lives to make this project possible. Throughout this process, our colleagues have provided us with valuable insights and feedback. Special thanks go to Melissa Holmes, Sheri Meredith, and Gisela Nash, who were steadfast in their attention to detail as they provided constructive criticism, helped us refine and clarify our thoughts, and encouraged us through to the end. Without their support, this project would still be an unfinished dream. We are indebted to Jennifer Brunenn, whose creative photographic outlook allowed us to capture in both pictures and words teachers' successful use of these strategies, and to Stuart Miller, whose statistical and analytical expertise helped us document the effective teacher practices supported by these strategies.

We also owe special thanks to the many administrators and teachers across the state of Kansas and in numerous other states who opened their school and classroom doors to us for extensive conversations regarding cultural and linguistic diversity in America's classrooms. Their continuous dedication to the field was a constant source of motivation. Their perspectives and their willingness to discuss both their challenges and their successes contributed tremendously to the heart and soul of this book.

Finally, to the many BESITOS students who have passed through the College of Education at Kansas State University and are continually striving in the field to provide all students with the education they deserve, regardless of current or past political agendas, your willingness to share your lives as advocates for students and families has certainly paved the way for generations of students to turn their dreams into reality.

PART I

Foundations and Framework

AS SCHOOLS and districts across the country race toward a continually moving target of increasing academic achievement for all, the students most in need of effective classroom instruction continue to be left behind with regard to both opportunity to learn and community membership. These realities manifest themselves in demonstrated gaps in learning and achievement among certain groups of students. For the last 2 decades, the Center for Intercultural and Multilingual Advocacy (CIMA) has posed the following questions in an attempt to identify what often keeps professional development from accomplishing its intended goals: educators' application of theory to practice or, more specifically, their higher levels of implementation of scientifically based strategies that support content and language learning for all students.

- What explicit supports do teachers need in order to be successful in diverse classrooms where students vary in level of language proficiency, cultural background, and academic foundations to learn?
- What do "opportunity" and "respect" look, feel, and sound like in classrooms that hold high expectations for all?
- In what ways can conditions be created for all learners to be active participants in the learning community?
- What implications do lesson activities and strategies have for student interaction, higher-order thinking, and academic achievement?
- How can a teacher utilize students' languages, cultures, and academic backgrounds to promote their higher-order thinking and support them in reaching high levels of participation, discussion, and learning?

These are but a few of the questions for which we have gathered data across the country for nearly 15 years. These data have informed our own teaching and learning and have provided us with evidence from classroom practice that gives us the confidence to say, "What you will find in this book works in classrooms!" This book was written for teachers, with teachers, and by teachers. In it, we present a comprehensive model for bridging between students' biographies and grade-level vocabulary and concepts, and for ensuring individual accountability in learning.

Why It's Important

Now, more than ever, there is a need to ensure that educators become decision-makers within their classrooms and that they are equipped with the best research, reflective about their practice, and dedicated to not just teaching but *knowing* and *reaching* their community of learners. Teachers in 46 states are now charged with implementing the Common Core State Standards. These standards ask teachers to increase the rigor in instruction, resources used, and assessment, and to promote higher-order thinking in every classroom, every day! All these expectations are imposed at the same time that our classrooms are becoming increasingly diverse in language, culture, socioeconomic status, mobility, and so much more.

For example, more than 400 languages are represented in U.S. schools. Although Spanish-speaking students make up 77% of the total K–12 CLD student population, Vietnamese, Hmong, Haitian, Creole, and Korean are among the other top languages, each constituting 1–3% of this remainder (U.S. Department of Education, 2002). According to the U.S. Census Bureau (2000), the diversity of languages and cultures will continue to impact educators across the United States, as an estimated 40% of school-aged students are expected to speak a language other than English by the year 2030. We choose to use the term *culturally and linguistically diverse (CLD)* to describe the students for whom this book is targeted. This term, for us, provides the reader with a more realistic picture of what classroom diversity looks like across the country. Within any classroom, one will find students who "wear" different labels and receive different services. For these students, and particularly for those whose first language is not English, the strategies in this book provide essential support systems that ensure critical scaffolding for their linguistic and academic learning.

Creating Proficient, Lifelong Readers and Learners

The Common Core State Standards (National Governors Association Center for Best Practices & Council of Chief State School Officers [NGA & CCSSO], 2010) have set the bar that "all students must be able to comprehend texts of steadily increasing complexity as they progress through school" (p. 2). Every classroom must be focused on ensuring that all students, regardless of background, spend more time reading in the content areas. The key to achieving these goals is an explicit focus on instruction in academic vocabulary in ways that move learners beyond being passive recipients of word explanations and definitions to being active constructors of word knowledge who understand how words work in different contexts and for different purposes. This type of academic language learning requires teachers to have a deep understanding of not only the instructional content but also their students' biographies. Teachers must create classroom conditions in which all members of the learning community see both their own background knowledge and ongoing discourse as central to generating ideas, testing hypotheses, reaching consensus, and applying their knowledge to the future.

At the end of the day, increasing student achievement is as much about the *how* of teaching and learning as it is about the *what*! The goal of this book is to provide preK–8 teachers with explicit strategies within a biography-driven model of instruction (Herrera, 2010). These biography-driven instructional (BDI) strategies assist teachers in providing all learners with the tools, skills, and knowledge necessary to support their own learning within a grade-level, standards-based, and standards-driven curriculum.

Making It Happen

Fundamental to moving forward in meeting the academic, linguistic, and social needs of all learners is understanding the paths they have traveled before they arrive in our classrooms. The "histories" they bring serve to inform our instructional practice in ways that allow us to better establish the necessary conditions for all learners to be part of a classroom learning community that together negotiates meaning, challenges positions, and constructs new meaning from text. This type of teaching and learning dynamic

begins with the single step of our creating opportunities for learners to make public both their personal and academic biographies.

CLD students come to school with a wealth of knowledge and experiences (Rea & Mercuri, 2006). As educators, we realize this, but we often fail to invite the learner in when we open our lessons. Asking students to share the knowledge they already possess related to the topic or vocabulary we are going to introduce is essential. When asked, most teachers agree that using prior knowledge in the lesson is critical for "hooking" students into learning. Yet we educators often fall short of holding every student accountable for sharing and documenting what he or she knows so that this knowledge is available for our joint use when we cross the bridge into the lesson with our students.

In our work with teachers, most share with us that they generally incorporate isolated, and at times fragmented, activities and strategies into their teaching, and they cite time constraints and scripted programs as the reason for not taking time to listen to every student's voice. They realize that they are missing opportunities to invite the learner into the lesson, yet they struggle to see how providing such opportunities will translate to greater learning outcomes. In this book, we challenge teachers to think of the "activation" of background knowledge systems (Herrera, Kavimandan, & Holmes, 2011) as a nonnegotiable phase of the lesson that validates the potential of every learner. This process of activating and accessing students' background knowledge is as important as interaction during the lesson and assessment of student learning at the end of the lesson.

We ask teachers to re-envision the opening moments of a lesson, moving beyond the typical KWL (know/want to know/learned), picture walk, or whole-group response to visuals and toward strategies that provide insights into every child's multiple layers of background knowledge. Applying strategies that provide a forum for every student to be an active participant at the beginning of the lesson increases the likelihood that teachers will use what students already know to take every learner to the zone of proximal development (Vygotsky, 1978), as well as validate, respect, and invite every learner into the lesson. When teachers have knowledge of what students know both in and out of school, they are better prepared to create conditions and situations that scaffold learning socioculturally, linguistically, cognitively, and academically.

A Closer Look at the CLD Student Biography

Building on the work of Thomas and Collier (e.g., 1995, 1997), Herrera and Murry have developed the concept of the *CLD student biography* (see Herrera, 2010; Herrera &

Murry, 2005, 2011; Herrera, Murry, & Morales Cabral, 2007; Herrera, Perez, & Escamilla, 2010). This book reflects thinking and learning about student biographies at two distinct levels: the school-situated biography and the home/community/personal biography of every learner. Each student has both an academic and an experiential/personal history that is uniquely his or her own. The more a teacher learns about the student, the more likely the two are to build a personal relationship, and the more likely it is that the teacher will understand the dynamic process through which the student is learning new vocabulary and content and making sense of new information.

Understanding the individual student is an essential component of both planning and lesson delivery. Following is a brief overview of the four interrelated dimensions we explore within classroom practice: the sociocultural, linguistic, cognitive, and academic dimensions. Biography-driven lessons incorporate structured opportunities for students to articulate their perspectives and to make connections between the past and the present. Because lessons are connected with each dimension of students' biographies, they promote lasting links to the content, language, and future applications of learning that are meaningful to students.

Sociocultural Dimension

The sociocultural dimension is at the heart of the CLD student's biography, as it reflects the student's funds of knowledge (home) and prior knowledge (community). It consists of the intersection between social institutions (e.g., home, school), affective influences (e.g., self-esteem, anxiety, motivation), and social interactive phenomena (e.g., bias, prejudice, discrimination). In short, the sociocultural dimension is about a student's life, love, and laughter (Herrera, 2010).

Socioculturally, the family and community in which the CLD student is being raised have a huge impact on how he or she initially defines literacy (Herrera et al., 2010). For example, a CLD student raised in a family where oral storytelling practices are woven into the fabric of traditions is no less literate than a student who spends hours each week at the library. Educators in schools, where the tapestry of learners is as rich and as varied as the stories they know, must begin to define "literacy" in ways beyond the act of reading from a book.

Teachers in biography-driven classrooms respect students for the varied backgrounds they bring and provide all learners with a "canvas of opportunity" for sharing the literacy opportunities they have at home. These opportunities may include visual representations of knowledge and learning. At the opening of the lesson, during the lesson,

and at the close of the lesson students are provided with multiple opportunities to "make public" their connections to the academic language and content being taught. Students' depth of understanding then becomes transparent not only for the learner but also for the teacher, who can then use these insights to guide each learner to higher levels of linguistic and academic development. In short, a teacher's working knowledge of the sociocultural dimension is contingent upon the classroom conditions that he or she creates to encourage students to share their knowledge and experiences and know that such contributions will be respected, valued, and capitalized upon in the learning process.

Linguistic Dimension

Educational perspectives that overlook or minimize the role of students' linguistic assets in their development of English language proficiency have led to classroom practices such as "teaching to the test" and drill-and-practice techniques to increase language and vocabulary development. Tests and more tests have been developed to monitor, sometimes on a weekly basis, the language growth of English language learners. Such an emphasis on testing leads to a narrowed curricular focus and frequently results in students remaining at the lower levels of thinking and learning. Resulting classroom practices do little to maximize L1 (native language) to L2 (target language, English) transfer, rarely allow students to use their native language to build a conceptual foundation for learning, and seldom focus on meaningful interaction. A shift in thinking can open doors for educators to understand how the native language, which is intertwined with a student's culture, influences how students comprehend, communicate, and express their knowledge, process thinking, and self.

The native language represents the core of each student, as it is the vehicle he or she first used to communicate and express his or her needs. Depending on the individual school and classroom, this native language is either acknowledged and validated as an essential part of the CLD student biography or is ignored and disregarded based on the belief that it inhibits the student's acquisition of English. However, research has shown that when the native language is used as a foundation for English language development, we are able to accelerate our students' acquisition of English (Cummins, 1981, 1989; Thomas & Collier, 2002). By encouraging students to draw upon their native language in their academic endeavors, we affirm their personal identities, support their expression of content understanding and learning, and promote the cross-linguistic transfer of literacy knowledge and skills needed to comprehend academic, grade-level curricula (Cummins, 1989; Herrera, 2010; Herrera et al., 2010).

Key aspects of any language that shape literacy development and that have implications for learning (Herrera et al., 2010) include

- **Phonology.** The sounds of the native language, which may or may not exist in the English language.
- **Syntax.** The order in which words are put together in the native language, which again can be very different from English word order.
- **Morphology.** The structure of words and the meaning of word parts.
- **Semantics.** The meaning of words in context.

Knowing about each of these aspects can support us as we approach literacy instruction with CLD students. The art of observing the student's ways of knowing and how this knowledge is expressed or made public has the potential to teach us about the cognitive paths the learner is taking. With these insights, we can better orchestrate instruction to ensure that each learner has the linguistic support necessary to achieve each lesson's goals.

Cognitive Dimension

The cognitive dimension highlights how students know, think, and apply. As defined by Gipe (2006), cognition refers to "the nature of knowing, or the ways of organizing and understanding our experiences" (p. 5). The lived experiences of CLD students vary greatly and dramatically influence the way they make sense of the world. For example, the lived experiences of a CLD student who has fled his country with a parent due to religious persecution are very different from those of a CLD student who was born and raised in the United States. Understanding how the experiences lived by each of these students provides him or her with a unique lens for interpreting events and information is critical.

As a result of individual differences in how they know and think, students also differ in the way they apply new knowledge. Consider the varied responses students might provide if asked to summarize a passage of text. Each student, based on how he or she knows and thinks about the topic, might perceive certain details to be of greater or lesser importance. Each of these processes—knowing, thinking, and applying—is influenced by the funds of knowledge, prior knowledge, and academic knowledge specific to each individual student.

- **Funds of knowledge** relate to "those historically developed and accumulated strategies (e.g., skills, abilities, ideas, practices) or bodies of knowledge that are essential to a household's functioning and well-being" (ERIC Clearinghouse on Languages and Linguistics,

1994, p. 1; see also Greenberg, 1989; Moll et al., 1992; Vélez-Ibáñez & Greenberg, 1992).
- **Prior knowledge** relates to the knowledge that students gain through their interactions with the community or communities in which they live and through their environments, including the natural world, recreational reading, television, and the Internet.
- **Academic knowledge** relates to the school-bound skills and knowledge students gain through their academic experiences in the United States, as well as those in the country of origin (or any other country in which the student received education). Students can also gain academic knowledge in unconventional ways, such as through informal apprenticeships. For example, a student who learns how to build a house from a parent might possess cognitive skills that can support him or her in solving mathematical problems. (*Note:* The same student may or may not have the academic vocabulary needed to verbally express the mathematical reasoning and problem-solving processes.)

Together, these existing knowledge systems make up a student's background knowledge, and they create unique pathways for the learner (Herrera, 2010).

Educators often talk about learning styles and learning strategies, yet we seldom connect how each of these may be molded by the language, culture, experiences, and academic background of the learner. Taking students to the zone of proximal development (Vygotsky, 1978) in the classroom requires us to ensure that they have a certain level of "struggle" and challenge. This constructive imbalance requires the learner to use all available pathways—new and old—to solve the problem. Learning results when students take information and make it their own. Our reward as teachers comes from seeing the student make meaning of the information and use it for more than simply answering a question on a test! Academic success begins with students knowing that they have learned something and that the effort they have put in was worthwhile.

Academic Dimension

The academic dimension of the CLD student biography encompasses students' access, engagement, and hope. It relates to both present and past school experiences, educational and support programs, and curricula that have played a part in a student's education. The climate of the educational settings in which a student has participated—as well as the attitudes, perspectives, and expectations of teachers—help form a student's perceptions about his or her abilities and place in school. Such factors play a pivotal role in the student's motivation to engage in the learning process. They also affect whatever degree of hope the learner has that his or her effort will lead to English language development and academic achievement.

When it comes to literacy development, the academic dimension plays a particularly pertinent role. Academic literacy, as defined by Gipe (2006), is the instructional literacy children have been exposed to through personal experiences with books and other forms of written or spoken language. As noted in our discussion of the sociocultural dimension of the CLD student biography, many CLD students may not have experienced the more traditional exposure to "text" that is recognized within the public school setting. Yet both literacy development and academic learning that are guided and supported by the teacher's reflective action, selection of materials, and orchestration of the community of learners have the potential to lead to the type of learning that is always moving students forward.

Meeting of the Minds: Students and Teachers as Equal Partners

Teachers are experts on their content areas; students are experts on their lives. The student and the teacher each possess knowledge and understandings that the other needs to reach the common goal of personal and professional (in the case of the student, academic) success. Before teachers can expect their students to gain the targeted concepts, vocabulary, and academic language from a given lesson, they must first activate students' existing knowledge. At this stage, the teacher acts as a participant observer, noting any insights or associations shared by the student that can be used as building blocks in his or her construction of meaning.

After activating students' existing background knowledge, the teacher then helps students make connections between their existing knowledge and the new content. The teacher supports learners as they extend their understandings and, as necessary, reroutes them to accurate understandings. Vygotsky (1978) asserts the importance of collaboration and interaction among peers during this process. He conceptualizes the *zone of proximal development* as the most effective instructional level, which is attained when the learner is stretched beyond his or her current independent level of skill through the help and interaction of more capable peers (along with the teacher). Similarly, Krashen (1985) uses the term *i+1* to describe the developmental process of language learning, whereby the learner begins at a particular level ("i") and is able to move to the next stage of development ("+1") when provided with comprehensible input. Building on the work of Krashen, we have adopted his "i" to identify the level of the student and used it to represent the "i"ndividual student biography.

Teachers who strive to provide students with comprehensible input frequently shelter their instruction by using the traditional components of hands-on activities, cooperative learning, guarded vocabulary, and visuals (Herrera & Murry, 2005). Although these instructional strategies have potential for making content more comprehensible at the surface level, they generally are insufficient for helping CLD students connect with the academic vocabulary and concepts on a personal level. Such individual schematic connections—or links to a student's sociocultural, linguistic, cognitive, and academic biography—are essential to a student's full understanding and ownership of the material (Anderson, 1999; Donovan & Bransford, 2005; Maria, 1990; Rumelhart, 1980).

Traditional methods of providing second language learners with comprehensible input can also fall short of developing students' academic literacy skills needed for success in the content-area classroom (Calderón, 2007). This means that students must acquire academic vocabulary. Without such vocabulary, CLD students are prevented from full participation in the curriculum, and their ability to discuss, interpret, analyze, critique, debate, and apply concepts (both orally and in writing) is hindered.

What is needed, then, is a re-envisioning of what it means to provide students with comprehensible input. The previously referenced means of providing comprehensible input (along with others that are discussed in the following section) must be implemented *in the context of the CLD student biography* and *with the explicit intent to build academic vocabulary*. The vocabulary development framework modeled in this book is grounded in the notion of transformative comprehensible input provided throughout the opening, work time, and closing phases of the lesson. As you read the strategies presented in this book, you will see many references to using visuals, grouping, guarded vocabulary, and hands-on activities. Through generous presentation of photos and real-world examples, we have attempted to help you *experience* what these four components of comprehensible input look, feel, and sound like in classroom practice when they are used to maximize learning!

Transformative Comprehensible Input

To ensure that content-area instruction promotes both students' personal connections to the content and acquisition of key academic vocabulary, teachers can employ strategic grouping configurations, revoice students' connections, and confirm/disconfirm learning throughout the instructional process. Essential to these processes, however, is a classroom climate that supports relationships among students and between the students and the teacher. Walqui (2000) describes an effective classroom environment as one in which "teachers and students together construct a culture that values the strengths of all participants and respects their interests, abilities, languages, and dialects. Students and teachers shift among the roles of expert, researcher, learner, and teacher, supporting themselves and each other" (p. 1). Our goal, then, is to create within our classroom a true community of learners.

Group Configurations That Teach

Planning for and using student groups to move the lesson forward requires teachers to be active/intentional facilitators in ways that lead them to place themselves in the "why" of student processing. The use and configuration of student groups are guided by the learning goals/objectives of the lesson and the situational talk that happens as a result of how students are processing what they are learning. The strategies in this book use the acronym *i+tpsI* to help teachers think about the "ebb and flow" of classroom talk that encompasses moving from learner (i = individual) to teacher, teacher to learners (t = total group), student to student (p = partners), and students in groups (s = small groups) debating, discussing, rationalizing, and coming to consensus on learning. Throughout the lesson cycle the teacher serves as a guide, scribe, facilitator, and supporter of student and classroom discourse. By the end of the lesson, individual students (I) are equipped to apply the new material in personally meaningful ways while demonstrating individual accountability.

When planning for student groups, teachers can reflect on each dimension of the CLD student biography by considering the following types of questions:

Sociocultural

- How can I capitalize on students' possible leadership and decision-making skills resulting from the roles they play in their families?
- How might each student's possible knowledge of community resources and challenges be used to make real-world applications to the text or lesson?
- How can I draw upon the insights that students might bring based on their countries of origin and/or knowledge of international travel?

Linguistic

- How can I best utilize and develop my students' levels of English language proficiency?
- How will I allow for cross-linguistic insights to be shared among the students given their native language proficiencies?
- How might I consider students' preferred modes of expression?

Cognitive

- How can I allow for cross-cultural perspectives on processes or events to be shared by students so that a deeper level of understanding is gained?
- How might I encourage students to use their inductive or deductive reasoning skills?
- How will I structure student groups to enhance learners' creative and imaginative thinking (and thereby enhance group motivation)?

Academic

- How can I capitalize on students' family literacy practices to make the process of academic vocabulary development more relevant?
- How will I provide opportunities for students' academic knowledge gained in another country to be used in the class's construction of knowledge?
- How might I encourage students to make text-to-text or text-to-world connections?

Putting students together in ways that advance each learner's holistic development requires "on-your-toes" thinking and planning and continual observation of student responses to evolving learning situations. Our responsiveness to students as we consider their biographies and the learning goals during lesson delivery becomes part of our habits of mind.

Revoicing Student Connections

Revoicing is the act of observing students, listening to what they have to say, and re-uttering their understanding through repetition, rephrasing, expansion, and reporting of what was shared (Forman, Larreamendy-Joerns, Stein, & Brown, 1998; Herrera, 2010). Revoicing allows teachers to combine their content-area expertise with their knowledge of individual students in order to help students successfully navigate the grade-level content and academic vocabulary. Although teachers can use revoicing throughout the lesson, it is predominantly employed as an instructional tool in the "work time" phase. Through revoicing, teachers acknowledge students' background knowledge and then use these insights to scaffold students' thinking to a greater depth of understanding.

As students share from their lived experiences and bring their funds of knowledge, prior knowledge, and academic knowledge into the public realm of the classroom, they look to their peers and their teacher for assurance that what they know is important to the construction of meaning. Revoicing acknowledges each student's membership in the intellectual community and has the potential to increase the individual's self-esteem (O'Connor & Michaels,

1996). Teachers use revoicing to help solidify and expand upon students' schematic connections to the content and vocabulary. This repetition of key conceptual relationships and academic terms provides students with opportunities to hear the concepts and terms multiple times and from multiple perspectives.

Confirming/Disconfirming Student Learning

Teachers confirm and disconfirm learning in the "work time" and "closing" phases of the lesson to validate students' thinking and effort while redirecting where needed. During the lesson, teachers are continually assessing students in informal ways to gauge their understanding of the content and related vocabulary. The manner in which we disconfirm learning is especially critical. We must strive to disconfirm misconceptions in ways that uphold the dignity of the student and encourage community members to learn from one another. We need to sensitively identify building blocks of student knowledge that can continue to be used in the construction of a more accurate understanding. In this way, we help students celebrate their incremental gains toward mastery of the content and language.

At the end of the lesson, teachers use authentic assessments to document what students learned. In doing so, they continue to keep in mind the CLD student biography. They consider the varied starting points of each individual learner. Progress matters! Every additional piece of knowledge and each additional vocabulary word committed to memory becomes another piece the CLD student can then use for future learning. Documenting student learning throughout the lesson provides both the learner and the teacher concrete evidence of what was learned. The strategies described in this book provide a framework that supports teachers in what we authors consider the *core* of learning.

A Framework for Linguistic and Academic Development

In this book we provide a strategy-based framework for linguistic and academic development. The proposed framework, depicted in Figure 1, is intended to help stimulate a discussion among paraprofessionals, ESL teachers, content-area teachers, administrators, and other educators regarding academic vocabulary development, comprehension, and acceleration of literacy and academic achievement of *all* students. The framework is meant to be descriptive rather than prescriptive, as it is not meant to replace existing curricular programs but rather to provide tools that more explicitly bring CLD students into the learning

equation. Toward this end, we describe what we see as essential components of effective instruction through the presentation of specific strategies that are used seamlessly from the beginning to the end of the lesson. Core to our work is that these strategies accomplish the following during lesson delivery:

- Invite learners into the lesson by providing a canvas of opportunity that allows all students to be active contributors in the classroom community.
- Provide the teacher with words/information from each student's background knowledge (funds of knowledge, prior knowledge, and academic knowledge) to use during the lesson.
- Provide the teacher with a frame for creating opportunities for academic talk throughout the lesson.
- Support students with a tool in their hand that they can use for building academic vocabulary and conceptual knowledge.
- Provide the teacher with concrete evidence of students' processing and learning throughout the lesson.
- Scaffold students' participation in the lesson and ownership of their learning.
- Incorporate a tool that the teacher can use to authentically assess and celebrate student learning.

Our framework supports attainment of these goals throughout the following three phases of linguistic and academic development within the lesson: Activation, Connection, and Affirmation. These phases of development align with the three general stages of the lesson: opening, work time, and closing.

Activation: A Canvas of Opportunity

In the *Activation* phase (opening of the lesson), the goal is to create a risk-free environment for our students so they can draw from their funds of knowledge, prior knowledge, and academic knowledge and identify links to the lesson. From the outset we must create conditions that encourage learners to take risks at their own pace without being judged for their linguistic variations or background knowledge. Although strategic grouping ($i+tpsI$) figures predominantly in the Connection phase, the design of student groups in the Activation phase is based on using our knowledge of students' biographies to promote student expression. We use our knowledge of students' cognitive and academic dimensions to consider differences in academic readiness. We also take into account possible differences in student perspectives resulting from influences of culture and community. Throughout this phase we assume the role of strategic observer, taking in whatever students

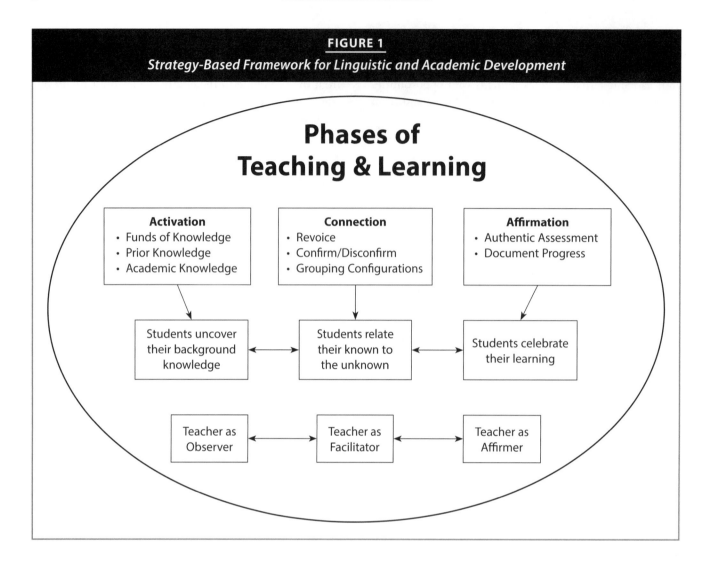

FIGURE 1
Strategy-Based Framework for Linguistic and Academic Development

Phases of Teaching & Learning

Activation
- Funds of Knowledge
- Prior Knowledge
- Academic Knowledge

Connection
- Revoice
- Confirm/Disconfirm
- Grouping Configurations

Affirmation
- Authentic Assessment
- Document Progress

Students uncover their background knowledge ⟷ Students relate their known to the unknown ⟷ Students celebrate their learning

Teacher as Observer ⟷ Teacher as Facilitator ⟷ Teacher as Affirmer

share and internally brainstorming ways we might be able to connect students' thoughts and ideas with the lesson.

By introducing the topic or vocabulary using visuals and specific strategies that activate students' background knowledge, we provide students with the opportunity to make public both their experiential and academic knowledge. A risk-free environment allows all students to represent what they know in words and/or in pictures and to use whatever language(s) are available as resources to express what they know. By documenting what every student knows and thinks, we make the information available for incorporation into the lesson. Using student voice for explanation of new vocabulary and making connections from what students have shared to text lead to greater levels of engagement and academic achievement. To motivate and engage learners, Activation first lets them see themselves as contributors to the lesson. Our responsibility as teachers is to be aware of what has been shared and to hold

ourselves accountable for using that information in constructive ways throughout the lesson.

Connection: The Broad and Narrow Strokes of Learning

In the *Connection* phase (work time of the lesson), we act as facilitators in students' construction of meaning and knowledge. Student knowledge/words from the Activation phase serve as links to the new lesson. This foundational knowledge and language support student connections to new vocabulary and concepts as well as their progress toward meeting the expected outcomes of the lesson. In this phase, we as teachers orchestrate the teaching–learning process by balancing individual students' biographies (identified assets and needs), the learning goals/objectives, and the community of learners. Selecting strategies that support this orchestration has the potential for decreasing the frustration that many teachers have with prescriptive programs, limited time frames, and communities of learners with diverse language and academic needs. Supporting students in making connections involves actions by the teacher that balance rigor, relevance, and biography.

As we teach and students negotiate their learning, we revoice the connections they make between their background knowledge and the content. As discussed earlier, our revoicing helps to ensure that all students receive the comprehensible input they need to achieve language learning at the *i+1* level as well as the cognitive and academic challenge they need to be stretched (via their zone of proximal development) to their highest learning potential. We confirm/disconfirm students' understandings of the relationships among content concepts and related academic vocabulary. We are able to model for students our own ways of approaching a task, thinking about a passage of text, or relating a vocabulary term to existing schemas. Through the strategies that we as teachers select, students are able to practice and apply various cognitive, metacognitive, and social/affective learning strategies, individually and with peers. Students come to understand which strategies can be used to achieve specific purposes. As a result, students are better able to internalize the strategies and apply procedural knowledge regarding their use to future applications within and across the content areas.

Affirmation: A Gallery of Understanding

In the *Affirmation* phase (closing of the lesson) students need to have evidence of what has been learned throughout the lesson. Positive self-concept related to learning, for many students, does not come from grades or periodic positive statements. Rather it comes from frequent words of affirmation and application of authentic assessments that evaluate what they have gained from the lesson. This type of assessment is both formative during the lesson and summative at the end of the lesson. Effective strategies can serve as tools for documenting both language and academic growth for every student. Students who are guided to make decisions about what is important throughout the lesson, and who are explicitly provided evidence of what they have learned at the end of the lesson, are more likely to be engaged and motivated to continue learning in the future.

Conclusion

In these introductory remarks, we have tried to provide a glimpse into an educational context where thoughtful reflection is the cornerstone of teaching. There is a need for all of us to critically examine our own perspectives about the students we teach and the learning opportunities we provide in our classrooms. The strategies that follow are meant to be a starting point—a resource to use as you gain new insights into your learning community and create an environment where students can explore meaning and find ways to connect with text.

Any kind of strategy application must begin with an analysis of the students' needs and one's own site-specific realities. As you read each strategy, contemplate how you might adapt the strategy or add your own creative spin to make it work for *your* students and *your* curriculum. We encourage you to make these strategies your own—reflecting upon your classroom at every step along the way and using the CLD student biography as the lens through which you view lesson planning, implementation, and assessment.

We encourage you to ask yourself, How can I use these strategies to set conditions that lead to more academic talk and higher-order thinking through the use of challenging activities? In our work, we have drawn from the Standards for Effective Pedagogy and Learning developed by the Center for Research on Education, Diversity & Excellence (e.g., CREDE, 2002). We encourage teachers to use strategies that lead to *joint productive activity* that involves teacher, students, and peers working jointly to produce evidence of learning and progress toward common learning goals. We strive to ensure that our classroom conditions and situations are driven by *instructional conversations* and the discourse that results by encouraging students to make their thinking public. We scaffold *challenging activities* that accelerate learning for all students, rather than remediating and dumbing down the curriculum. Finally, every lesson is grounded in *language and literacy development* and *contextualized* in the lives of the students we teach. Our research has documented the great promise that biography-driven instruction has for increasing the academic success of CLD learners. When strategies are implemented consistently, students and teachers become equal partners in learning.

PART II

Vocabulary Development Strategies

IN PART II, we provide the reader with strategies that can be used by K–8 educators to support CLD students in attaining the academic vocabulary needed for comprehension and application of literacy concepts. The strategies are organized into three chapters:

- *Chapter 1: Images as Catalysts for Predictions and Connections.* This chapter includes strategies that use images to spark students' imaginations and ignite students' connections with their background knowledge (i.e., funds of knowledge, prior knowledge, and academic knowledge). These strategies also support students in making predictions about the content they are studying.
- *Chapter 2: Words and More Words.* This chapter includes strategies that use words as the basis for student thought and reflection. The starting words are either generated by students or selected by the teacher for their usefulness in explaining the essential concepts of the lesson.
- *Chapter 3: From Word Knowledge to Comprehension.* This chapter includes strategies that provide the teacher with insights into students' levels of knowledge about academic vocabulary. These strategies also guide students to greater depths of understanding related to literacy concepts and enable them to more effectively monitor their own learning.

The description of each strategy follows the same organization and includes the following introductory elements:

- *Strategy Artifact.* Each strategy elaboration begins with one or more photos that reflect a "moment in time" during implementation of the strategy.
- *Teacher Testimonial.* A K–8 teacher shares his or her thoughts regarding implementation of the strategy and its benefits for students.

- *Where Theory Meets Practice.* Each strategy is founded on key theories and current research regarding literacy development, culturally responsive pedagogy, second language acquisition, teaching/learning dynamics, and brain-based learning.
- *Materials Needed.* A list of materials needed to perform each strategy is provided. Many strategies employ only basic classroom materials. For others, a template provided in the strategy description is also used as a worksheet for students.

The same guiding elements are provided for each strategy to help educators follow the flow of strategy activities. As described in Part I, the three phases of a lesson are *Activation* (opening), *Connection* (work time), and *Affirmation* (closing). In like manner, implementation of the strategies progresses through these three phases. For each phase, we provide:

- A separate set of directions.
- A visual depicting a student artifact or student involvement related to the particular phase of strategy implementation.
- Letter icons (**T**, **P**, **S**, and **I**) identifying the *i+tpsI* group configuration(s) used in the lesson. The icons are intended to help teachers plan their responsive groups for the various activities in each phase of the strategy. The *i+tpsI* mnemonic, as explained in Part I, reminds teachers to always consider the sociocultural, linguistic, cognitive, and academic dimensions of their students' biographies when making grouping decisions.
- A section that explains the benefits of the strategy activities for CLD students.

Where applicable, sections of "Author Talk" are also included to provide educators with opportunities for critical reflection on classroom practice as well as insights that teachers across the country have shared with us regarding practical adaptations and modifications of the strategy.

Finally, each strategy includes the following wrap-up elements:

- *Spotlight: Early Literacy Connection.* This feature demonstrates how the strategy can be used to promote CLD students' early experiences with oral language, reading, and writing. Because these experiences vary considerably from one child to another, this feature allows educators to promote important literacy connections in the home.
- *Biography-Driven Response to Intervention.* Given the need to differentiate instruction for CLD students, this section explains how each strategy can be used within a response to intervention (RTI) framework. Applications for Tiers 1, 2, and 3 of tiered instruction are highlighted.
- *One Classroom's Perspective.* This element uses words and pictures to capture the progression of the strategy from one classroom's perspective. The featured teacher provides a first-hand description of his or her implementation of the strategy with students throughout the lesson to target the critical concepts and academic vocabulary.
- *Student Voices.* This feature captures CLD students' responses to use of biography-driven instructional strategies in their classrooms.
- *Templates.* Some strategies require templates for use during the lesson. When applicable, the template specific to the strategy is provided at the end of the strategy description. The templates are also available for free download and printing from www.tcpress.com.
- *Rubrics and Checklists.* Sample assessment tools for some strategies are provided in the Appendix. Student assessment rubrics and student academic behavior checklists are provided as examples of formative and summative assessments that can be created for use in conjunction with the strategies presented in this book. The rubrics and checklists are also available for free download and printing from www.tcpress.com.
- *Video Clips of Exemplary Teaching.* A DVD of video clips highlighting teachers' implementation of select strategies is provided with each copy of this book. (The clips can also be viewed online at www.tcpress .com/AcceleratingLiteracyVideos.html.) Each clip illustrates an educator's use of a biography-driven strategy with diverse learners in a grade-level classroom. The clips exemplify the Activation, Connection, and Affirmation phases of the lesson. They provide an inside look at how teachers have used the strategies to meet the needs of individual learners in their site-specific classrooms. Just as no two classrooms are alike, the implementation of a particular strategy as modeled by the teacher in a video clip might not reflect how you would choose to implement the strategy with your learners. We challenge you to use the modeled strategies as a source of inspiration for your own ideas about how best to implement these strategies in your professional practice.

We realize that, for some teachers, the amount of information provided for each strategy may initially be overwhelming. We also understand that some teachers prefer a "nutshell" overview of strategies they are considering for implementation with their particular group of learners. To accommodate the varying needs and purposes of our readers, we have provided all information that is essential to carrying out each strategy in boxes. We can assure you that everything you absolutely need is *in the boxes*. The full strategy description provides the elaboration, details, and nuances of classroom application that teachers are continually requesting when we share these strategies in the field. Use those elements that you find most applicable, return to others as needed, and share with others what works for you!

CHAPTER 1

Images as Catalysts for Predictions and Connections

THE STRATEGIES PRESENTED in this chapter explore the power of images as catalysts for vocabulary development. Research has shown that when used in instruction, images can ignite students' connections with existing background knowledge about the topic, concepts, and academic vocabulary of the lesson (Harvey & Goudvis, 2000; Herrera, 2010; Tompkins, 2007; Wormeli, 2005). Our experiences in elementary classrooms across the United States consistently validate this, and the following example shared by Mrs. Foster, a 4th-grade teacher, provides an illustration of the phenomenon:

It was the first day Joaquin had ever attended school in the United States. Joaquin had attended school in Puerto Rico, but he was just acquiring English and was in the intermediate fluency stage. I knew that Joaquin would benefit from having visual cues about key vocabulary terms from the story that we would be reading, *The Great Kapok Tree*. Therefore, before starting the main reading lesson for the day, I showed the students six pictures. Each picture represented a key vocabulary word from the story. I wanted to pre-assess what the students knew about the vocabulary terms. So, as each picture was shown, I had Joaquin and his peers individually draw a picture in response to the visual. I made sure the paraprofessional translated the directions in Spanish so Joaquin knew that he could draw whatever he thought of or felt in response to each visual. Knowing that he could simply draw made this activity safe for Joaquin, and it was wonderful to see how engaged he became in drawing his own pictures. In fact, I was amazed to see the pictures that Joaquin came up with. For example, one of the pictures I provided showed the canopy of the rain forest. In response to this picture, Joaquin drew a house. Not quite understanding the connection, I asked him why he had drawn a house.

Joaquin answered me by saying, "This picture reminded me of my home in Puerto Rico so I drew our house there." Having this insight into Joaquin's thought process and connection not only provided me with invaluable insight into his personal life and culture, it also gave me the opportunity to tap into his first-hand knowledge of the rain forest and make him our class "expert" when it came to this lesson!

As demonstrated in this example, the pictures used by Mrs. Foster served several purposes. Among these was providing her with a window into Joaquin's personal connections based on his background experiences. They also supported her ability to differentiate subsequent instruction in response to the information she had gained.

A Picture Is Worth a Thousand Words

As demonstrated in the example shared by Mrs. Foster, a picture can be worth (metaphorically at least) a thousand words. The phrase can be taken even more literally when we think of the support that images provide to culturally and linguistically diverse (CLD) learners as they communicate in a second language. When teachers such as Mrs. Foster incorporate visual cues before the lesson even begins, they are able to see how each student might interpret key concepts and academic vocabulary based on his or her individual background and cultural lens. With this simple type of preassessment, the teacher is able to gain the most accurate understanding of students' background knowledge before it is influenced by what their peers, teacher, or textbooks have to say (Herrera et al., 2011).

Once the information has been gathered, the teacher can use what was learned about the students' existing knowledge, skills, and experiences as a bridge to the new content and language of the lesson. One of the best ways to support connections between the known (background knowledge) and the unknown (new material) is by having students share their initial connections with their peers. This sharing process helps to bring to light the similarities and differences in students' perspectives, cultural backgrounds, and so forth, as evidenced by their various interpretations of the same image. By purposefully observing and listening to students as they share with one another, the teacher also is able to gain insights into the best ways to scaffold instruction during the lesson.

Scaffolding is a component of high-quality sheltered instruction and includes the use of visuals to help provide CLD students with comprehensible input (Echevarría, Vogt, & Short, 2010). To ensure that the input students receive is indeed comprehensible, it is important to revisit their interpretations of the visual cues throughout the lesson. Because interpretations are based on context, which is often culture-bound, some students might require redirection. Opportunities to confirm and disconfirm connections allow students to refine their understanding of academic vocabulary and concepts and develop a sense of appropriate contextual use.

Mental Pictures: Bringing Words to Life

Knowledge is stored both linguistically and nonlinguistically. Traditionally, teachers present knowledge by having students listen to or read new information. This linguistic approach to instruction is not very effective for CLD students because they cannot rely solely on linguistic ability to learn and retain knowledge in a new language (Hill & Flynn, 2006). On the other hand, knowledge that is stored nonlinguistically can be stored in the form of mental pictures. The mental pictures that students create are highly dependent on their individual schemas, or background knowledge. Proficient readers create mental images from all of their senses when they read (Harvey & Goudvis, 2000; Tompkins, 2007). By using nonlinguistic cues during literacy lessons, we are able to facilitate CLD students' ability to combine the author's words with their own background knowledge to create mental images that enhance their understanding of the text and bring the words to life (Harvey & Goudvis, 2000). In other words, we are able to help our students activate their background knowledge, which in turn enhances their comprehension of key vocabulary and the overall text. According to Marzano, Pickering, and Pollock (2001), educators can further this process

by asking students to explain and justify their nonlinguistic representations.

At the outset of the lesson, visuals help CLD students connect to the content by providing them with concrete links to the text. By actively engaging students in hands-on activities such as creating graphic organizers, drawing pictures, or using visuals, educators can enhance their abilities to demonstrate and elaborate on their existing knowledge. Key considerations when working with CLD students include

- The schemas that CLD students bring to a text or lesson may not match those of the author, the teacher, or their peers.
- For background knowledge to be useful, the student must be able to locate it and then apply it (Fisher & Frey, 2009).

In *Brain Matters* (2001), Pat Wolfe writes that the human brain needs to be primed so that it can pay attention and determine what is meaningful in any text or experience. To help CLD students reap the most benefits of using visuals during learning, Herrera et al. (2010) suggest the following:

- Select visuals from a variety of cultures so that all students can relate to them.
- Have students bring visuals from home that illustrate the content or concept being presented.
- Refer back to visuals and extend students' knowledge through discussions and activities associated with the visuals.
- Link key vocabulary to visuals.

Strategies in Practice

In this chapter you will find descriptions of the following seven strategies, which explicitly create conditions that encourage learners to use visuals to further their content and language learning and to support their active engagement in the lesson:

- Linking Language
- Picture This
- Pictures and Words
- Mind Map
- Tri-Fold
- Listen Sketch Label
- Story Bag

STRATEGY

Linking Language

The CLD students were excited about the Linking Language strategy. They were comfortable with the fact that they could draw pictures if the words they wanted to express were too difficult for them to write down. The CLD students drew pictures, which demonstrated their background knowledge. My Samoan student and my Spanish-speaking student could identify with the picture of the waterfall, trees, and greenery. They had each come from countries where they had seen that sort of environment/vegetation. I observed written words as well as pictures being drawn by the CLD students. For example, my Spanish-speaking student wrote "mariposa" on the Linking Language poster of a butterfly.

—*Cathy Hollis, 1st-Grade Teacher*

Where Theory Meets Practice

CLD students have the dual task of learning academic English language and content simultaneously. Although CLD students may have the cognitive capacity to grasp the material, they may not have the English language proficiency to comprehend explanations of academic concepts. When teachers use contextual clues such as visuals, hands-on activities, and other nonverbal accommodations to make their instruction comprehensible, they increase CLD students' ability to understand complex academic concepts and the language used to explain them (Bredekamp & Copple, 1997).

Pictures offer a powerful visual stimulus when used in instruction, particularly for CLD students. Research by Curtis and Bailey (2001) found that pictures provide students with something to talk about and take the focus off the language learner during the discussion by turning attention to the picture. In addition, pictures provide CLD students with a concrete link to the content material being studied. To enhance these links, it is important for teachers to be strategic in their selection of pictures so that they tap into students' funds of knowledge, prior knowledge, and academic knowledge (Herrera, 2010).

Linking Language is a strategy that builds on the research noted above to support CLD students' academic literacy development, understanding, and content-based connections. To implement this strategy, the teacher uses pictures from the specific content being taught to elicit connections, activating students' existing knowledge and vocabulary prior to instruction. The pictures are used as a bridge between the content and CLD students' background knowledge. As such, Linking Language can help educators link home and community culture to school culture to reinforce children's self-worth, sense of belonging, identity, and achievement (García, 2005; Nieto, 2002; Osterman, 2000).

This strategy can be used with a whole class, small groups, pairs, or individuals to initiate CLD students' inquiry about the words as they begin adding them to their vocabulary. When pictures are used as a stimulus for reading, writing, and word study, CLD students can further deepen their understanding of the new vocabulary and the content material. In summary, Linking Language incorporates cooperative learning, writing, vocabulary, and concept development as a means of assisting CLD students' academic understanding.

A video clip illustrating implementation of this strategy appears on the DVD included with this book and is available for viewing online at:

www.tcpress.com/AcceleratingLiteracyVideos.html

Materials Needed: Blank poster paper • pictures for key vocabulary words • vocabulary words on precut strips of paper • sticky notes • paper • markers/colored pencils

---

 ACTIVATION: A Canvas of Opportunity

Directions:

- Select three or four pictures that illustrate key concepts from the lesson (pictures can be taken from the Internet, clipart, or magazines, or actual textbook pictures can be used).
- Tape each picture to the center of a large piece of poster paper (if using the textbook, place the textbook in the center of the poster paper).
- Give each student a marker or pencil of a different color (this way, you can confirm that every student contributed something).

- **S** Place students in groups of three to five and station one group at each of the posters.
- **I** Instruct the students to individually write down everything they think of, see, or feel when they look at the picture (be sure to encourage CLD students to write in the native language or draw if they prefer).
- Allow only 1–2 minutes for students to write.
- **S** Then have all of the groups rotate to the next poster.

- Continue until all groups have been to each picture.

Author Talk: Activation

One of the single most important assets we have in our classrooms today are the students! Each and every one of them brings a unique set of experiences and background knowledge that he or she can share. The key is to find ways to access these experiences and expose students' background knowledge so that they are empowered to become active members of a learning community. As observers in preK–6 classrooms across multiple states, we have been privileged to witness the power of Linking Language in providing students full access to the curriculum and classroom community.

The more we observed this strategy in practice, the more we noticed the "energy" change within the classroom as the teacher prepared the students for application of the strategy. We immediately noticed students becoming more alert as the teacher explained the directions for the strategy. It was almost as if students were undergoing a mental shift as they saw that this was their opportunity to tell the teacher what they knew. And because they all understood that there was no "right" or "wrong" answer, the stress that

is usually associated with a pre-test to determine what students know about a topic was nowhere to be found. Close observation of the CLD students revealed that they often had an even higher level of confidence because they were allowed to draw or write in their native language. By removing the pressure to produce something in English, particularly if they were not yet proficient in English, their affective filters were lowered and their motivation was high.

In talking to teachers, we learned that this strategy provided them with a great deal of insight about their students. Many of them commented that if it had not been for the Linking Language strategy, they would not have known half the things they did about their students' background knowledge. In fact, several teachers indicated that once they learned how much their students already knew about a particular topic, they were able to spend significantly less time on identified vocabulary in the curriculum and focus on other academic vocabulary that the students did not know. Using insights into students' background knowledge as a springboard to instruction inspires students as well as the teacher to fully engage in the lesson.

Activating the "*i*"
How does this process activate CLD students' existing knowledge?

- **Sociocultural:** The visual cues provided to students in this strategy prompt immediate and student-specific sensory responses based on their own experiences.
- **Linguistic:** Students at all levels of language proficiency can participate in this strategy because they are allowed to use their native language, pictures, and simple labels in English.

- **Academic:** Linking Language provides students with a vehicle for demonstrating their existing knowledge about the academic content being taught.
- **Cognitive:** The activation activities encourage students to cognitively stretch their imagination and make schematic links to content.

 CONNECTION: The Broad & Narrow Strokes of Learning

Directions:

- **S** Once all groups have returned to their original posters, have them review all of the information that was placed on the poster and identify common ideas/vocabulary by circling them and linking them with a line.
- As students complete this activity, make sure to note the academic vocabulary they already have on their posters and listen in on their discussions.
- **T** Share with students the target vocabulary for the lesson. As you say each word, tape its strip of paper to the chalkboard/wall for all to see.
- **S** Have students discuss in their group which of the target vocabulary words best matches the picture on their poster.

- **T** As a class, discuss ideas about the best match for each poster. Upon reaching a consensus, have a student representative from each group come up to remove the appropriate word's strip and tape it to his or her group's poster.
- **S** Ask students to look for connections between the target vocabulary and the common ideas/vocabulary they recorded on their poster.
- **T** Have each group share out these connections, as well as other links they made, to the rest of the group.
- **I** Have all students continue to work individually to add to the Linking Language posters throughout the lesson by using sticky notes to

add new information (e.g., specific vocabulary words, new concepts) they learn.
- Encourage students to refer back to the posters for key vocabulary throughout the lesson.

Connecting to the "*i*+1"
How does this process move CLD students from the known to the unknown?

- **Sociocultural:** In the connection phase, the teacher should use the information students put on the poster during the activation phase as the bridge for promoting students' comprehension of new content.
- **Linguistic:** Having students discuss the vocabulary terms on the poster and make links between common ideas/vocabulary engages student in hands-on practice of all four literacy skills: listening, speaking, reading, and writing.

- **Academic:** Linking Language enables students to think about content and vocabulary in a more visual and creative manner. They are also actively engaged in learning key academic content and vocabulary.
- **Cognitive:** Students are continually developing their metacognitive processes as they monitor their own learning by building upon existing knowledge.

AFFIRMATION: A Gallery of Understanding

Directions:

- **T** Model this activity with the whole class before releasing students to do the activity on their own. As a whole class, select 10 words from the Linking Language posters. Use the selected words to write a whole-class summary on a large piece of poster paper as an example.
- **I** Next have students individually transfer 8–10 key vocabulary words from the Linking Language posters onto a blank sheet of paper. Encourage students to select those words that were most meaningful to them.

- Tell students that they now are going to write a summary of what they learned over the course of the lesson. They are to use the key vocabulary words they just wrote down on the sheet of paper to help them construct their summary.
- Transfer of the group activity to the individual activity may not be automatic for all students. Carefully attend to indications of the need for additional modeling and support.
- **P** Encourage students to share their final summaries with a partner to show all that they have learned.

Affirming Student Ownership: *"I"* Get It!
How does this process celebrate CLD student learning?

- **Sociocultural:** Linking Language supplies students with a visual representation of the progression of learning. Posting students' completed posters at the end of the lesson or unit is great affirmation of their background knowledge and learning.
- **Linguistic:** After completing the activity, students are able to summarize their thoughts in a more effective manner with the support of key vocabulary to refer back to when discussing or writing about the topic.

- **Academic:** This strategy ensures that CLD students have access to academic vocabulary and content knowledge throughout the lesson. The act of individually summarizing their learnings also allows each CLD student to demonstrate what he or she has learned.
- **Cognitive:** Linking Language enhances CLD students' metacognitive awareness by supporting the transition from visual connections to the key concepts/vocabulary to written documentation of their individual learning at the end of the lesson.

SPOTLIGHT: Early Literacy Connection

As early childhood instructors, we know that skills such as alphabetic knowledge (letter recognition), phonological awareness (e.g., rhyming, alliteration), and vocabulary are precursory skills for learning to read (Shonkoff & Phillips, 2000). We are challenged to teach young children the literacy skills that are essential for success in school and life, particularly for increasingly diverse learners.

Linking Language is a visual strategy that can help teachers incorporate critical early literacy skills in English by accessing students' background knowledge and existing vocabulary regarding a particular picture from a story. All children, regardless of their backgrounds, have strengths that we can build on. As teachers, we need to know precisely what skills each child controls and plan instruction accordingly.

To modify the Linking Language strategy for young CLD students, teachers can engage them in the following activity:

Activation:

- Select one picture from the story that you can share with the whole class that previews key information from the story. Have this picture photocopied and taped to the center of a large piece of chart paper.
- Tell students to look at the picture and think of all the things they see in the picture.
- Then have the students share what they see with a partner.
- After sharing with their partner, have the students orally share what they see with the teacher and the rest of their classmates.

Connection:

- As the students are sharing, write their observations around the picture on the chart paper for the whole class to see. As you are writing, be sure to model the sounds and spelling of the each word.

- In this way, CLD students will begin to focus on and internalize the phonetic and structural patterns of the English words.
  - By highlighting common features in the words such as beginning consonants, rhyming words, and letter patterns, you are providing an introduction to basic phonics skills in English.
- After recording your students' observations, have them find words that begin with the same sound.
  - In this way, CLD students are explicitly practicing phonemic awareness skills by attending to the sounds of the English language in context.
- To further connect this activity to visuals and the key vocabulary words in the story, you could have a picture for the word on one side of a 3×5 note card and the word on the other side. Give every student a card before reading the story and have them hold up their card when they hear the word read aloud.
  - To challenge students, have them listen for the words on the chart as you read the story aloud. Have them raise their hand if they hear one of the words.

Affirmation:

- To assess students' understanding, give them a copy of the book and have them work with a partner and look for words that start with the same letter, thereby practicing phonics skills in context.
- As students find these words, have them write them down in a list.
- At the end of the lesson, the lists can be turned in for you to review and revisiting the next day.

Note: These purposeful, meaningful activities allow all of the students to hear and practice the sounds of the key vocabulary words they will hear in the story. For some CLD students, they will be hearing these sounds for the first time.

Biography-Driven Response to Intervention

Linking Language is a strategy that can help students connect with content at their own linguistic level. Because visuals can provide additional context for students, this strategy works well for making content comprehensible for *all* learners, especially at the Tier 1 level. When you plan your Tier 1 instruction, allow all of your students to connect with visuals as they negotiate the meaning of the academic vocabulary. As you proceed with the lesson, provide adaptations to students by having them self-monitor their comprehension of the lesson.

One Classroom's Perspective

Activating:

I knew that my students had been exposed to multiple experiences/opportunities within our own classroom setting that allowed for repeated use and application of some of these words. However, I tried to find pictures that they may not be really familiar with in order for them to focus on reactions through feelings rather than trying to find the "right word." Considering the biographies of my students, I knew that by allowing them to draw pictures I would be able to discover the depth of their understanding of key vocabulary as the pictures were shared and discussed as a whole group. It also ensured 100% participation. After the modeling it would be time to release. My plans considered the groupings so that students were not grouped by academic achievement levels but by background experiences. I planned to have the largest variety possible in each group for the students to expand upon. The decision to use small groups supported my speech-emergent students by giving them opportunities to practice the vocabulary in meaningful context.

Connecting:

The students moved from predicting what our next unit would be about, to small groups where they wrote or illustrated their thoughts, to the whole group where we compared our thoughts and explored cognate recognition/identification to support the academic dimension. The pictures were an effort to take students from the known to the unknown. They explored their own concepts by using vocabulary without fear of grammatical errors, and then as a group we compared our thinking with the true definitions. During their discussions I was able to listen to determine which students were learning new words and which students were learning new concepts. As a group, we identified words that were repeated in order to create meaning through repetition. As the students tied the vocabulary from this activity into their own experiences, I knew they were that much closer to tying it into their permanent memory. The strategy allowed each student to apply their words independently and at their own level.

Affirming:

We had an engaging discussion based on the pictures and words recorded on the posters, focusing our attention on those that were the same and those that were different. As we elaborated on the meaning of the words, the students were using the words in a new way. The student-to-student and student-to-teacher interactive learning supported them in their efforts to create a deeper understanding through connections to their prior knowledge. This was due in part to their discussion within their small social networks. Once the words were identified, we discussed our experiences that prompted those ideas or concepts, generating a connection between self and the vocabulary. I read the book *Under One Rock* by Anthony Fredericks to underscore the text-to-self concept.

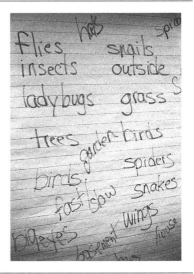

Student Voices

I like Linking Language because I can share what I know with my English-speaking friends in my own language and by using pictures.

—*ELL Student*
Speech Emergent

I had seen the rainforest before from Samoa. I was able to draw and write a lot about this picture. My friends really liked hearing about the rainforest. It was neat to talk about it since most of them have never been to the rainforest!

—*ELL Student*
Speech Emergent

I liked the picture of bugs because we go camping a lot. I was able to tell my friends that when I go camping, I get "eaten up" by bugs! That's why I don't like bugs—they bite!

—*ELL Student*
Intermediate Fluency

STRATEGY

Picture This

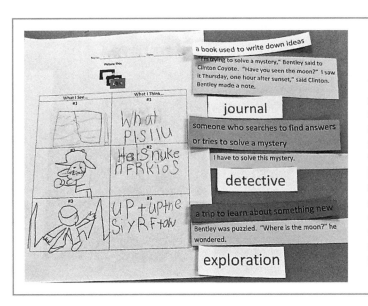

This strategy builds on the strengths and background experiences of my CLD students. Students were able to express their individual ideas of the meaning of the vocabulary word so they could correct or affirm their own knowledge. The strategy also encourages the acknowledgment and celebration of diversity among all students in the classroom. Each time, five different students were allowed to share with the entire class, putting them in the spotlight.

—*Kari Ritter, 2nd-Grade Teacher*

Where Theory Meets Practice

Making word meanings and relationships visible is a powerful way to involve students in actively constructing the meaning of words. For CLD students, this ability to connect to a word visually is critical. However, it is important to remember that simply using a visual is not enough. Discussion of the visual among peers is also needed to help students construct word meaning (Blachowicz & Fisher, 2006; Stahl & Vancil, 1986). Linking this discussion to text is also essential, because such contextualization further supports CLD students as they work to fully understand the meaning of target vocabulary.

Picture This is a strategy that promotes the use of visuals and peer discussion, as described above, to foster student understanding and contextualization of target vocabulary. Oxford's (1990) System of Learning Strategies would categorize Picture This as a cognitive learning strategy that deals with *analyzing and reasoning* because students are asked to reason inductively and analyze expressions to figure out how a picture and its corresponding clues can be used to determine the meaning of key vocabulary terms.

In the Picture This strategy, CLD students engage in a four-step process. First, they are introduced to visuals that represent key vocabulary. Using the visuals, students apply their background knowledge to engage in an inductive task by determining *what they see* and *what they think*. After completing the task, students are given dictionary definitions of each of the three words on strips of paper and are asked to use their background knowledge once again to determine which definition matches each picture and align them accordingly. The process is repeated with sentences from the text that relate to each vocabulary word in terms of sentence content but do not use the specific word. Finally, students are given the actual vocabulary words and asked to align them with the three visuals that started the lesson.

While engaged in this process, CLD students have opportunities to discuss their connections with their peers at each step. By working through this process of analyzing and reasoning, students draw upon their own background knowledge, experiences, and inductive reasoning skills to determine what each word means.

Materials Needed: Three pictures from the text, the Internet, magazines, newspapers, library books, picture cards, etc. • "What I see, What I think" template (one per student) • dictionary definitions for each vocabulary word on precut strips of paper (one set per student) • sentences from the text that illustrate the definition of each vocabulary word but do not state the vocabulary word on precut

strips of paper (one set per student) • vocabulary words for each student on precut strips of paper (one set per student) • paper • pencils/pens

ACTIVATION: A Canvas of Opportunity

Directions:

- Select three appropriate pictures to support students' acquisition of key vocabulary terms.
  - You can project pictures for the whole class to see, make copies for small groups to share, or have a copy of each picture for each student. The pictures can be taken directly from the text or from other sources (e.g., the Internet, magazines, newspapers, library books, picture cards).
- **T** Show students the preselected images one at a time.
- **I** Have students individually record on the "What I see, What I think" template what comes to mind as they

look at the picture. In the first column they will draw a picture of what they see, and in the second column they will write all the words they think of when they see the picture.
  - Encourage students to reach deep into their "permanent memory folder" to record as many words as possible.
  - Use questioning techniques as students work. Ask them to describe all the things they see in the picture as well as what they think of when they look at the picture.
- Repeat this process for each picture.
- **P** After students have completed documenting their individual

responses on their templates, have them share what they have written with a partner.

Activating the "*i*"
How does this process activate CLD students' existing knowledge?

- **Sociocultural:** CLD students have the opportunity to individually brainstorm and document background knowledge and experiences based on their interpretation of the pictures. They also have the opportunity to engage in discussion with peers and hear their interpretations, which may spark additional connections.
- **Linguistic:** Students' use of nonlinguistic representations to demonstrate what they see reduces the stress associated with writing, particularly for CLD students in the initial stages of second language acquisition.

- **Academic:** Activities during this phase help the teacher create a low-risk academic environment and set the stage for all CLD students to be active participants in the learning process as they make individual connections to content-based pictures.
- **Cognitive:** The peer discussions incorporated in this strategy create conditions that allow students to share multiple ways of knowing and thinking about each picture.

CONNECTION: The Broad & Narrow Strokes of Learning

Directions:

- **I** Pass out the set of strips with the dictionary definitions for the words and have students individually match them to the pictures and descriptions they drew on their template.
- **P** **S** Again, be sure to have students discuss in pairs or small groups how they are matching the definitions before the whole-group discussion begins.
- As students are matching the dictionary definitions, circulate around the room and observe what they are doing. Ask students to provide the rationale for their matches.

- **T** Next, read the text as a whole group.
- **I** Pass out the set of strips with the sentences from the text. Once again, have students individually match the sentences to the pictures and descriptions they recorded on their template.
- **P** **S** Have students discuss their matches in pairs or small groups before beginning the whole-group discussion.
- As students are matching the sentences, circulate around the room as

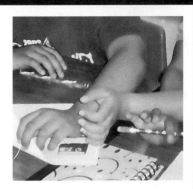

before and observe what they are doing. Again have students provide the rationale for their matches.

Connecting to the "*i*+1"
How does this process move CLD students from the known to the unknown?

- **Sociocultural:** Students are actively engaged in discussions with peers to support meaningful content connections during the lesson as they share insights based on their own perspectives and understanding.
- **Linguistic:** Having CLD students engage in active discussion with their peers helps them process their thoughts as well as articulate their content understanding.

- **Academic:** This strategy creates conditions that allow students to express *multiple ways of knowing* during the course of the lesson.
- **Cognitive:** The way in which students organize their definitions and sentences provides a lot of insight into what they are thinking as they listen, interact, and work with their peers and the information that is presented in the lesson.

AFFIRMATION: A Gallery of Understanding

Directions:

- **I** Pass out the set of strips with the vocabulary words and have students individually match them to the pictures and descriptions they drew on their template.
- **P S** Be sure to have students discuss in pairs or small groups how they are matching the vocabulary words before beginning the whole-group discussion.
- As students are matching the vocabulary words, circulate around the room and observe. Ask students to provide the rationale for their matches.

- **T** Discuss as a whole class what vocabulary words match each picture and why.
- **I** To conclude the lesson, have students individually write on the back of their "What I see, What I think" template a sentence for each vocabulary word that defines the word and incorporates the information and clues they were given (i.e., the picture, dictionary definition, sentence from text, and actual vocabulary word). (*Note:* Some teachers

have included a section for writing a class sentence as well.)
- **P** Have students share their sentences with a partner.

Affirming Student Ownership: *"I"* Get It!
How does this process celebrate CLD student learning?

- **Sociocultural:** This strategy helps students synthesize multiple perspectives about the lesson's vocabulary and concepts into a personally meaningful statement that reflects their understanding.
- **Linguistic:** Students' use of academic vocabulary is stretched to the *i*+1 as they develop their own meaningful sentences to demonstrate their understanding of the vocabulary words.

- **Academic:** Each student's individual sentences demonstrate the level of internalization and knowledge he or she has gained for each vocabulary term.
- **Cognitive:** CLD students use a variety of cognitive, academic, linguistic, and even sociocultural skills to synthesize in their own words the meaning of each vocabulary term.

Author Talk: Affirmation

Each CLD student brings a unique set of experiences and background knowledge to the classroom. However, depending on what stage of second language acquisition (SLA) they are in, students differ in their ability to share their knowledge in English. For example, a CLD student in the preproduction stage of SLA (the first stage) is able to provide only one- or two-word responses. On the other hand, a student in the early production stage of SLA (the second stage) is able to respond in short sentences. The more teachers know about the linguistic biographies of their CLD students, the better equipped they are to differentiate their instruction and support their students' academic achievement (Herrera, 2010). This strategy enables students at all

levels of language proficiency to actively participate in the process of inductively determining the meanings of the vocabulary words.

Some teachers who implement this strategy admit to initially thinking that their CLD students would not be able to successfully complete the various tasks of the strategy because they require students to engage in higher-order thinking. Yet teachers have all found that this strategy actually enables their students to better retain the meanings of the vocabulary terms because they are not told the definitions at the outset. Rather, students must work out the definitions by using their own background knowledge, rationalization, and peer support. Consequently, Picture This has proved extremely effective in stretching students' critical thinking skills.

SPOTLIGHT: Early Literacy Connection

Research findings indicate that children's success in reading and writing depends on a solid background in the development of oral language skills (McGee & Richgels, 2003). At the preschool level, oral language development not only contributes to children's literacy success but also plays a pivotal role in their academic and social development. Young children generate language when their beginning efforts are accepted and reinforced. According to the National Research Council (1998), language development during the preschool years—in particular the development of a rich vocabulary and of some familiarity with the language forms used for communication and literacy—constitutes an important domain of preparation for formal reading instruction.

Providing meaningful opportunities for oral interaction is one way teachers can foster vocabulary acquisition for young CLD students. To help these children catch up with their peers who are native English speakers, we need to provide comprehensive instruction that includes oral language activities, language activities, and direct teaching of key vocabulary and language structures. The Picture This strategy is a structured oral language activity in which students are able to develop their oral English language skills.

To modify the Picture This strategy for young CLD students, teachers can perform the following activity.

Activation:

- Select two pictures that represent two of the key vocabulary words from a story you are going to read aloud.
- Rather than having the students individually try to draw or write what they see when they look at each picture, post each picture at the front of the room on a large piece of poster paper or on a white board.
- To keep the two pictures separate, we recommend displaying the pictures as a T-Chart. Tell the students they are going to play a game called "I Spy!"
- Explain that it is their job to "spy" or name all the things they see in the picture. Give students a few minutes to look at each picture and then have them share all the things they spied with a partner.
  - If possible, try to pair CLD students who speak the same native language (L1) so they can communicate in that language if they choose.

- Next, ask students to orally share with their partner one thing they spied in each picture until all partners have shared. Be sure to write students' comments below the corresponding picture.
  - If students choose to share in their L1, write their responses in the L1 (if possible) and in English.
- You can also invite students to come up to the poster paper or white board and draw what they see. As you are writing, talk about the words and labels given by the students to promote their oral language development.
- After recording what the students see, ask them what they feel when they look at the picture.
- Have students share with a partner before recording group responses on the T-Chart.
- Once again, focus on highlighting the oral language used by the students to describe their feelings.

Connection:

- Finally, show the students the two vocabulary words and have them predict which word belongs with which picture and why. Explain to the students that they are making a guess based on the clues they have so far.
- Once the class has reached a group consensus, tape the vocabulary words under the corresponding pictures and tell the students that it is their job to listen for the words in the story.
- Begin reading the story. Tell the students that when they hear the words from the story, you will stop reading. Then the whole class will check to see if they matched the correct vocabulary word to each picture.

Affirmation:

- After you have read the story, revisit the two pictures and vocabulary words from the story.
- Put students into small groups of three or four. Explain that each group will generate two sentences for each of the vocabulary words. Each sentence will be written on an individual sticky note.
- After each group has written their two sentences, bring the whole class back together. Each group will read their sentences and place the sticky note on the appropriate picture from the story.
- Continue this process until all of the groups have shared their sentences.

Biography-Driven Response to Intervention

Picture This supports students' connections to content by allowing them to use visuals as a way of constructing knowledge. Students activate their background knowledge as they record "What I see" and "What I think." The strategy can be taken toward tiered instruction or used as an extension to tiered instruction. Picture This helps students work with the target words in multiple contexts, understand how context clues work, and explore formal definitions. These aspects of literacy are critical for systematic instruction of the core curriculum. As an extension of Tier 1, the same visuals used at the beginning of the strategy can be used again for added intervention as students continue to practice the words and apply their learning.

One Classroom's Perspective

Activating:

Our reading series has three vocabulary words each week that students focus on. Vocabulary is a crucial part of comprehension, and my students come to me with limited vocabulary. They are often able to draw a picture and describe a word but fail to know the word itself. Sitting at their desks in teams of three, students had to discover three new vocabulary words. They did this through the Picture This strategy. First, students were directed to turn over a picture and draw what they saw and write down any thoughts that came into their heads.

Connecting:

Second, students were given the dictionary definitions of the vocabulary words and had to match them to the correct picture. Third, students were given short paragraphs or sentences from the text we were going to read and were instructed to match them to the correct picture and definition. Then, students were given the vocabulary words and had to match them with the correct definition, picture, and text passages. Throughout this lesson students were able to communicate with their teammates and bounce ideas off each other. The implementation of this strategy provided me with the insight that many of my CLD students use the context to figure out the meaning of new vocabulary words. They also benefited from the use of pictures and dictionary definitions. I was impressed with their ideas and thoughts.

Affirming:

After the vocabulary lesson strategy, students partnered to read the story with their new vocabulary words in context. Students were asked to create new meaningful sentences with their partners using the vocabulary words. I felt that this lesson went well. I do believe my students benefited from the strategy. Students were able to successfully give definitions and use the vocabulary words correctly in context. All CLD students were able to use the text, pictures, and definitions to discover the correct vocabulary word. The students were excited and engaged throughout the activity.

Student Voices

I liked using the picture. It helped me understand what the word meant.

> —*ELL Student*
> *Speech Emergent*

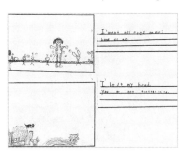

Being able to write down what the word means to me really helps me remember. I got to talk to my friends about the words too. That really helps a lot!

> —*ELL Student*
> *Intermediate Fluency*

I really liked being able to figure out the word using all the clues! It was a lot more fun than just writing down the definitions, and I really had to think about what meanings would go with what pictures. I hope we get to do this activity again!

> —*ELL Student*
> *Advanced Fluency*

TEMPLATE: Picture This

Name: _____

Date: _____

Picture This

	What I See . . .	What I Think . . .
Picture #1		
Picture #2		
Picture #3		

STRATEGY

Pictures and Words

I think this lesson really benefited each of the students because they were able to draw what they were thinking and then put words to their pictures. For many of the students, doing the drawing first really helped them to be able to come up with the words that matched their drawing. The students really reacted positively to the lesson because they were able to use their creativity. I also think that having the students come back together at the end and share what they drew and the order in which they drew it really helped to emphasize the point of retell.

—*Kristin Fisher, 4th-Grade Teacher*

Where Theory Meets Practice

Student motivation plays a large role in facilitating our success as educators. Lessons that are relevant and interesting keep students engaged in the learning process and increase student motivation (Routman, 2003). Herrera (2010) notes that it is easy for us as educators to "get stuck in what has been researched or prescribed within our own teaching cultures and pay little attention to the cultural context of the student or the role of individual motivation in the learning process" (p. 53). By building upon CLD students' existing knowledge, educators are more likely to motivate and engage their students in the learning process. As Jensen (2008) emphasized in his research, "in order to get learners to be creative and have greater subject interest, higher self-esteem, and the ability to be reflective, there must be intrinsic motivation" (p. 124).

Additionally, it is important to provide CLD students the opportunity to make meaningful connections between what they know and new knowledge they are going to learn. In high-performing schools, these connections are explicitly made throughout the lesson to enhance student understanding (Gunning, 2006; Langer, 2001). To promote and make effective use of these connections, a variety of factors need to be in place:

- All students need to be held accountable for participating in the activity.
- All students need to be provided access to participate in the activity, regardless of their language proficiency level.
- Students' background knowledge and interests need to be captured at the onset of the lesson.
- Students' initial connections between their existing schemas and new content need to be documented.
- The activities used throughout the lesson need to reinforce (and further ignite) students' connections to the new material being held in working memory.
- Finally, students need to be able to use the text to make and articulate connections to the key concepts and the content-specific vocabulary used within the lesson (Herrera, 2010).

The power of the Pictures and Words strategy is that—by meeting all of the conditions identified above—it provides CLD students with the opportunity to make meaningful connections to text. Students are immediately asked to make and document connections to the text based on their own background knowledge. As the lesson proceeds, students reconceptualize their initial connections to reflect key content vocabulary and new content presented in the text. The ongoing restructuring stretches students both academically and cognitively as they continually refine their understanding. By having students document their evolving understanding as the lesson progresses, the strategy helps students develop a concrete tool for demonstrating their learning.

Materials Needed: Pictures and Words template (one per student) • sticky notes • books to share with the whole class • pencils/pens

ACTIVATION: A Canvas of Opportunity

Directions:

- **T** Begin the activity by first sharing with students the academic vocabulary of the lesson. When selecting the academic vocabulary, focus on the six to eight most important words that will communicate the essence of the story/topic for the lesson.
- **I** As you share the vocabulary with students, ask each one to write the words on a sheet of paper or in his or her vocabulary notebook. After students have written the words:
  - Have them individually rate their understanding of each word by putting a plus sign (+) next to the word if they think they know it and could use it in a sentence or a minus sign (–) next to the word if they do not know it.
  - For words with a plus sign, have them use the word in a sentence or write its definition in their own words next to their rating.
  - For words with a minus sign, still encourage them to try to use the

word in a sentence or come up with a definition for it.

- **P** Once all students have finished the self-assessment task, have them discuss the words with a peer. This will help students make initial links between their background knowledge and the academic vocabulary.
- During the peer discussions, listen to the connections students are making and note the words they indicated in their notebooks they do not know.
- Next, share the title of the story/topic that the class is about to explore.
- **I** At this point, provide each student with a copy of the Pictures and Words template and four sticky notes (one sticky note for each box on the template). Have students place the sticky notes over the boxes.
- Ask students to think about the academic vocabulary for the lesson as well as the title of the story/topic and then use their background knowledge to predict what they think the

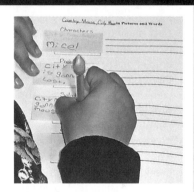

story/lesson will be about. Have them draw a visual representation for or write (in their native language [L1] or in English) four concepts, characters, events, etc. (one for each sticky note) that represent their predictions.

- **P** Have students do another quick turn-and-talk to share their predictions with a partner. As they do this, circulate around the room and listen to the ideas the students are sharing with each other.

Activating the "*i*"

How does this process activate CLD students' existing knowledge?

- **Sociocultural:** Engaging students in academic talk with their peers about the key vocabulary and their individual predictions from the outset of the lesson promotes culturally relevant and biography-driven connections to the text.
- **Linguistic:** Academic discussions among peers provide all students the opportunity to check their understanding one on one, which keeps affective filters low. When students are strategically paired, they also have the opportunity to provide and receive L1 support as needed.

- **Academic:** Previewing key vocabulary before the lesson and having students define it in their own words provides a springboard from which they can make connections to key content.
- **Cognitive:** Asking students to predict what they think the story is about based on the academic vocabulary helps build CLD students' ability to draw on their background knowledge when completing academic tasks.

CONNECTION: The Broad & Narrow Strokes of Learning

Directions:

- **T** Once students have finished discussing their predictions, bring them back together and share with them that they will be confirming/disconfirming their predictions as the class proceeds with the story/lesson. If the class is using a text, students will transfer sticky notes with accurate predictions to the pages that confirm those predictions. (All sticky notes with disconfirmed predictions will simply be removed from the template.)

- Begin reading the story/text and stop when you encounter any of the academic vocabulary words. Ask for volunteers to share their own sentences/definitions of the word. Using the context cues in the text, determine as a whole group what the meaning of word is and have all students write

it down on a piece of paper or in their notebook.

- As you read the story or cover the topic with the students, stop at predetermined points and model your own mental imagery/conceptual connections regarding that section of material. You may choose to share a text–self connection, text–text connection, or text–world connection by saying, "This section reminds me of _____."

- **I** After providing this initial modeling, at relevant points in the the the lesson have students stop and record their own mental images/connections to the different sections of the story or aspects of the topic by drawing in the template boxes. Have students use the lines beside the boxes to write associated details.

- **P** Periodically allow students to do a turn-and-talk with a partner regarding the specific section of the story/topic and have them share their mental images with each other. Remind students that they can share text–self, text–text, and text–world connections.

Author Talk: Connection

Pictures and Words is ideal for supporting teachers in aligning their instruction with the Common Core State Standards (CCSS), especially with regard to the type of text they have their students read. For example, several teachers have focused on using Pictures and Words with informational text, which is an emphasis of the CCSS. This emphasis is due in large part to the disproportionate percentage of narrative text versus informational text taught at the elementary level. Narrative text is often easier for CLD students to visualize. Pictures and Words prompts CLD students to visualize what is occurring in informational text as well, and thereby supports teachers in providing scaffolding that allows all students to access and understand more challenging informational text. Initial implementation of this strategy with narrative text and subsequent use with informational text will promote CLD students' strategic use of visualization across text types.

The adaptability of this strategy has allowed highly successful implementation by classroom teachers. In fact, I am continually surprised by the ways in which teachers at multiple grade levels have adapted and used Pictures and Words. For example, teachers have used it as a strategy to get to know their students at the beginning of the school year, by having their students write about their lives in Pictures and Words. With younger students, the teacher might use three boxes and ask the students to draw the following:

- *Picture 1:* Family and/or important people in the student's life
- *Picture 2:* Favorite activity or hobby
- *Picture 3:* Favorite thing about school or something that makes school challenging

For older students, the teacher might use six boxes and have the students identify six things about their biography. Teachers who have used Pictures and Words in this way report that it has been one of the best ways for them to get to know about the lives of their students.

Connecting to the "*i*+1"
How does this process move CLD students from the known to the unknown?

- **Sociocultural:** Explicit modeling by the teacher during the lesson helps CLD students continue to make schematic connections throughout the lesson.
- **Linguistic:** The use of oral discussion between peers, along with the hands-on application of writing their individual connections on the Pictures and Words template, empowers CLD students to articulate their evolving understanding and connections to text.

- **Academic:** Picture This promotes students' concrete connections to text. When students formally articulate text–self, text–text, or text–world connections, the content becomes more culturally relevant.
- **Cognitive:** By sharing their own mental images/conceptual connections with peers, CLD students are exposed to multiple perspectives and are able to redefine their understanding as necessary.

 AFFIRMATION: A Gallery of Understanding

Directions:

- **S** Have students in small groups discuss their mental images/connections so they can see that, even though they all heard the same content, their mental images/ideas/connections differ due to their unique perspectives.
- **S** Ask the members of each group to work together to create a group statement that summarizes the essential aspects of the story/topic.
  - Remind students to use within their summaries the academic vocabulary they have learned and recorded throughout the lesson.
- Once the groups have finished their summaries, have them share the summaries with the class.

- Allow students to display their completed templates on the wall (if they wish) so that the class can see the various interpretations/connections of their peers.
- **I** Students also can use the Pictures and Words template at the end of the lesson to summarize their learning by including images related to the critical content in the boxes and incorporating the target vocabulary in their written descriptions. Students can then use their completed templates to write individual summary paragraphs.

Affirming Student Ownership: "*I*" Get It!
How does this process celebrate CLD student learning?

- **Sociocultural:** Students' completed Pictures and Words templates represent their biography-driven understanding and interpretation of the text.
- **Linguistic:** Sharing their completed template with peers allows CLD students to articulate their cognitive understandings and biography-driven connections in their own words. Hearing peers' interpretations of the text also provides CLD students with the opportunity to learn from their peers.

- **Academic:** The completed Pictures and Words templates and group summaries provide concrete evidence of students' academic understanding.
- **Cognitive:** Through peer discussion and collaboration, students are challenged to apply new learning and articulate knowledge gained at a much higher cognitive level than if asked only to complete the task independently.

SPOTLIGHT: Early Literacy Connection

Pictures are universal stimuli to aid learning that provide a starting point for language sharing in the classroom. As Curtis and Bailey (2001) have stated, "Pictures provide something to talk about. They take the focus off the language learner during oral practice and turn it to the picture" (p. 11). Teachers can use pictures containing familiar objects to elicit words from children's listening and speaking vocabularies. Because pictures can be used as a stimulus for reading, writing, and other literacy activities, they have much potential for use with CLD students.

Early childhood teachers can use pictures to introduce and reinforce key vocabulary words that are relevant to the topic the class is learning. A picture can evoke mental images to help second language learners recall a term or concept. Pictures can be used with any and all languages, are easily accessible, and can be used to reinforce literal, critical, and creative thinking.

To modify the Pictures and Words strategy for young CLD students, teachers can do the following activity:

Activation:

- To use this strategy with young children, use a book that has vivid pictures that students can readily connect to during a read-aloud.
- Begin the lesson by sharing three vocabulary words. Write the words on the board, pronounce them, and have students echo them back. Then have students briefly discuss the words with a partner.
- Next, rather than having each student predict what he or she thinks the story is going to be about by writing on individual sticky notes (as these are much too small for them to manipulate), have the students look at the cover of the book and talk to their partner to make a "partner prediction" (guess) about what they think the story will be about.

- Then, have the partners work together to draw their prediction on a piece of paper that they can share with the whole class before reading the story. As students share their pictures, post them at the front of the room and label the objects in the picture.
  - If time is limited, have each set of partners orally share their predictions with the whole class and document these on a large piece of chart paper at the front of the room.

Connection:

- To ensure that students are actively involved in the reading of the story, tell them that they will be listening to the story to see if their predictions (guesses) are right.
- Explain to students that they also will be listening for the three vocabulary words. If they hear one of the words, their job is to raise their hand to let the teacher know so he or she can stop reading and everyone can talk about what each word means in the context of the story.
- After this discussion for each word, have students use the Pictures and Words template to draw a picture related to the meaning of the word and use the lines provided to write the word.

Affirmation:

- After reading the story, ask the students to look at their pictures again.
- Explain to the students that they can make any changes to their original prediction pictures to make their predictions correct.
- After the students have revisited their prediction pictures, have them share with each other their predictions and the changes that were made to the pictures.

Author Talk: Parental Use of the Strategy

The Pictures and Words strategy is an activity parents can do with their children in their home environment. Employing the strategy in the home setting promotes language development in students' native language, with the parents providing their own biography-driven perspectives to their children. Parents can point to various objects in a picture and label them in their native language. This helps to build critical background knowledge as well as maintain the development of their children's native language. Encouraging parents to explore language through pictures in their native language also promotes English language acquisition, because abilities and knowledge developed in the first language often transfer to the second language.

Biography-Driven Response to Intervention

As we consider modifications required for specific responses to intervention, we need to think specifically in terms of students' individual needs. One way to focus on students' needs is through the Activation phase of Pictures and Words. For students requiring intensive English language development at the level of Tier 2 or Tier 3, the teacher can have them use the strategy as a framework for connecting their understanding of the vocabulary words to their individual backgrounds. With its focus on individual predictions recorded on sticky notes and then discussed with peers, the strategy can be used to tap into students' cultural and linguistic schemas.

One Classroom's Perspective

Activating:

Before the lesson I first thought of the group of students that I would be working with and their background. I decided to first look at their language skills, because this is a reading lesson that is focusing on fluency and comprehension. I knew that I had three CLD students in my group whose L1 is something other than English. When taking this into consideration I knew that I needed to go over some key vocabulary words before the students read the passage, which was about plants. Next I looked at the students' cognitive abilities and what information they might already know about plants. I knew that in 3rd grade the students had studied about how plants grow and the things they need to be able to grow. I also knew that in 3rd grade they did some experimenting with plants. Finally, I thought about what type of academic experience the students have and what would be the best way to engage them in this academic assessment with retell and comprehension. From working with these students this year, I know that when I give them a list of things to do they tend to get frustrated and at times shut down. After thinking about this response, I decided to take the lesson one step at a time: I would have them read first, then we would talk about the

reading, and finally I would have them put what we talked about into pictures and words. In addition, I took into consideration the students' sociocultural background. I tried to think about what types of situations stress these students academically to the point they are unable to do their best work.

Connecting:

After having the students read the passage about plants silently, I called the whole group back together. Once the group was reassembled, I showed the students how to retell what they had just read by having them each give me a detail about the passage. After we did this as a whole group, I had the students get together with their shoulder partner and tell that person the first thing they were going to draw and write about on their Pictures and Words template. After the students shared with their partners, they got into their small groups and did a round robin to check to see if everyone had something similar to the others about the first retell Picture and Words. Finally, I had the students work independently on filling out the rest of the Pictures and Words boxes.

One Classroom's Perspective (continued)

Affirming:

Once the students had finished all of their drawings and words to go along with the drawings, I had them get back with their small groups. At this point, the students then shared their drawings and writings in the order in which they did them. Also during this time, I walked around the room and had some of the students in each group summarize what the group had discussed about the retell and the order in which it went. I assessed the students by looking and listening to how they put the details about plants and what the plants needed in order. The students really reacted positively to the lesson because they were able to use their creativity. I also think that by having the students come back together at the end and share what they drew, and the order in which they drew it, really helped to emphasize the point of retell. This also helped some of the students who may have been struggling with the order in which to put things to see how or in what order the other students put things.

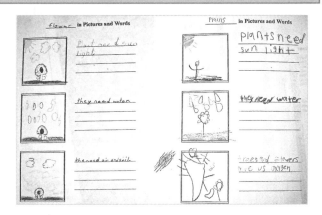

Student Voices

Before we drew the picture I did not like the reading part very much because I am not very good at reading, but I really liked the drawing part because I am really good at that.

—ELL Student
Intermediate Fluency

It was really helpful to be able to write sentences to explain my pictures. When I read them to my friend, she said she could tell I really knew what the words meant and how they went with the story. That made me feel really good!

—ELL Student
Intermediate Fluency

I really liked being able to put the sticky notes into my book because it helped me to see where the information was in the book. I was able to see if my predictions were right too!

—ELL Student
Advanced Fluency

TEMPLATE: Pictures and Words

Name: _____

Date: _____

_____ in Pictures and Words

STRATEGY

Mind Map

This strategy gave my students a chance to organize their own thoughts before being taught new content. They were each allowed to enter the lesson on their own level. They had the choice of writing or drawing their thoughts on the page. Next, my students were able to meet their social needs by having role models in the classroom during partner and small-group discussion. Students of all abilities were able to participate in this lesson on their level while learning important grade-level content.

—*Kerry Wasylk, 4th-Grade Teacher*

Where Theory Meets Practice

A mind map consists of words and pictures that are linked and arranged around a central key concept. Mind maps are generally used to generate, visualize, structure, and classify thoughts, and can serve as an aid in study, organization, problem solving, and writing (Buzan, 1989). Mind maps provide a great visual, especially for students who are in the process of learning English as a second language. They allow students to use colors, drawings, and powerful key words in English or their native language to represent concepts and relationships (Buzan, 1989).

For CLD students, mind maps are much more than just nonlinear representations of a text, story, or presentation. They are tools that can be used to promote learning and language development throughout a lesson. Educators first use mind maps to understand each student's background knowledge and ways of expressing that knowledge (Herrera, 2010). During the lesson, mind maps can help educators "tap into what students are thinking as they listen, interact, and work with the information that is shared during the lesson" (Herrera, 2010, p. 54). Teachers explicitly

model links between the new information that students add to their mind maps based on the lesson and the information that the students initially placed on their mind maps. Students make meaningful connections between the topic and the key content vocabulary, as well as connections among the vocabulary words (Blachowicz & Fisher, 2000).

Ultimately, mind maps help make students' ways of knowing and thinking public. The sharing that takes place among students as they work in small groups is particularly powerful, as the information shared among peers adds depth to their individual understanding of the topic. The completed mind maps serve to document the entire learning process.

A video clip illustrating implementation of this strategy appears on the DVD included with this book and is available for viewing online at:

www.tcpress.com/AcceleratingLiteracyVideos.html

Materials Needed: Blank sheet of paper (one per student) • poster paper • colored pencils/markers • pencils/pens • sticky notes (optional)

ACTIVATION: A Canvas of Opportunity

Directions:

- **I** Before you begin the lesson or cover the concept with the students, give them the topic and ask them to conduct a "What's in your mind?" regarding the topic. To do this, have students individually brainstorm about the topic for a minute, putting their results on a blank sheet of paper.
- Explain to the students that as they brainstorm, they should think in terms of both words and pictures, since the mind uses both linguistic (English and L1) and nonlinguistic representations. At this point, it is important to emphasize that there is no right or wrong answer.

- **S** Once the students are done their individual brainstorming, have them share their ideas in small groups.
- Next, give each group a piece of poster paper on which to draw their mind map. Have students write the concept in the middle of the poster paper and then ask all group members to add their individual ideas to their group's mind map using colored markers.
- Give students 3–5 minutes to individually illustrate or write something on the group's mind map.

- **T** Bring the class back together and have each group share their mind map with the class. When the groups have finished sharing, proceed with the lesson.

Author Talk: Activation

One of the questions I am most frequently asked when working with teachers of CLD students is, How can I make sure I am engaging all my CLD students in the lesson? With the Mind Map strategy, teachers have an immediate tool for monitoring CLD student engagement in multiple ways. First, all students brainstorm and document what they know about the topic before meeting in small groups. Teachers can gather these individual CLD students' responses to see what prior knowledge they brought to the lesson. Second, by allowing student responses to be linguistic and nonlinguistic in nature, CLD students at all levels of language proficiency are able to actively participate in the process and document their responses. Third, hav-

ing students share their ideas in small groups and once again document responses on the group's mind map gives the teacher another opportunity to actively engage CLD students in the learning process.

Teachers who have implemented the Mind Map strategy with CLD students have found that having students share responses in small groups also keeps their affective filters low because they are allowed to learn from one another as they discuss vocabulary words and lesson concepts. By providing the option to continue using linguistic as well as nonlinguistic representations, the teacher can ensure that all CLD students still have equal access to the activity. To help monitor student engagement and increase individual accountability, the teacher can have each student within each group use a different color of marker.

Activating the "i"

How does this process activate CLD students' existing knowledge?

- **Sociocultural:** Mind maps enable each student to quickly draw or write his or her own connections to the topic.
- **Linguistic:** Students at all levels of language proficiency are able to engage in this learning experience. The students are able to record their content knowledge using their own symbols and codes in a visual representation.

- **Academic:** Students are able to make links and connections to the topic in a systematic format. Because words do not always represent thoughts, this phase frees students from the "academic" constraints they often feel at the onset of a lesson.
- **Cognitive:** The Mind Map strategy supports students in quickly retrieving from memory, organizing, and documenting diverse pieces of information.

CONNECTION: The Broad & Narrow Strokes of Learning

Directions:

- **S** As you do the lesson, stop at regular intervals and have students in their small groups talk to each other about the different concepts being explained.
- **I** After students have finished discussing their ideas, have them individually add new information to the group's mind map using sticky notes or a marker of a color different from the one they used to record their initial understandings. By doing this, you will be able to distinguish brainstormed associations from new learning throughout the lesson (which may span several days).

- **S** You can further expand upon this task by asking students to work in their small groups to connect their new learning with their initial ideas on the mind map (as applicable).
- As students record and expand upon connections among the group concepts, informally monitor their work and listen to their conversations. During this time, note the following:
  - ○ Connections between students' existing knowledge and the topic that you can build upon within the lesson to make content more comprehensible to the students.
  - ○ Preexisting content vocabulary.

- ○ Key concepts/ideas that students are struggling with.
- **I** Have students individually continue to add words to clarify, elaborate, or incorporate content concepts on the mind maps throughout the lesson.

Connecting to the "*i*+1"
How does this process move CLD students from the known to the unknown?

- **Sociocultural:** More meaningful connections to the lesson are promoted among students when CLD students' experiences and knowledge, as shared in the Activation phase, are linked to the key content and vocabulary of the lesson.
- **Linguistic:** CLD students' connections are enhanced when they are allowed to engage in meaningful discussions with peers about the content/concepts on their mind maps.

- **Academic:** Because mind maps enable students to think about lesson content/concepts in a more visual manner, they remain more engaged in the learning process.
- **Cognitive:** Students continually support their metacognitive processes as they monitor their own learning by building upon existing knowledge and creating links with the new information.

AFFIRMATION: A Gallery of Understanding

Directions:

-
- **I** Allow students to individually use their mind maps to complete curricular tasks, end-of-chapter tests, or cloze exercises.
- Throughout this phase of the strategy, students are able to transfer their thoughts and connected ideas into a piece of writing. (**Note:** Transfer may not be automatic for all students; additional modeling and support may be needed to ensure that students are successful with the task.)
- Students can also individually write a summary at the end of the lesson, connecting all the ideas on the mind map.
- **P** Encourage students to share their final products with a partner to show all they have learned.

Affirming Student Ownership: *"I"* Get It!
How does this process celebrate CLD student learning?

- **Sociocultural:** The mind map is a visual representation of the progression of learning throughout for the students. Posting students' completed mind maps at the end of the unit is a great affirmation of both their background knowledge and their learning.
- **Linguistic:** Students are able to summarize their thoughts in a more effective manner, as they have the completed mind map to refer back to when discussing or writing about the topic.

- **Academic:** Mind maps provide CLD students with an easier way to learn and retain the information they will be assessed on, because it first originated from the language/symbols the students were most familiar with.
- **Cognitive:** Mind maps are a creative way for students to monitor their own learning.

SPOTLIGHT: Early Literacy Connection

Tabors, Roach, and Snow (2001) found that many factors impact the development of early literacy skills, including the amount of extended discourse at home, the density of rare or sophisticated words in home conversations, and parental support for literacy activities (e.g., book reading). To support parents in developing these early literacy skills with their children, it is important to provide them with concrete strategies they can use in the home with their children when engaged in literacy activities.

Families must be seen as an asset in the schooling process, and all families regardless of socioeconomic status, race, language, or culture can be important contributors to their children's success and to their children's school (Violand-Sanchez, Sutton, & Ware, 1991). Parents of CLD students may or may not be literate in English, but they can apply the Mind Map strategy immediately with their children regardless of the language in which the literacy activity is conducted. Mind Map enables CLD families to play an instrumental role in their children's academic success.

To modify the Mind Map strategy for young CLD students, teachers can do the following as a home–school connection:

Activation:

- To help parents of CLD students promote early literacy skills at home, you can send home bilingual books or books in the students' L1 before reading them in the classroom.

(continued on the next page)

SPOTLIGHT: Early Literacy Connection (*continued*)

Activation (*continued*):

- Ask the parents to read the book to their child and then encourage them to do a mind map with their child about the book.
- Write directions on how to make a mind map for the parents.
  - In the directions for the parents, tell them to label the mind map images as their children draw them to help the children associate the word with the picture (Buzan, 2003).
  - The parents can write the labels in whichever language they are most comfortable writing.
  - By performing this strategy in the native language, parents are supporting their children's future transfer of knowledge from the native language to English because they are providing the foundation in the L1.
- Send the necessary materials, such as paper and pencils, for the children to complete the project at home.
- When the children return to school the next day, encourage them to share their mind maps with you and/or the whole class. Even if the information is shared in the students' L1, you will have visual cues to the initial connections they made to the story.
- You can then work with the whole class to create a class mind map on the topic.
- To create the class mind map, have the students look at the cover of the book you will read from and talk to their partner about what they see and the connections they make to the picture.
- Then ask students to share aloud with the rest of the class one of their connections.

Connection:

- In creating the mind map for the whole class, use a large chart paper or the entire white board. This ensures that everyone can see the mind map and that there is room for everyone to add their connection.
- As students are sharing, have them come up one at a time and write or draw the related word or image on the class mind map.
- Have each student use a different-colored writing implement when marking on the mind map.
- Continue this process until all of the students have added their connection to the mind map.
- In pairs, have the students talk about the connections other students made on the mind map.
- Read the story aloud to the students. As you read the story, stop at specific points and draw the students' attention to the connections they made on the class mind map.

Affirmation:

- After reading the story, revisit the class mind map.
- Ask the students if there are any new connections they want to add.
- If there are new connections:
  - Have students talk to each other about the new connections they have formed and about some of the old ones that are already on the mind map.
  - Add students' new connections by putting the connections on sticky notes and adding them to the class mind map.

Biography-Driven Response to Intervention

As you work on the Mind Map strategy, have students create their individual mind maps on computers. These can be saved as evidence for targeted and intensive intervention. The same mind maps can serve as a tool for data collection and progress monitoring as you informally observe your students "during the process." Ask students to use their own words as well as the academic vocabulary as they add new ideas to the mind map on the computer. This will allow you to see whether students are able to use the academic vocabulary along with their own language. Further, you can use a checklist or a rubric to track your students' progress.

One Classroom's Perspective

Activating:

To promote the best possible learning for each of the CLD students in my classroom, I designed a lesson that took into consideration their experiential knowledge as well as the knowledge some of the students exhibited about nature and habitats. I needed to know what the students really new about habitats and nature prior to exposing them to a variety of animal habitats and diverse groups of animals within nature. I broke the students into multi-tiered groups in order to promote success for each of the students within his

or her cognitive ability. Through team collaboration, the "higher-level learner" was able to utilize expressive language to convey his or her knowledge of the subject matter. The ability to collaborate lowered the affective filter for the CLD students due to the stimulation of the peer-to-peer mentorship. The academic language facilitated the interaction between the peers. The ability of the students to access knowledge through engagement and excitement about learning was insightful. To authentically assess the knowledge the

students had prior to the lesson, I asked them to write what they knew about habitats and nature before conversing with their peers.

Connecting:

The students were brought together as an entire class to view a documentary about habitats and nature. I utilized the documentary to stimulate conversation and provide visual aids to the CLD students who had not been exposed to the concept of habitats. To reinforce cognition, I displayed pictures on the ELMO projector to help the students to connect with the vocabulary as well as habitats of animals we had viewed. While sitting on the carpet they shared their knowledge on the subject matter.

The students were asked to give responses as I questioned them about habitats, nature, and who lives where. We acted out various types of animals that live in nature. A few of the students wanted to be a tree, a cave, ... The access of knowledge, the engagement, and the excitement/hope of seeing real habitats (such as "log hotels") was evident. The students returned to their small groups to add information to their mind maps. Students worked with a partner to peer tutor as they wrote.

Affirming:

I used the Mind Map strategy to assess the students' learning by monitoring throughout the lesson their understanding of habitats and "log hotels." The students demonstrated their academic knowledge by writing a paper about living in a log hotel: "If I were a . . . living in a log hotel, I would . . . ." The written text from each student portrayed cognitive growth as they wrote about "slithering through a log hotel," "curling up in a log hotel," and "finding bugs in a log hotel and eating them for dinner." The ability of the students to see the log hotel as a "hotel" for animals in nature was clearly demonstrated and

depicted through their writings. The students participated in crawling, slithering, creeping, sliding, crunching, . . . as they entered a "log hotel" I created in our classroom. The students added more detail to their mind map after they participated in the kinesthetic activity—they took on the role of the animal in nature in order to clearly define its habitat. Students collaborated on who they were in the log hotel and what they did. Students shared their work on the ELMO and their peers politely added comments, praise, or suggestions. While outside, they now constantly find "log hotels."

Author Talk:
One Classroom's Perspective

It is important to connect to our CLD students' *ways of knowing,* for it is in these connections that we find the wealth of information they bring to the classroom. Catherine Hollis, the 1st-grade teacher who contributed the One Classroom's Perspective for this strategy, discusses the kinds of insights students shared from their background knowledge:

> The students were able to demonstrate their learnings by drawing in personal experiences from their culture in order to relate (make a connection) to the content and vocabulary being studied. For example, two of my students are from Puerto Rico, and they discussed habitats by the beach in Puerto Rico and how they were different. The students asked the students how they were different (i+1) and they were able to reference water animals versus land animals and habitats—who would live in a log hotel and who would not. My student from the Philippines discussed how different the "log hotels" looked in his country. The students asked him several questions in order to get a "mind movie" of the habitat in the Philippines.

When we help students make their knowledge public, their peers can benefit and learn from this knowledge as well.

Student Voices

I like mind mapping because I can see what other kids are doing. I can learn from what they are writing or drawing on the mind map paper.

—*ELL Student*
Intermediate Fluency

Mind mapping is cool because you can put down stuff you know about and add new stuff you learn about.

—*ELL Student*
Speech Emergent

Mind mapping is fun because I can color pictures or write words. I can ask my friends what they are writing about and we can help each other learn!

—*ELL Student*
Intermediate Fluency

STRATEGY

Tri-Fold

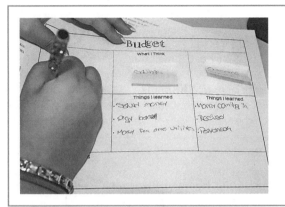

The Tri-Fold strategy provided me with evidence of student learning from the beginning of the lesson through to the end. I had a clear understanding of what the students brought to the lesson in the way of prior knowledge because of their initial sticky notes. Students were really able to make deep connections between what they read and what they already knew by reevaluating their ideas.

—*Reesa Darby, 5th-Grade Teacher*

Where Theory Meets Practice

According to research by Gregory and Kuzmich (2004), sequencing is an important thinking skill for students to develop because it helps them with the writing process and in being able to relate a series of events. To be successful at sequencing information from text, students should first understand the structure of the text. Tompkins (2007) recommends that teachers "consider the structure of the text as they decide how to introduce an informational book, what type of graphic organizer or diagram to make to help emphasize the big ideas, and what points to emphasize in discussions" (p. 318). By first evaluating the text in this way, teachers are able to provide their students with a structured approach to reading and analyzing the material. With such guidance, students have an opportunity to focus on the big ideas in the text rather than becoming overwhelmed by less important information.

The key to such an approach is to provide students with strategies for working with the text that will increase their comprehension and internalization of key content. Summarization is one such strategy that can be especially helpful when working with CLD students, some of whom may not be familiar with the expectations traditionally associated with summarization in U.S. schools. Herrera (2010, p. 55) recommends the following:

- First identifying key concepts from a passage or lesson and then asking students to locate textual explanations/ support for each concept or to record points of the lesson related to each concept.
- Providing explicit instruction on how to differentiate key information from supporting details.
- Incorporating opportunities for students to work together to practice differentiating essential information from nonessential details.
- Supporting students in individual summarization tasks by providing a graphic organizer to help guide their thinking.
- Providing students with examples of written summaries and modeling for students how information contained on a graphic organizer can be used to develop a written summary of content knowledge.

The Tri-Fold strategy provides CLD students with a concrete tool that can be applied in the classroom to explicitly model the process of summarization. In addition to following the recommendations outlined above, the Tri-Fold strategy incorporates the use of visuals, peer learning, and hands-on tools to enhance CLD students' comprehension and engagement. Furthermore, because students are able to apply the strategy throughout the lesson to explore sequences of ideas/events, they are able to see that vocabulary and concepts are interrelated.

Materials Needed: Tri-Fold template (one per student) • vocabulary words on precut strips of paper (one set per student) • textbook • sticky notes • paper • pencils/pens

45

ACTIVATION: A Canvas of Opportunity

Directions:

- **S** Organize students in groups of four or five students, and give each student a Tri-Fold template.
- **I** Depending upon the skill/topic of the day, ask students first to individually think of any concepts or images they associate with the topic.
- **S** After students have individually brainstormed ideas, have them discuss their ideas within their small group.

- As the groups are discussing ideas, circulate around the room to gather some of the ideas students are sharing.
- **I** Next, have students individually draw or write (using L1 or L2) their key ideas on three to six sticky notes (one idea per sticky note). The number of sticky notes used might vary depending on the topic.

- Have students place their sticky notes on the middle part of the Tri-Fold under "Our Connections."

Author Talk: Activation

As educators, it is easy to approach instruction with specific expectations in mind. Yet when working with CLD students, it is important to remember that their cultural background serves at their "template for the organization of knowledge" (Byers & Byers, 1985, p. 28). In other words, the cultural background of CLD students largely influences the way they individually think about the academic content presented to them in the classroom setting. Being aware of this, and using students' culturally driven understanding as a springboard from which to build greater depth of understanding, greatly enhances their comprehension. Teachers are most effective at implementing the Tri-Fold strategy when they listen closely to what their students are saying. Specifically, they need to note the verbal as well as the nonverbal cues of their students and build upon these. Teachers need to look for patterns in their students' responses, because these patterns are indicative of students' understanding as well as their areas of confusion.

Activating the "*i*"

How does this process activate CLD students' existing knowledge?

- **Sociocultural:** What students think and how they express it is situated in their cultural identity, which may conflict with traditional school expectations. The Tri-Fold strategy provides CLD students with an avenue to express their culturally bound perspectives in an academic way.
- **Linguistic:** Students' oral sharing of their initial connections allows them to express their biography-driven understanding in a safe environment.

- **Academic:** Students are held accountable for making connections to the topic when they are asked to document their ideas in the "Our Connections" portion of the Tri-Fold template.
- **Cognitive:** CLD students are learning to process and document their understanding in a systematic way.

CONNECTION: The Broad & Narrow Strokes of Learning

Directions:

- **T** Continue with the lesson and explain to students that they are going to focus on sequencing ideas/events related to the topic.
- **S** If desired, you can ask students to do a jigsaw of the text to look at the events covered. For the jigsaw, have each student in the small group take a different part of the story/chapter and silently read it.
- After students have finished reading the text, have them come back together and share with the small group their understanding and ideas about the text. Have students pay particular attention to the order of events/ideas. If students read the text using the jigsaw, have them share with the group the events/ideas from their part of the story/chapter.

- Next, have students evaluate the ideas they included on the sticky notes to determine whether they reflect one of the critical events discussed in the text. If the idea on a sticky note is not a key event, have students remove the sticky note from the Tri-Fold.
- **I** After students have evaluated their original ideas, have them individually use what they learned from their group discussion about the text to add additional key events on sticky notes (one event per sticky note) for a total of at least three events.
- Have students individually rearrange the "event" sticky notes and place them on their Tri-Fold in the order in which the events occurred in the text to create a sequence.

- As students place the "event" sticky notes, have them also add details regarding those events in the "Things I Learned" column of the Tri-Fold.
- **S** When students have finished adding ideas, have them talk with their group members to share their added learnings.

Connecting to the "*i*+1"
How does this process move CLD students from the known to the unknown?

- **Sociocultural:** Students' ongoing discussion with peers to check understanding and determine key events helps make learning more meaningful for CLD students because past experiences are being shared and new perspectives are being added and understood.
- **Linguistic:** Careful consideration of your CLD students' linguistic proficiency when dividing the text for the jigsaw activity can allow you to differentiate the amount of reading each student receives to reflect each individual's linguistic abilities.

- **Academic:** All students are held accountable for taking part in the learning process and reporting key information from the reading back to the group.
- **Cognitive:** The group interaction during application of the Tri-Fold strategy prompts students to engage in ongoing monitoring of their own understanding of the text so that they can articulate key concepts with their peers.

AFFIRMATION: A Gallery of Understanding

Directions:

- **I** After students have finished sharing their additional learning with their group, have the students individually create a short summary connecting their personal ideas together. Have them record their work in the "Summary" column of the Tri-Fold.
- **S** Next, have group members work together to create a timeline of their combined events on a separate sheet of paper.
- Have students in their groups talk about cause and effect using the ideas on their Tri-Folds and the group timeline as a reference.
- Finally, have students as a group write a paragraph summarizing one or more aspects of their group discussion or overall learning from the lesson.

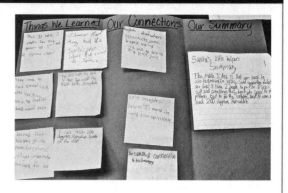

Affirming Student Ownership: *"I" Get It!*
How does this process celebrate CLD student learning?

- **Sociocultural:** CLD students work collaboratively to express their combined perspectives, which promotes respect and appreciation for one another as individuals and as fellow learners.
- **Linguistic:** CLD students are engaged in practicing and using grade-level, content vocabulary throughout the lesson, which promotes their academic English language skills.

- **Academic:** All CLD students are held to the same high expectations as their monolingual English-speaking peers.
- **Cognitive:** CLD students are actively conceptualizing and documenting their understanding of curricular concepts and the relationship between these concepts and key content vocabulary.

 SPOTLIGHT: Early Literacy Connection

Recognizing sequencing and the correct order of events in a story is a critical skill for young students to develop. Identifying the beginning, middle, and end of a process helps children to remember the procedure and understand that most steps have a logical sequence. However, for young learners, the concept of sequencing can be very abstract. You can best teach the concept in a hands-on activity. The Tri-Fold strategy is a great tool for making sequencing more concrete and understandable. When the students seem to understand the sequential structure of a reading, you can move on to using specific details to describe the characters, setting, problem, etc.

Young CLD students need the opportunity to learn through hands-on activities as a way of enriching the learning experience. CLD students learn while discussing, investigating, creating, and discovering with other students. As CLD students become familiar with the beginning–middle–end structure, they begin to make decisions about content and process, requiring less teacher support and allowing more interactive learning experiences to occur (Cooperstein & Kocevar-Weidinger, 2004).

To modify the Tri-Fold strategy for young CLD students, teachers can do the activity described on the next page.

(*continued on the next page*)

SPOTLIGHT: Early Literacy Connection (*continued*)

Activation:

When initially teaching this strategy for understanding the sequential elements of beginning, middle, and end, start by having students complete the sequence of an event from their own lives.

- Fold a piece of chart paper into three different sections.
- Explain to the student that they are going to learn about the concept of beginning, middle, and end.
- On the folded chart paper, start in the middle section and draw something that you did before school this morning (i.e., brush your teeth). Then write a sentence at the bottom of the page describing that picture.
- Next, move to the first section (beginning) and draw an event that happened directly before the event that was drawn in the middle section. Again, write a sentence at the bottom of the page describing the picture.
- Finally, move to the last section (end), and draw something that happened directly after the middle event. Again, write a sentence at the bottom of the page describing the picture.
- Explain to the students that they are going to create their own Tri-Fold of their own personal event.
- Brainstorm with the students on possible personal events that they could write about in their Tri-Fold.
- Have the students share their ideas with the whole class.

Connection:

- Have the students fold a piece of paper into three different parts.
  - Depending on the age and abilities of the students, you may have to fold the paper for them.
- After the students have their folded piece of paper, explain that they are going to draw a picture of a per-

sonal event in the middle section and leave space at the bottom of the page for writing.

- In the first section (beginning), have the students draw something that happened directly before the event they drew in the middle section. Again, they need to leave space at the bottom for writing.
- In the last section (end), have the students draw an event that happened right after the one depicted in the middle section, leaving space at the bottom for writing.
- After the three pictures are drawn, have the students verbally share their sequence of events with a partner.
- Next, have them write a sentence for each picture.
  - If the students struggle with writing, they can dictate their sentence to you or another adult.

Affirmation:

- After the students have completed their Tri-Fold, have them share their personal event with two other students in the classroom.
- When all of the students have shared their Tri-fold story, have them reassemble as a whole class.
- Explain to the students that they are going to write a short personal narrative from the information on their Tri-Fold.
- On a blank sheet of paper, have the students write each of the sentences from their Tri-Fold in the order of beginning, middle, and end. This creates a story of their personal event from the Tri-Fold activity.

Note: When students are comfortable with the tasks and processes of this strategy, you can implement the strategy with fairy tales, folktales, and fiction stories such as "Goldilocks and the Three Bears," which will help to reinforce the concept of beginning, middle, and end.

Biography-Driven Response to Intervention

Tri-Fold is a strategy that can support students as they take their initial thoughts about a topic toward a more thorough understanding of the content. This strategy is a great way to help students build on their original thoughts regarding the topic and connect them to the learning gained during the Connection phase. When the strategy is used as part of an intervention plan, teachers can look for evidence of growth and language enhancement in the completed Tri-Fold page. The tool itself provides students with meaningful repetition of the content, an important aspect of core instruction.

One Classroom's Perspective

Activating:

I know that my students enjoy learning more about new subjects and are very curious by nature. These students bring various types of background knowledge to our class discussions, and because of this I knew that their group discussions would be rich. The Tri-Fold activity allowed students to tap into their schema about the topic of working with satellites before they were expected to learn more and share their knowledge. This gave some of my hesitant learners a chance to get comfortable with the topic at hand before instruction began. The students were given the opportunity to think individually about the prior knowledge they had about the topic and use sticky notes to record that knowledge. I made sure to explain to the students when introducing the activity that they would be adding to their knowledge of the subject and that their thinking might change as we continued.

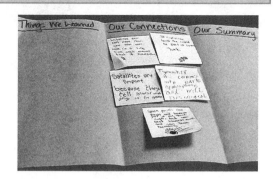

Connecting:

During the lesson, students were placed in four groups, each containing four students. I selected group members by using data on the students' reading comprehension and fluency levels. Because the students were grouped for mixed abilities, the arrangement allowed for some peer teaching to occur. After students had created an individual list of their prior knowledge, they shared with their teammates.

The reading for the day was divided among students in each team using the jigsaw method. Students were given pages to read in their book, and then after all were done reading, they were asked to come up with no fewer than three key ideas they had learned from their reading. They also were asked to reevaluate their prior knowledge on the sticky notes.

I had a clear understanding of what the students brought to the lesson in the way of prior knowledge because of their initial sticky notes. I was also able to determine how their thinking changed because they were asked to reevaluate their learning and move their "prior knowledge" sticky notes if they felt they did not relate to the topic after they had done their reading. By tracking

the students' self-evaluation, I was able to see how well they had read the information in the book, and could see where I needed to fill in the gaps in their knowledge.

Affirming:

Finally, each group created a team summary of their learnings. The student summaries helped by providing a conclusion to what the students knew and had learned through their reading for the day.

Student Voices

It was good because it took a lot of teamwork to combine our ideas together, and it made us think more about what we read.

—*ELL Student*
Intermediate Fluency

It helped us learn because we had to rethink what we read and what we already knew. We really had to remember what we had learned and what we read in the book.

—*ELL Student*
Intermediate Fluency

It exercised teamwork and helped tell if you were paying attention. It helped learning because writing down helps you remember what you read better.

—*ELL Student*
Advanced Fluency

TEMPLATE: Tri-Fold

Tri-Fold

Things I Learned	Our Connections	Summary

STRATEGY

Listen Sketch Label

I implemented this strategy to explain the concept of figurative language. Students were able to discuss and explain how they determined the meaning by using isolated words as the basis. Other students shared previous schema from other lessons to help identify connections between core content and the idiom represented. The diverse ideas of isolated words demonstrated the background and "social world" of each student. This strategy really helped students understand that language—whether present day, past, or from another culture—can mean more than one thing.

—*Devin Beursken, 1st-Grade Teacher*

Where Theory Meets Practice

When students encounter words and phrases in text, it is important for them to be able to determine the correct meaning of each. Many have both literal and figurative meanings. According to Tompkins (2007), "literal meanings are the explicit, dictionary meanings, and figurative meanings are metaphorical or use figures of speech" (p. 182). There are three main types of figurative language: similes, metaphors, and idioms. A simile is a comparison signaled by the use of the word *like* or *as*. An example of a simile is *The water is like the sun*. A metaphor compares two things by implying one is something else, but the terms *like* or *as* are not used. Rita Mae Brown authored one of the most powerful metaphors related to language and culture: *Language is a road map of a culture. It tells you where its people come from and where they are going.* An idiom is a phrase in which the combined words have a meaning different from the dictionary definitions of the individual words: for example, *Easy as ABC*. While this idiom is meant to imply that something will be as easy as learning the ABCs, for second language learners this is not necessarily a simple task. This idiom is difficult to understand figuratively, and it might also be literally incorrect for CLD students!

The use of figurative language occurs quite naturally in everyday conversation as parents and teachers talk with children. For the most part, children who are native speakers of a language are very adept at inferring the meaning of figurative phrases based on the context of conversations. However, for CLD students, the meaning of such language is not always clear. In fact, CLD students in the early stages of second language acquisition are inclined to translate these phrases literally, which causes even more confusion. Consider the following idiom: *It's raining cats and dogs!* Translated literally, a CLD student would expect to walk outside a building and see cats and dogs falling from the sky. Therefore, it is important to provide students with concrete strategies they can use to break down and clarify the meaning of various forms of figurative language.

Listen Sketch Label is a strategy that takes CLD students through a step-by-step process of determining the meaning of figurative language. The strategy incorporates the skill of visualization as well as multiple opportunities for student collaboration. Students are encouraged to share examples of figurative language from English as well as their native language. Combined with opportunities for illustrating the meanings of various phrases, this strategy is sure to pique students' interest and keep them engaged throughout the lesson.

A video clip illustrating implementation of this strategy appears on the DVD included with this book and is available for viewing online at:

www.tcpress.com/AcceleratingLiteracyVideos.html

Materials Needed: Listen Sketch Label template (one per student) • index cards (one per student) • copies of short passages that include the use of figurative language (idioms, metaphors, similes) • pencils/pens

---

ACTIVATION: A Canvas of Opportunity

Directions:

- Identify books/poems that you can use to teach different types of figurative language.
- **S** Place students in groups of three or four students and give each student a Listen Sketch Label template. (*Note:* The template can be copied on both sides to double the number of boxes for student response if desired.)
- **T** Explain to the students that they are going to do a strategy that will help them understand the actual intent of figurative language. Scaffold students' understanding of the concept of figurative language by providing two or three examples of figurative language (e.g., It's raining cats and dogs; It's as big as a whale; It's a thorn in my side) using visuals or written phrases.

> ## I'm so hungry I could eat a horse.

- **S** In their small groups, have students discuss what they see in the visuals or understand from the particular written phrase.
- **T** Bring the class together and discuss with them how the intended meaning of the visuals/phrases differs dramatically from the literal meaning and emphasize the importance of always keeping this is mind when working with text.
- **I** Next, have students individually brainstorm and draw or write on the back of their templates other examples of figurative language that they have heard or that they know in their native language or in English.

- **S** Have students share their examples and their related meanings with their small groups.
- As students are sharing, circulate around the room to gather examples you can revoice for the rest of the class.

Activating the "*i*"

How does this process activate CLD students' existing knowledge?

- **Sociocultural:** When students are allowed to discuss with a peer what they think each phrase might mean, they are provided with a low-risk opportunity to share aloud their initial thoughts.
- **Linguistic:** As students record other examples of figurative language, they are able to draw upon their native language as a resource and practice English.

- **Academic:** When students share their ideas with each other, they are able to hear numerous examples of how the meaning figurative language differs from the literal meaning of the individual words.
- **Cognitive:** Students' sharing of their initial interpretations of the phrases promotes curiosity and subsequent engagement in the remainder of the lesson.

CONNECTION: The Broad & Narrow Strokes of Learning

Directions:

- Choose a book with figurative language infused throughout.
- **T** Explain to students that they will be further exploring figurative language by looking at phrases in the context of text (e.g., book, poem).
- **T** Depending on the length of the book, read aloud the passage/part of the book in which the phrases appear. Remind students to actively **listen** for the figurative phrases.
- **I** As you come across an example of figurative language, have students individually write the phrase above one of the boxes on their template.
- As students write the phrase on their templates, make sure to write the same phrase on the board for students to refer to.
- To help students understand the phrase within the context of the text and to help them move away from its literal meaning, ask them to individually visualize what they think the phrase means by keeping in mind:
  - the context of the text,
  - individual words within the phrase, and
  - any information from their own background knowledge that can help them infer the meaning.

Note: During the first few implementations of this strategy with students, you may need to model the skill of visualizing when trying to infer the meaning of a phrase within the context of a text.

- **S** Next, allow students to discuss the phrase in their small groups and come to a consensus about what they think the particular example of figurative language means.
- **T** Ask one group of students to share their interpretation of the figurative language with the whole class. (Ask a different group to share for each example of figurative language you examine.)
- Discuss as a whole group whether the meaning provided by the small group works or needs to be modified.
- **I** Once the class has decided what a specific phrase means, or the author's intent behind the phrase, have students individually **sketch** a picture in the corresponding box on the template to illustrate the meaning.
- Have students use the lines beside

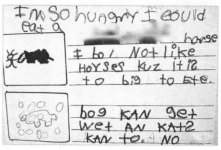

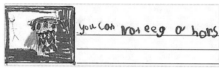

the box to record/**label** the meaning of the phrase.
- Repeat the process for each passage/phrase you encounter in the text.
- Once you have covered the whole book or text selection and students have drawn and labeled the intended meanings of the phrases, have them post their completed templates on a classroom wall for continued reference.
- If applicable to the selected text, you can also have students compare their illustrations of the phrases with those provided in the book.

Author Talk: Connection

The Common Core State Standards call for students to use precise language and techniques including metaphors, similes, and analogies to manage the complexity of academic topics (NGA & CCSSO, 2010). This is a particularly important skill for CLD students, who might approach figurative language literally unless explicitly taught how to identify and interpret the different types of figurative language they might encounter in text or daily conversations. Listen Sketch Label is a wonderful strategy for teachers to use to provide this type of explicit instruction.

Teachers have commented on the fact that Listen Sketch Label not only helps their students understand the actual meaning of figurative language but also helps keep them actively engaged in the learning process. As one 3rd-grade teacher shared, "My students love this strategy! They are always asking when they get to draw the meanings of the sentences again and talk about them with their friends!" When asked why she thought her students enjoyed the strategy so much, this teacher commented that she felt like her students took ownership of the activity. They were the ones deciding what to draw and how to explain what each phrase meant to their friends; she was not giving them the answer.

By turning over the responsibility to the students, this strategy enables them to be in charge of their own learning. More and more, what students and even what teachers control about the curriculum is restricted, but as this strategy clearly illustrates, the more we give our students ownership of their learning the more they get out of the process.

Connecting to the "*i*+1"
How does this process move CLD students from the known to the unknown?

- **Sociocultural:** Engaging CLD students in small-group and whole-class conversations about their individual interpretations builds valuable cooperation and negotiation skills.
- **Linguistic:** The Connection phase integrates practice of English listening, speaking, reading, and writing skills.

- **Academic:** Using both contextual cues from the text and visuals helps CLD students connect to grade-level material in meaningful ways.
- **Cognitive:** Having to justify their interpretations of the phrases within their small group engages CLD students in the application of key cognitive skills, including elaborating on prior knowledge, using imagery, and making inferences.

 AFFIRMATION: A Gallery of Understanding

Directions:

- **I** To assess whether students have been able to understand the idea of figurative language, give each student an index card. Have them individually select a phrase from the lesson (that you have already written on the board) and write the phrase on one side of the card and its meaning on the other side of the card. Erase the phrases from the board after the students have written them on their index cards.
- **S** Explain to students that they will be doing an interactive activity in their small groups. For this activity, one person from the group gets to share with the group his or her *interpretation* of one of the figurative phrases *but not* the actual phrase. When the interpretation is shared,

the group members have up to a minute to talk with each other about which phrase matches the interpretation. Once the minute is up, the group gets to share the answer. If the answer is correct, then the next person in the group gives his or her interpretation of the phrase, and the rest of the members follow the same process. If the answer is wrong, then the original person gets to tell the actual phrase. Repeat this process until all of the phrases the group members have written on their cards have been discussed.

- **T** When all of the groups have finished sharing their interpretations and phrases, bring the class back together. Explain the need to always look beyond the individual words of

sentences and consider the larger context of the passage/text in order to understand the actual meaning of figurative language.

- **P** Further, you can have students work in pairs to select three or four phrases of figurative language from the lesson and write an amusing short story using those examples.

Affirming Student Ownership: *"I" Get It!*
How does this process celebrate CLD student learning?

- **Sociocultural:** Having students discuss the phrases and their meanings with multiple peers provides a shared learning experience that supports them in seeing one another as valuable members of the learning community.
- **Linguistic:** The ongoing practice of articulating the phrases and their meanings provides CLD students with valuable practice in using English.

- **Academic:** By the end of the Affirmation phase of the lesson, students have had many opportunities to solidify and demonstrate their understanding of the examples of figurative language.
- **Cognitive:** Students are continually challenged to think critically about each phrase and evaluate their own understanding as they discuss and listen to their peers' interpretations/meanings of the phrases.

SPOTLIGHT: Early Literacy Connection

Gentry (1987) identified six developmental stages for spelling: precommunicative, semiphonetic, phonetic, transitional, conventional, and morphemic/syntactic. When approaching the instruction of spelling with young children, it is important to be aware of these stages as they influence how students spell words. For example,

- The spelling of a student at the precommunicative stage looks like a bunch of scribbles and drawings of caricatures (Boyd-Batstone, 2006).
- Students at the semiphonetic stage of spelling are able to write letters (mostly consonants) that indicate the dominant sounds at the beginning or the end of a word.
- Phonetic spellers include all the sounds featured in a word, but their spelling is typically inventive in nature (Boyd-Batstone, 2006).

Research by Schickedanz and Casbergue (2004) found that "it is rare for preschool children to move beyond the beginning stages of semiphonetic spelling, and most will not progress to fully phonetic spelling until kindergarten" (p. 40).

For young CLD students, spelling can be difficult because they are working with sounds that are not present in their native language or that exist in their native language but in a different position. CLD students need to be engaged in lots of conversations to build up their vocabulary and understanding of the English language. To support CLD students in their movement from semiphonetic spelling to phonetic spelling, the teacher can use a modified version of the Listen Sketch Label strategy.

Note: For this variant of the strategy, you can use consonant–vowel–consonant (CVC) pattern words that are critical for young CLD students to understand. The CVC pattern is that when a single vowel occurs between two consonants, the vowel is pronounced as a short vowel sound.

To modify the Listen Sketch Label strategy for young CLD students, teachers can do the following activity:

Activation:
- Write three CVC words (including pictures of the words) on the board.
- Ask the students to think about the words on the board and share any thoughts about them.
- After the students have shared their thoughts about the CVC words, explain to them that these are *CVC words.*
- Model how to say each word and pronounce each sound.
- Ask the students the following questions: What is the first sound? What letter makes that sound? As you do this, have students think of any words in their own language that start with that sound. Circle the first letter of each word in green.
- Then ask the students about the middle sound, with the following questions: What is the next sound? What letter makes that sound? Again, make connections to the same sounds in the students' native language. Circle the second letter of each word in yellow.
- Finally, ask the students about the last sound in the word, with the following questions: What is the last sound? What letter makes that sound? Circle the last letter of each word in red.
- Review each of the words in the following format: Read the word, say each sound in the word individually, and read the word again. Point to each word as you say it.
- Have the students read the words with you.

(continued on the next page)

SPOTLIGHT: Early Literacy Connection (*continued*)

Connection:

- Read a book that has many words that follow the CVC word pattern (e.g., cat, dog, pig).
- Give each student a Listen Sketch Label template worksheet.
- Choose four words from the story that follow the CVC pattern. Have students listen as you say each word and then have them echo the words back to you.
- After saying each word one time, go back to the beginning of the list and read the first word.
- After saying the first word the second time, have each student draw a picture in one of the boxes to represent the word.
- Next to the box, have the students spell the word by writing down the sounds they hear as you sound out the word for them.
- Repeat this process until all of the pictures and words have been completed.
  - If time allows and/or students are able, encourage them to write the words in their native language as well. By doing this, you are promoting your CLD students' transfer of knowledge from the L1 to the L2.
  - This can also be an L1 activity you send home and ask parents to complete with their children. Then have the students share the words in their native languages the next day.

Affirmation:

- After the students have completed the Listen Sketch Label sheet, split the students into small groups of four, giving each student in the group a sheet of paper with one of the CVC words on it.
- Have each student write a sentence using the word on their sheet of paper. After they have finished, they pass their papers to the left. They keep on writing sentences and passing papers until all of the papers have made it around the circle once.
- After the students have received their original CVC paper back, have them read the "stories" that the other group members helped them write.
- You can ask each group to share one of the stories with the class.

Biography-Driven Response to Intervention

Listen Sketch Label is a strategy grounded in the belief that, with appropriate support, students can self-regulate their own learning. All students are exposed to the same input as they listen to the content information; however, the output expected from individual students can be varied and differentiated, depending upon their cognitive, academic, and linguistic needs. This strategy allows students to use sketches to support their understanding and retention of the lesson material. To extend students' learning, the strategy can be used during tiered instruction to provide a focus on self-monitoring and self-evaluation.

One Classroom's Perspective

Activating:

My students love to do this strategy because it gives them a chance to show me what they already know about the vocabulary words before the lesson even starts. I began the lesson by having the students write down all the words in their vocabulary notebooks. They then had to rate their knowledge of the word by putting an "x" next to the word if they already knew what it meant. To find out if they could apply the word, I also asked my students to add a second "x" if they thought they could use the word in a sentence. Then I passed out the Listen Sketch Label templates and had each student draw a picture for each of the six phrases I read aloud to show me what they thought the phrase meant. They would then write what they thought the word's definition was based on their pictures.

I loved seeing the pictures the students came up with for the different phrases! I really got to know what background knowledge my students had by looking at their pictures.

To help students make connections, I encouraged them to share their drawings with their peers. This sharing really helps my CLD students because they get to see other points of view. I also found it gave them a sense of pride, since they were able to share their interpretations with their peers. By sharing one-on-one, they are not intimidated like they would be if they had to share in front of the whole class. As students were sharing in pairs, I watched for those who really got the meaning of the phrases and asked them if they would be willing to share with the whole class.

Connecting:

After students had shared with the whole class, we began reading our text. As the phrases were encountered in the text, I had students confirm the actual meanings of the phrases by using context clues from the story. If the students did not have the right meaning, they added their new learnings to their Listen Sketch Label handout.

Affirming:

At the end of the lesson, they used their handouts to write a summary of what they had learned. I was impressed with the added detail students included in their summaries. This strategy really made a difference for all of my students!

Student Voices

We drew pictures to tell the teacher what the sentences are. It was fun to draw the picture about a lot of snot going out my nose to tell the teacher what "My nose is running" is.

—*ELL Student*
Speech Emergent

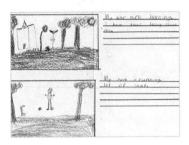

I draw really good pictures, so I like being able to draw. The teacher said my pictures were really good because she could really tell that I knew what the words meant! My friends liked my pictures too! I hope we get to do this again!

—*ELL Student*
Intermediate Fluency

I really like being able to talk to my friends about the meanings of the phrases during the lesson! I had not heard a lot of them before, so I did not know what they meant and they did not make a lot of sense to me. But thanks to my friends, I know what they mean now and I can explain them to my teacher!

—*ELL Student*
Advanced Fluency

TEMPLATE: Listen Sketch Label

Name: _____

Date: _____

Listen Sketch Label

STRATEGY

Story Bag

The Story Bag strategy was a perfect way to get the class motivated and excited about learning new words. The implementation of this strategy gave me the chance to see that the working vocabulary my students had been building throughout this unit was becoming established and comfortable. Students raised their hands to reply to questions and to offer their thoughts about the story. I was pleased to see their level of participation high and their motivation strong.

—*Shilo Burnham, Kindergarten Teacher*

Where Theory Meets Practice

Good readers use pictures, titles, headings, text, and background knowledge and experiences to make predictions before they begin to read. Predicting involves thinking ahead and anticipating information and events in the text. After making predictions, students can read through the text and refine, revise, and verify their predictions (Duke & Pearson, 2001).

Making predictions activates students' background knowledge about the text and helps them make connections between the new, unknown information and the known information they already possess. By making predictions about the text before reading, students use their existing knowledge and what they think might happen to connect to the text. In addition, predictions encourage active reading and keep students interested throughout the story/text.

Story Bag is a strategy adapted from the work of Lado (2004) that helps CLD students establish a purpose for reading as they make predictions about pictures and objects that will and will not appear in the text. The strategy begins as a teacher-directed activity and evolves into a student learning strategy through repetition and meaningful contact with vocabulary words and academic concepts. Story Bag is a strategy that can help teachers capitalize on student differences, and at the same time it provides a single tool that supports predictions, word building, and meaning making. Strategies such as this that convey respect for student differences become the basis for meaningful relationships and favorable academic results (Gay, 2000; Irvine, 1990; Ladson-Billings, 1994).

Materials Needed: Story Bag • pictures/objects that are and are not in the story • poster paper or white board to post T-chart • brown paper bags (one per student)

ACTIVATION: A Canvas of Opportunity

Directions:

- **S** Place students in small groups of three to four students.
- **T** Have the students examine the front cover of the book, and explain that they will make predictions about the objects that will or will not be in the story.
- To support students in making their predictions, write the following on a white board or a large piece of poster paper:

In the Story	Not in the Story

- **S** One by one, pull objects/pictures out of the Story Bag and ask the students to predict whether the item will be in the story or won't be in the story. Have students discuss their predictions in their small groups.
  - As students are predicting, have them explain why they think the item will or will not be in the story.
  - Circulate around the room to listen to student conversations about their predictions and related rationales.
- **T** After students have had a chance to discuss their predictions in their small groups, bring the discussion to a class vote for the first item. Then tape/place the item under the appropriate column. Alternatively, you can also have students write the name of the item in the correct column.

  - If students are not sure whether an item will or will not be in the story, you can place the item on the line between the two columns. Alternatively, you can add a "Maybe" column and have students place the items there.
- Repeat the voting and posting process for each object/picture.

Activating the "*i*"

How does this process activate CLD students' existing knowledge?

- **Sociocultural:** By asking students to provide a rationale for their predictions, Story Bag strategy allows students to make their background knowledge public.
- **Linguistic:** The Activation phase promotes awareness of academic language connected to the topic as CLD students hear peers' articulation of rationales for their predictions.

- **Academic:** Story Bag promotes comprehension from the very onset, as students have exposure to visuals that connect to the text prior to their reading the material.
- **Cognitive:** The CLD student uses his or her background knowledge and clues from the cover of the text to make logical predictions.

Author Talk: Activation

As teachers, we know that our students come to us with varied experiences. Consider how Ms. Berg used the Story Bag strategy to learn more about the backgrounds of her students:

As Ms. Berg pulled pictures out of her bag and students predicted which would or would not appear in the story, the conversations were typical for a 2nd-grade classroom. Often kids would laugh at the pictures that would come out of the bag. Occasionally, a student would make a deeper connection to a picture and say something like "That's a picture of a war. . . . Where I come from, there was a lot of fighting and wars. It was really scary and not safe for our family. That's why we moved here." As soon as Ms. Berg heard comments such as this, she opened up the discussion to the class. As students later discussed their ideas in groups, Ms. Berg walked around the room to listen to the students talk. Later on, when she started reading the story, she made a point to revoice some of the ideas the students had shared, thereby creating a true community of learners where everyone's ideas were being valued and brought to life.

As you use this strategy, consider ways you can create conditions and situations in the classroom that will allow students to share their many culturally bound understandings. A few tips that teachers have shared with us include

- As you pull a picture from the bag, have students talk in pairs first about why they think the picture is critical for the book and second about how the picture relates to them as individuals.

- Have students in pairs or small groups use the pictures that were shared at the beginning of the lesson to create their own stories revolving around the topic. As appropriate, this can be used as a summative assessment for comprehension.

- Have students individually or in pairs use computers to search the Internet as an added resource after you have finished reading the story. They can look for pictures and objects that could be added to the story.

CONNECTION: The Broad & Narrow Strokes of Learning

Directions:

- **T** As the text/story is read, call on students to verify the objects/pictures as they appear in text. This can by done by having students come to the front of the room and determine whether the objects/pictures are in the correct column. If they are not, have the students move the objects/pictures to the appropriate column.

- As a student verifies or moves an object/picture, have the class members talk to each other about the way the object/picture is used within the context of the story to help them understand the notion of context

clues. Guiding questions you might ask your students include:
  - Were our initial predictions correct? Why or why not?
  - What does this mean for us as readers?

- **S** As you continue reading the text, stop at key points and have students discuss the text/story in their small groups.

- **I** As an extension, have students write in their notebooks the names of the objects/pictures as they appear in the text. When the reading has been completed, students can retell the story using these words.

Connecting to the "*i*+1"
How does this process move CLD students from the known to the unknown?

- **Sociocultural:** The visual nature of the activity allows students to use their personal schema to connect to the text and make meaning for themselves.
- **Linguistic:** Students are able to practice their selective listening skills as they listen for the mention of specific objects while the text is being read aloud.

- **Academic:** Students are able to broaden their understanding of contexts in which given objects/pictures might be relevant.
- **Cognitive:** Students are able to become "constructively responsive" readers (Pressley & Afflerbach, 1995) as they think about the initial placement of the pictures/objects in the columns and then finally place the item in the correct column based on the text.

AFFIRMATION: A Gallery of Understanding

Directions:

- After the story has been read, place students in pairs and pass out the objects/pictures, giving one object/picture to each pair of students.
- **P** Have the students work with their partner to find the page in the story in which the object/picture appears, or be prepared to tell the class that the object/picture did not appear in the book.
  - For the objects that did not appear in the story, stretch your students cognitively by asking them to explain why they initially thought they might appear in the story.
- Next, pass out story bags to each student. Inside each story bag, have the individual pictures reflective of the story for students to manipulate.
- **I** Have students individually sequence the pictures in the order in which they appeared in the story.
- Finally, have students individually write a summary of what they remember about the story on the outside of their story bag.

Affirming Student Ownership: *"I" Get It!*
How does this process celebrate CLD student learning?

- **Sociocultural:** As students interact with their partner and report to the class, they have an additional opportunity to develop their collaboration skills and share their background knowledge (if their object/picture was not in the text).
- **Linguistic:** The visuals in the story bag provide non-linguistic support for students' writing process.

- **Academic:** As students work to explain which objects/pictures are and are not in the text, they solidify their understanding of the text.
- **Cognitive:** Students are able to gain ownership over their learning as they employ sequencing and summarizing skills.

SPOTLIGHT: Early Literacy Connection

Story Bag is an effective strategy that allows students to predict whether or not various objects or pictures are going to appear in a text that is read aloud by the teacher. Because predictions vary based on the background knowledge and experiences of the student, this strategy is ideal for highlighting sociocultural elements of students' biographies. Story Bag provides the frame for the following activity that students can do at home with their parents and then replicate for their peers in the classroom.

As young CLD students enter our classrooms, each one brings a unique set of experiences and skills. Some students may have strong academic backgrounds and know how to read in their native language. CLD students' home language and previous cultural and educational experiences give them a sense of belonging and support their ability to learn a new language and so should not be subtracted from the learning of English (Wong Fillmore, 2000).

To modify the Story Bag strategy for young CLD students, teachers can set it up as a home–school connection. When students are familiar with the routine of the Story Bag strategy and have used the strategy multiple times, they should be encouraged to create their own Story Bag activity for their peers with help from their parents, as described on the next page.

(*continued on the next page*)

SPOTLIGHT: Early Literacy Connection (*continued*)

- The students can choose a book from their home library or a book from the classroom that they can check out to take home.
  - The selected book should be one the student is familiar with or one that is at the individual's independent reading level.
- Explain to the students that they will be creating a Story Bag activity with their parents at home, and that they will then bring back their story bag and conduct the activity with their classmates.
- You will need to create a story bag board for the students. The story bag board is a piece of paper with two columns, the headings of which read "In the Story" and "Not in the Story."
- The students will use the story bag board to classify objects that are in or not in their story.
- With their parents, the students will select objects from the story that will be used, as well as some other objects that do not belong in the story.
- Students can draw or cut pictures out of magazines to represent objects that will be included in their story bag. The pictures need to be small enough to fit on the story bag board.
- After the students and their parents have completed preparing the story bag, have the students share their book and story bag with their classmates in small groups.

Activation:

- Have the students separate into small groups of three or four.
- Each student will have a chance to be the leader in the group. The leader will share the story bag he or she created at home with the other students.
- Have the leader show the cover of the book to the group and ask the group members what they think the story will be about.
- Each group will discuss what they think that story will

be about. After a brief discussion, have the leader start to show one object at a time from the story bag.
- As the leader pulls out each object, have the group members do the following:
  - Take turns in saying the beginning and the ending sounds of the name of the object/picture.
  - Take turns in sharing any other words associated with the object/picture. Students can also share the word in their native languages.
  - The leader will ask if the object will be "in" or "not in" the story. After the group comes up with consensus on where to place the object, the leader will listt that object on the two-column paper the teacher provided.
- This process will continue until all of the objects have been placed on the two-column chart.

Connection:

- If the leader can read the story, have him or her read it aloud to the other students in the small group.
  - If the student is not able to read the story aloud, have an adult (older book buddies, office staff, paraprofessionals) read the story for him or her.
- As the story is read, the students can change the objects to the proper category if necessary.

Affirmation:

- After the story has been read, have the leader check to see if the objects from the story are in the correct category.
- Then have the leader ask the other students what their favorite part of the story was and explain why it was their favorite part.
- Lastly, have the leader share his or her favorite part of the story and tell why it was the favorite.
  - As an extension, you can also have the groups write a few sentences retelling the story in their own words.

Biography-Driven Response to Intervention

Story Bag is a strategy that can be implemented across all three tiers to help students not only connect with the vocabulary words but also develop the skills of prediction and retelling. As you implement the strategy, the three phases of the lesson help students monitor and manage their own learning as they focus on the placement of the pictures, either within their individual bags or in their small groups. As an extension to your core instruction, you can further connect the pictures to students' biographies by asking them how the pictures relate to their family backgrounds. Depending on the intervention required at Tier 2 and Tier 3, you can have students use their individual story bags to create sentences, work on letter sound combinations, create stories, and more.

One Classroom's Perspective

Activating:

As I was preparing for this lesson, I thought carefully about my students' experiences with the Latin music and dancing that is known as Salsa. I knew that I could use the experiences of my para-educator, Mrs. Oliver, with Salsa dancing to help my students see and learn what this kind of dancing was like. I chose vocabulary that I knew would need clarification and extra practice. I also chose some vocabulary with dual meanings to provide extra practice with homophones. I wanted the activity to be engaging and relevant. The only English language learner (ELL) child that I have is Vietnamese. I knew that this language and information would possibly be very new to him. All of the students were excited when then found out they would get to help decide what pictures would be in the story, and they eagerly volunteered to help tape them up on the white board.

Connecting:

The grouping for this activity was whole group; however, I feel I did a responsible job of asking the children to think/pair/share and have alternate ways of responding and thinking. At one point in my lesson, I asked students to try the Salsa dance with our para-educator. I knew that the Story Bag strategy would provide an exciting and motivating experience for my students to practice and potentially learn new vocabulary. They were invested and highly curious about the vocabulary words that I pulled out of the bag at the beginning of the lesson. I asked the students to put their finger on their nose, or their hand on their head each time they heard the word(s) in context as I read. As we encountered these words, I had students come up and put a star on the picture to show it was in the story. For the pictures that we had originally placed in the "Not in the Story" column, we moved them to the "In the Story" column before putting a star on them. I was very pleased with the group participation and their responses.

One Classroom's Perspective (*continued*)

Affirming:

After the lesson, I engaged the students in a brief discussion about the story so I could do a quick check of concepts and vocabulary. These conversations are extremely powerful for me, as I am able to do some basic assessment and observation about the students' comprehension and learning. Because I teach kindergarten, this is one of the most important ways I am able to gather authentic information about my learners. I asked the students to engage in further thinking by doing a short writing activity in response to the story. I wanted to see what further evidence I could gather about their understanding from the book and the new vocabulary practiced and learned. Overall, I was very pleased with their learning and the results of my observations.

Student Voices

This year I want to write a lot so that I can teach my mom how to write sentences in English. I loved using paper bags at the end to form my sentences because I got to take them home and my mom copied sentences from there in her own notebook.

—*ELL Student*
Intermediate Fluency

I like the picture of grandpa in the park. He had a dress on. We looked at Japan on the map and I got to keep the pictures in my own paper bag!

—*ELL Student*
Early Production

The best part of the story was when the grandfather was raising the birds. I like to go see birds in the zoo. I took a picture of a bird and put it in my paper bag. Tomorrow I am going to write a story about birds on the computer.

—*ELL Student*
Advanced Fluency

CHAPTER 2

Words and More Words

ONE of the questions we as educators are most frequently asked is, "How do you know what vocabulary is most important for your CLD students to learn?" Before addressing this question, let us look carefully at what is being asked. What *vocabulary* is being referred to in this question? For teachers across the country, the objective of developing academic language (i.e., the decontextualized language of schools; the language of academic discourse, of texts, and of formal argument) is at the heart of vocabulary instruction (August & Hakuta, 1997; Beck, McKeown, & Kucan, 2002; Gersten, Dimino, Jayanthi, Kim, & Santoro, 2007; Tompkins & Blanchfield, 2004; Vaughn & Linan-Thompson, 2004).

The strategies presented in this chapter focus on teaching students how to interpret and internalize academic language, including academic vocabulary, so that it becomes personally meaningful to them. Personalized contextualization of the vocabulary, according to research by Blachowicz and Fisher (2000), not only helps to increase students' understanding but also promotes their retention of the new words. A study by the National Reading Panel (NRP) (2000) identified vocabulary instruction as an essential element for promoting improvement in reading achievement among students. Vocabulary knowledge also has been said to be the "great predictor" of school success when it comes to reading (Reutzel & Cooter, 2010). In fact, vocabulary knowledge has been shown to account for 80% of the variance in students' reading comprehension scores on standardized measures of achievement (Reutzel & Cooter, 2012). Given such statistics, it is not surprising that the education literature offers multiple frameworks and models for helping teachers identify key vocabulary to teach and providing them with systematic procedures to follow in teaching that vocabulary (see Marzano, 2004, Beck et al., 2002, and Calderón, 2007, for examples).

Selection and Instruction of Vocabulary Words

Students need to learn an enormous number of vocabulary words, and it is impossible to teach all of these words directly. However, not all words need the same attention. Beck et al. (2002) recommend choosing vocabulary words by determining their usefulness, their frequency, and the ease with which a student can restate their meaning in his or her own words. Researchers distinguish among three different tiers of vocabulary words.

Tier 1 words are basic vocabulary words—such as *cat, dog, clock,* and *jump*—that are heard frequently in social conversation and are seen in numerous contexts. These words rarely require direct vocabulary instruction in the school setting.

Tier 2 words represent more sophisticated vocabulary. These are words such as *consistent* and *assume* that mature language users employ in conversation and that are seen frequently in written text and standardized assessments. Tier 2 words also are encountered frequently in multiple content areas. Beck et al. (2002) feel that teachers need to target their direct vocabulary instruction on Tier 2 words because of the impact these words have on reading comprehension and because of their prevalence throughout a student's schooling.

Tier 3 words are content-specific words that appear in isolated situations and are rarely used in daily conversation. Tier 3 words are often regarded as the vocabulary of the academic knowledge domain, and they are learned in highly specialized contexts such as chemistry, geometry, and physics. These are the words that students are least likely to be familiar with from daily life because they are so domain specific. As such, they are most frequently the focus of explicit instruction.

Selecting vocabulary words for CLD students requires a different approach from what is needed for native English speakers. Kinsella (2005) asserts that because vocabulary knowledge plays such a pivotal role in the overall school success and mobility of CLD students, all grade-level teachers must devote more time and attention to selecting vocabulary words. Teachers must explicitly teach the vocabulary that will enable CLD students to meet the demands of today's standards-based curricula.

Calderón et al. (2005) modified the three-tier system of Beck et al. (2002) for use in vocabulary instruction with CLD students. According to Calderón and colleagues, Tier 1 words for second language learners are words that represent concepts typically already known by CLD students in their native language. The students may simply need the correct English label to make the connection with their background knowledge. Teachers can also make connections with cognates in the students' native language.

Tier 2 words for CLD students include many words with multiple meanings, which can be especially difficult for second language learners (August, Carlo, Dressler, & Snow, 2005). Unless CLD students are taught a word's multiple meanings, their limited background knowledge of the word might lead them away from a full and accurate understanding of its meaning in a particular context. Because Tier 3 words are, by definition, low-frequency words, these terms often can be translated to CLD students in their native language.

Biography-Driven Vocabulary Instruction

According to Herrera (2010), we as educators need to approach instruction from a biography-driven perspective in which we use information about students' sociocultural, linguistic, cognitive, and academic dimensions as a guide for creating the learning conditions in our classrooms. Each student has learned specific vocabulary and other background knowledge within the home, community, and school contexts he or she has experienced. A student's background knowledge is constantly changing in response to facts, social customs, experiences, and emotions that are encountered and/or learned (Marzano, 2004). To support CLD students in making connections between their existing knowledge and the academic vocabulary of a lesson, we first need to identify the assets—especially the linguistic assets—that our students bring to the classroom and use those assets as the starting point for instruction.

Research has shown that a critical element for students in their acquisition and retention of vocabulary knowledge is their ability to make connections between their existing background knowledge and the new material being presented in a lesson (Gunning, 2006; Langer, 2001; Nagy, 2003). For CLD students, who face extra challenges linguistically and culturally, support in making these connections is essential. Thus, effective vocabulary instruction must go beyond applying a "formula" for selecting key vocabulary words. Rather, the task must be approached from a biography-driven perspective in which our knowledge of individual students drives our selection of vocabulary words and guides our instructional efforts throughout the lesson.

A meta-analysis of the most successful methods of vocabulary instruction by Reutzel and Cooter (2010) produced the following list of principles for effective vocabulary instruction, which was based on the research of Stahl (1999), Rasinski (1998), and Coyne and colleagues (Coyne, McCoach, Loftus, Zipoli, & Kapp, 2009):

- *Principle 1.* Vocabulary should be taught both explicitly and incidentally.
- *Principle 2.* Learning how to construct vocabulary from rich contexts is valuable.
- *Principle 3.* Effective vocabulary instruction must include depth of learning as well as breadth of word knowledge.
- *Principle 4.* Multiple meaningful exposures are important for learning new vocabulary. (Reutzel & Cooter, 2010, pp. 226–227)

Building on Principle 1, the strategies described in this chapter provide a structure in which vocabulary is taught both explicitly and incidentally. The strategies begin by explicitly providing students with a stimulus or introduction to the new vocabulary in a way that actively involves each student in the learning process through listening, speaking, reading, or writing. Students are directed to attend to the topic, concepts, and vocabulary of the lesson and make immediate personal connections to them. As the lesson proceeds, students are engaged in the incidental use and application of the lesson vocabulary and other academic words.

Principle 2 emphasizes the importance of the student learning how to construct vocabulary from rich contexts. In our work with CLD students, we have seen that vocabulary knowledge expands when students have numerous opportunities to encounter new words in rich and varying contexts. The key issue in extending students' background knowledge is making specific connections between what they already know and the new material (Wessels, 2008). Without such connections to vocabulary words, the new information will not make it into storage in students' permanent memory (Swinney & Velasco, 2006). Working memory has the ability to activate information from both the sensory and the permanent memory. If students have sufficient multiple meaningful exposures to the vocabulary while it is in working memory, the information will move into permanent memory. The strategies introduced in this chapter are designed with this goal of retention in mind.

Building on Principle 3, the strategies have been designed to address depth of learning as well as breadth of word knowledge. The Activation phase of the strategies provides students with avenues for developing a "conceptual hook" (Young & Hadaway, 2006) to the information already in their permanent memory, which gives them access to all of their previous connections to that specific information (Svinicki, 1991). During the Connection phase, students engage with texts, hands-on materials, and peers in order to make connections between their background knowledge and the new vocabulary. Because students activated their schemas in the Activation phase, the previously established connections allow them to think more deeply about the meaning of the vocabulary words, which increases their metacognition (Wessels, 2008). A continual focus on students' use of academic language throughout the lesson ensures their exposure to (and practice with) a wide variety of words. Finally, during the Affirmation phase, students are provided with structured opportunities to use academic language, especially the key vocabulary, to demonstrate their learning.

Principle 4 highlights the need for students to have multiple meaningful exposures as they learn new vocabulary. A foundational component of each strategy is collaboration among students. By employing strategic grouping configurations that reflect consideration for students' individual biographies, teachers are better able to ensure that when students discuss academic vocabulary in pairs and in small groups, they will be able to gain new and deeper contextual understanding of the words and concepts through the sharing of ideas. The structured opportunities for student collaboration yield innumerable opportunities to hear and practice a wide range of words in authentic communicative tasks. As students use the vocabulary to make predictions, confirm/disconfirm initial associations, express ideas, and summarize learning, they become more likely to store the meanings of vocabulary words in their permanent memory, where they can be accessed, consciously or unconsciously, whenever needed (Stahl, 1999).

Strategies in Practice

In this chapter you will find descriptions of the following seven strategies, which explicitly create conditions that encourage learners to value and expand upon their preexisting vocabulary knowledge and linguistic abilities:

- DOTS Chart
- Vocabulary Foldable
- Tic-Tac-Tell
- Vocabulary Quilt
- Thumb Challenge
- Magic Book
- IDEA

STRATEGY

DOTS Chart

D etermine what I know
O bserve
T alk to peers as we elaborate
S ummarize what we learned

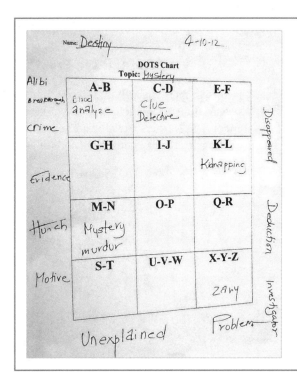

From the DOTS chart I was able to determine the knowledge gained by the students as well as whether or not they were able to connect what they learned to real-world situations. In the beginning, students were only able to relate the key vocabulary to themselves and were not able to see the bigger picture. Through my assessment of the students I was able to see that they were able to identify the key vocabulary. Students were able to think outside the box or provide examples for any key vocabulary that they may have forgotten or had difficulty explaining.

—*Miles McGee, 2nd-Grade Teacher*

Where Theory Meets Practice

The *interdependence hypothesis* suggests that the acquisition of a first language (L1) and of a second language (L2) is intertwined (Cummins, 1981, 2000). Given this hypothesis, literacy development can be greatly enhanced when teachers embrace the value of the native language and the role it plays in students' literacy development in English (Herrera et al., 2010). Accessing CLD students' native language is particularly pertinent when they are first learning English, as they go through various stages in the development of their English language proficiency and literacy skills. These stages are preproduction, early production, speech emergence, intermediate fluency, and advanced fluency (Krashen & Terrell, 1983). Given the fact that it can take 5–7 years for

a CLD student to develop cognitive academic language proficiency (CALP) commensurate with that of their monolingual English-speaking peers, using strategies that allow students to demonstrate what they know in their L1 and L2 can give teachers a much greater insight into what their students understand about specific topics (Goldenberg, 2008).

The DOTS Chart is a unique strategy that uses an A–Z chart, or Alpha Boxes, as they were originally termed by Linda Hoyt (1999). The strategy allows CLD students at all levels of English language proficiency to demonstrate their knowledge about a specific topic. In addition, this strategy explicitly teaches CLD students how to develop and apply metacognitive, cognitive, and social/affective learning strategies. The DOTS Chart strategy does this by asking students to:

D Determine what they know

O Observe and listen to make connections between the new content and the known (i.e., their funds of knowledge, prior knowledge, and background knowledge)

T Talk to their partner or group to confirm or elaborate on their understanding.

S Summarize their learning.

The "**D**" in DOTS first has students *determine* what they know and consider how it might be related to the topic of the lesson. This process of reflecting on what they already know about a topic stretches CLD students to use cognitive strategies, as they have to think about what they already know and how they know it, and then apply it to the DOTS chart. Cognitive strategies support reading comprehension for CLD students by providing them with specific, concrete tools they can manipulate and use (Herrera et al., 2010). As students make associations with the topic by writing down the specific words and experiences they think of in relationship to the topic, teachers can gain insights into the sociocultural connections students are making. These personal connections to the content and vocabulary better enable students to take ownership of the material (Blachowicz & Fisher, 2000).

The "**O**" moves students toward metacognitive strategy use by asking them to skim information and *observe* how their original thoughts about the vocabulary are connected to their new learning. Research indicates that when students are encouraged to link new content to past experiences or learning (i.e., their funds of knowledge, prior knowledge, and background knowledge, which they identified in the "D" step), there is an increased likelihood that they will learn and retain the information (Greenwood, 2001; Nagy, 2003). By using their selective attention skills as direct instruction proceeds, students are guided to make explicit links between the key vocabulary in the text and their initial thoughts about the topic (Chamot & O'Malley, 1994; Jensen, 2006).

The "**T**" highlights the importance of *talk*. When CLD students are encouraged to talk to their peers and ask questions for clarification, comprehension is increased (Chamot & O'Malley, 1994). Talk is a critical component of social/affective strategies. The DOTS Chart strategy teaches students how to mediate their learning with peers by engaging in discussions about the topic and exchanging ideas (Marzano, 2004; Wolfe & Brandt, 1998). In addition to providing a chance for students to learn from their peers, focused talk between peers can lower students' anxiety and help them learn more efficiently (Jensen, 2006; Vail, n.d.).

The "**S**" in DOTS reminds students to *summarize* what they have learned. The cognitive strategy of summarization is one of the most documented student strategies for increasing comprehension (e.g., Bean & Steenwyk, 1984; Hill & Flynn, 2006; Moore, Alvermann, & Hinchman, 2000). By having students summarize what they learned, the DOTS Chart strategy can be used to reinforce CLD students' understanding and application of the learned information in concrete ways. Research studies have concluded that such reinforcement and application of learning in practice increase student comprehension (Cooper, 1986; Cunningham, Moore, Cunningham, & Moore, 1995; Peregoy & Boyle, 2001; Rasinski & Padak, 2000; Vacca, Vacca, & Gove, 2000).

Materials Needed: DOTS Chart template (one per student) • paper • colored pencils/markers • pencils/pens

---

Note: The "standard" version of the DOTS chart (shown at the end of this strategy discussion, page 80) includes 12 boxes. A simpler version with only 6 boxes (three rows of 2 boxes, or two rows of 3 boxes), each covering more letters of the alphabet, might be more appropriate for K–1 students. The 12-box version provided can be used as a model for a simplified chart.

ACTIVATION: A Canvas of Opportunity

Directions:

- **I** Give each student a blank DOTS chart before the lesson begins.
- Have students place the name of the topic/concept that will be taught at the top of the chart.
- **T** To begin the "**D**" portion of the lesson, explain to the whole class that they are to *determine* what they know by individually thinking of words or pictures associated with the topic. *Tip:* To help students start brainstorming, encourage them to create a visual representation in their mind of their past experiences or learnings related to the topic.

- **I** Ask students to individually write their words or draw their pictures in the appropriately lettered boxes. For instance, if they have thought of the word "salamander" (related to the concept of *Amphibians*), then they would write "salamander" in the box with letter "S."
- Allow 3–5 minutes for students to individually write (in English and/or their native language) and draw on their charts as many ideas and words as they can think of.
- As the teacher, act as a silent observer so that students will feel comfortable

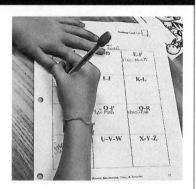

taking risks and sharing what they know. *Tip:* Document words from students' individual DOTS charts onto a master chart for later use.

Activating the "*i*"

How does this process activate CLD students' existing knowledge?

- **Sociocultural:** By explicitly connecting to the words and knowledge they bring to the lesson, students can make critical connections between the known and the unknown to promote comprehension.
- **Linguistic:** Allowing students to respond in their L1 ensures that all of them can actively participate in the lesson, regardless of their current stage of second language acquisition. When explicit links are made between the L1 and the L2, the transfer of knowledge and skills across languages is also promoted.

- **Academic:** Unlike group activities in which only a few students share what they know, beginning the lesson with CLD students individually documenting what they already know about the topic ensures that each student's voice is "heard," even if only on paper.
- **Cognitive:** The DOTS Chart strategy helps CLD students ignite their understandings of the topic and prepares them to monitor their personal links to the key vocabulary being taught in the lesson.

CONNECTION: The Broad & Narrow Strokes of Learning

Directions:

- **P** Once the students have finished writing, pair students and allow them time to share their ideas and look for connections. *Tip:* Allow students to "borrow" words from their peers during this time by writing down borrowed words with a pencil of a different color from what they had originally used.
- **I** Introduce the target vocabulary by having students individually write 8–12 key vocabulary words for the lesson around the edges of their DOTS chart.
- In the "**O**" portion of the lesson, you as the teacher need to support the students in connecting to the curriculum what they wrote during the Activation phase, helping them **observe** for connections by engaging in the following activities:
  - Connecting the DOTS. During the lesson, have students individually draw lines between their words and the target vocabulary they

wrote around the edges of their charts.
  - Reading the text and adding to their charts additional related words in colored pencil.
  - Adding the page number in the text where target vocabulary words are encountered beside those words on their charts.
  - Adding the curriculum definitions of the vocabulary words to the back of their charts.
  - Reading aloud and stopping at different points to discuss the curriculum words in context. Encourage the students to add new words to their charts. *Tip:* Ask students to signal to their partner whenever they hear key vocabulary words to promote their use of selective attention.
- **S** As the reading continues and the lesson enters the "**T**" portion, provide students with multiple opportunities to **talk** within small groups about

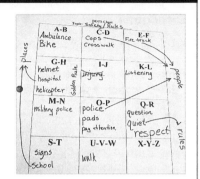

their associations between the words they individually (and as a community) have generated and the target vocabulary words. *Tip:* This sharing within groups enables students to discuss their ideas in ways that enable them to form valuable connections to the target vocabulary words.
- Throughout the lesson, return to both the target vocabulary and the student-generated words to clarify, elaborate, or review content concepts.

Connecting to the "*i*+1"
How does this process move CLD students from the known to the unknown?

- **Sociocultural:** Students make links to existing knowledge and share associations to make the topic more meaningful and comprehensible for themselves and for their peers.
- **Linguistic:** Continually returning to students' original words and ideas demonstrates to them that their cultural knowledge and L1 abilities are paramount in their development and conceptualization of new ideas.

- **Academic:** Having students make physical connections between their words and the academic vocabulary (by drawing lines on their charts) reinforces their schematic links between the known and the unknown vocabulary.
- **Cognitive:** Allowing students to talk about their learning with their peers gives them a chance to clarify understandings, make additional connections, and remain focused and engaged throughout the lesson.

AFFIRMATION: A Gallery of Understanding

Directions:

- During the "**S**" phase portion of the lesson, students are asked to take a more summative look at learning as they *summarize* what they have learned.
- **P** Before using the DOTS chart for individual accountability, teachers may wish to review by:
  - Having students, in pairs, write a paragraph discussing a connection between their own words and the academic vocabulary of the text. This activity provides students with one more opportunity to "connect the dots" and extend their learning.
- **I** For individual accountability, have students do one or more of the following to summarize their learnings:

- Use the DOTS chart as a tool to write individual definitions of the academic terms. Students should be encouraged to use their own words and pictures as a reference for coming up with these definitions.
- Write sentences using the target vocabulary as it relates to the topic of the lesson.
- Use the vocabulary on the chart to complete a fill-in-the-blank/cloze exercise. To do this, create sentence stems or a cloze paragraph in which you leave blanks for the vocabulary words.
- Use the vocabulary from the DOTS chart to write a paragraph that

summarizes the key ideas and details from the lesson.
- **P** **S** Have students share their definitions, paragraphs, etc. with peers and/or their small group.
- Return to the CLD student biography to make decisions related to affirmation of students' learning.

Author Talk: Affirmation

Throughout the presentation of the DOTS Chart strategy, we have emphasized the importance of validating and building upon CLD students' native language proficiency. The DOTS chart provides educators with the perfect vehicle for such validation by encouraging students to provide information in their native language, through pictures, or even in isolated English words. By allowing students such a range of ways to express themselves, educators can more accurately determine what each individual student knows and brings to the lesson. To maximize this knowledge gathering, we recommend that teachers carefully observe students as they are completing their DOTS chart and ask them questions about what they are writing. The students' answers combined with your own observations will help you make decisions about which students to partner together (e.g., which students might benefit most from hearing a particular peer's thoughts) during the lesson.

Continually revisiting the DOTS chart throughout the lesson helps CLD students make critical links between the words they brainstormed (the known) and the words they hear when the teacher is presenting the lesson (the unknown). One of the most effective strategies we have seen for employing the DOTS chart is for teachers to display a poster-sized version of the chart at the front of the class. As the lesson begins, the teacher adds words that the students wrote on their individual charts. During the lesson, new words are added to reinforce students' comprehension of the

preselected vocabulary. Whenever possible, we encourage teachers to explicitly model for the students how connections can be made between the words students shared on the group chart and the key vocabulary as it is encountered throughout the lesson. Teachers who have implemented the DOTS Chart strategy in this way have reported that this approach has indeed promoted the most powerful connections for both their CLD and their monolingual English-speaking students.

During the summative portion of the lesson, educators must make multiple decisions related to their own use of the DOTS chart. Of course, there are endless opportunities for informal assessment of students' learning throughout this teaching and learning process. However, for summative assessment, think of these options:

- Use the "S" portion of the DOTS activity to review and solidify the content with the students, and then return to your curriculum-required assessment tools.
- Create a checklist or a rubric that sets clear expectations for students' understanding of the vocabulary words or the paragraphs they create. As you develop the checklist or rubric, consider the variations that students will exhibit due to their individual stages of language acquisition.

As you implement this strategy, remember that it is about "connecting the dots" between what the individual student knows and his or her new learnings related to the topic.

Affirming Student Ownership: *"I" Get It!*
How does this process celebrate CLD student learning?

- **Sociocultural:** The final sharing phase of this strategy allows for meaningful demonstration of CLD students' learning as they are able to draw upon their personal knowledge of the topic to support their demonstration of key learnings.
- **Linguistic:** The flexibility inherent to the assessment phase of the DOTS Chart strategy allows all students, regardless of their language proficiency, to be assessed

on their engagement with and *progress* on the grade-level curriculum.
- **Academic:** The Affirmation phase ensures individual accountability for learning as students incorporate their own voice into their writing.
- **Cognitive:** The variety of assessment tools that can be used with this strategy provides students multiple avenues to demonstrate their learnings.

 SPOTLIGHT: Early Literacy Connection

Children come to school with a wide range of literacy and language skills in their first language, and these skills impact their ability in the second language (August, 2004). While native English speakers have been hearing the sounds (e.g., phonemes, intonation) of the English language on a daily basis since birth, many CLD learners are hearing these sounds for the first time. For this reason, learning to read can be challenging for young CLD students; it is often difficult for them to recognize the distinct sounds of the English language. The DOTS Chart strategy can be used to demonstrate how sound matches to print in the students' native language and in the English language. When children understand that there are relationships between the letters of written language and the individual sounds of oral language, their literacy skills are greatly enhanced (Freeman & Freeman, 2000).

The Power of Native Languages
To highlight connections between sounds and written symbols using the DOTS chart, choose a topic students

will work with as they complete their chart—first at school, and then in their homes. Send a blank DOTS chart home and ask parents to write on it meaningful words from their native language that relate to the chosen topic. Alternatively, parents can use their child's completed English version of the chart and simply add words from their native language. This activity (1) exposes students to ways in which the sounds of different languages match to print and (2) helps students create conceptual links between their native language and the information newly learned in the classroom. When the students return to school, allow time for them to discuss with a partner or small group their comparisons between the English words and the words in their native language version. If there happen to be cognates (i.e., words that are similarly spelled and have similar meanings) between the words in the student's native language and in English, they can locate the similarities and differences in the word's spelling and pronunciation in the two languages.

Biography-Driven Response to Intervention

The DOTS Chart is a strategy that provides students with structured opportunities to practice language. Teachers can employ the strategy to help differentiate their instruction, because it can be used to practice vocabulary with partners or small groups. At the same time, other students can use the DOTS chart to write sentences with the same vocabulary words. The same processes can be used during core instruction and tiered instruction. Thus, this strategy can be readily used with any subject material to help students add more and more words to their vocabulary.

One Classroom's Perspective

Activating:

This is the beginning of a new Literacy By Design reading unit on farming. I decided to use the DOTS Chart strategy to determine students' prior knowledge on the topic of farming. I also felt that using the DOTS chart would give all students the opportunity to share their prior knowledge without feeling any anxiety. I began the lesson by having all the students write the topic at the top of their page. Then I instructed them to write (including in their native language) and/or draw anything and everything they knew about the topic. They were given 5 minutes to write/draw. I walked around and observed as they did this. I was really impressed by some of the connections I saw my CLD students make. I knew some of them had lived on farms in Mexico, and it was clear that they brought a lot of insight that my monolingual English-speaking students did not have.

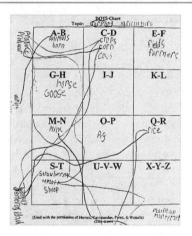

Connecting:

I then put the students in teams of three or four. I wanted to see if they could make connections to, and build on, the target vocabulary. So I introduced the target vocabulary by having the students write the key vocabulary words with red pencil around the outside of their DOTS chart. To make sure I supported/validated the native languages of my Spanish-speaking CLD students, I had all my students put the Spanish translation of each word next to the English version of the word as well. I then asked my students to associate their words, pictures, and ideas with the key vocabulary words on the outside of the DOTS chart by drawing lines to link any connections they saw using their blue pencil. We did a couple of examples of what some links might be, but I wanted to see what the students would come up with, so I told them their task was to make five links with their partner and be able to tell me why they made the links they did if asked. In essence, I wanted the students to solidify their thinking and connections. After completing this activity, I read the book *Farming* to the class. During the reading, we continued to discuss the vocabulary as it appeared in the book and was reinforced via the visuals/pictures. The class also created a list of words they had learned about farming. They added these words to their DOTS chart with a blue pencil and drew additional lines making new connections.

Affirming:

To assess the students' learning and understanding of the topic (farming), I had students pick an apple (a paper apple cutout with a task written on one side) and go to their desk and do what it said by drawing/writing (even in their native language) examples, writing the meaning of the vocabulary word, or using the vocabulary word in a meaningful sentence. The students had 5 minutes to complete their task. After the students had finished writing, they had a chance to share their work with a peer or the whole class. As they worked independently, I was able to listen and see how they were using the vocabulary words. It was great to see that most of the students were able to successfully use the words in context, particularly since they were able to refer back to their DOTS chart if they needed additional support.

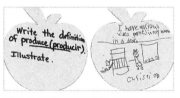

Student Voices

My Grandpa has a little farm in Mexico: pigs, geese, chickens. It was fun to learn, not boring.

—ELL Student
Speech Emergent

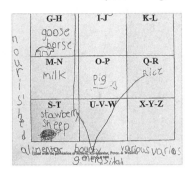

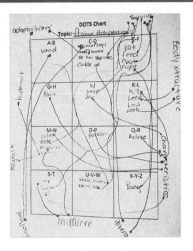

This was a fun activity because we got to show what we learned in a lot of different ways. The best part was getting to "connect the words" and show the teacher what I already knew!

—ELL Student
Intermediate Fluency

Seeing the words my partner used helped me think of new ways to match our vocabulary words.

—ELL Student
Early Production

TEMPLATE: DOTS Chart

Name: _____

DOTS Chart
(Determine, Observe, Talk, Summarize)

Topic: _____

A–B	C–D	E–F
G–H	**I–J**	**K–L**
M–N	**O–P**	**Q–R**
S–T	**U–V–W**	**X–Y–Z**

Note: A simpler version of the DOTS template with only 6 boxes (three rows of 2 boxes, or two rows of 3 boxes), each covering more letters of the alphabet, might be more appropriate for K–1 students. This version can be used as a model.

Available for free download and printing from www.tcpress.com

STRATEGY

Vocabulary Foldable

Foldables are an engaging activity that provides children the opportunity to demonstrate the knowledge they have previously held or gained through instructional teaching. The method of breaking down the assignment helps lower my CLD students' anxieties and sets all students up for success. My class this year tends to rush through assignments and not apply their previous knowledge to assignments or assessments. The information in the foldable is made comprehensible in manageable and meaningful units of information put in a very tactile and hands-on format. Through the use of foldables students were able to apply their learning in a format that demonstrated knowledge and understanding while lowering the anxiety that assessments oftentimes generate.

—Cheryl Werth, 3rd-Grade Teacher

Where Theory Meets Practice

One characteristic of effective vocabulary instruction is meaningful use. To accomplish meaningful use it is not sufficient that educators rely on classroom discussion as their sole means of vocabulary instruction (Bromley, 2002). Rather, meaningful use among students involves collaborating with peers and engaging in multiple types of activities that reinforce students' understanding of the target words. Research by Marzano and Pickering (2005) indicates that a systematic approach to academic vocabulary instruction is critical for CLD students. In earlier studies, Marzano (2003) and Crow and Quigley (1985) found that the most effective strategies for promoting the acquisition of academic vocabulary through content do the following:

- Separate relevant information from nonrelevant information for formulating a definition about the word
- Combine text, oral, and visual cues to develop a working definition
- Relate the new word to prior information already stored in students' long-term memories

The Vocabulary Foldable is a hands-on strategy that meets these conditions and allows students to use all four language modes—listening, speaking, reading, and writing—throughout the lesson.

In this strategy, students listen to the teacher and peers as they discuss their predictions about the vocabulary. They also talk about what they have learned or provide examples of the vocabulary words in use. Students are continually reading the vocabulary words in context, thinking about the new meanings they are learning, and comparing the new ideas to their initial understandings. As the lesson proceeds, students frequently revisit their vocabulary foldable to record new information that reveals their greater understanding of the words and related concepts. Such repeated practice not only promotes student learning but also builds high interest in future vocabulary study (Scott & Nagy, 1997).

The Vocabulary Foldable strategy is ideal for ensuring that students have multiple, meaningful opportunities to use the target words. The visual and kinesthetic nature of the strategy appeals to multiple learning styles. Because this strategy provides learners with a "tool in their hands," it promotes their engagement and mental processing of the content.

Materials Needed: Paper (four or five pieces per student; multicolored paper optional) • markers/colored pencils • pencils/pens

ACTIVATION: A Canvas of Opportunity

Directions:

- **T** Share the overarching topic of the lesson with the whole class.
- **S** Divide the class into groups of three or four students.
- **I** Before you share the vocabulary words, have the students individually create a foldable according to the directions at the end of this strategy description (page 87).
- Once the students have finished assembling the foldable, have them individually write the vocabulary words/concepts on the top of each flap (one word/concept per flap).
- Next, have students create a three-column grid on each flap, as shown below.

- Ask students to individually write or draw their predictions regarding each word in the "My prediction" column.
- **S** Have students share in their small groups what they already know about each word based on their individual predictions.
- As the students share, walk around the room and listen to the discussions they are having.
- Allow students to add to their individual predictions based on what is shared during the group discussion. Have students circle or underline any new information that is added so you will know it came out as a result of the group discussion.

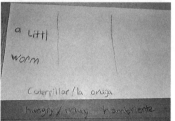

My prediction	What I learned/ Examples of the word	My definition

---

Activating the "*i*"

How does this process activate CLD students' existing knowledge?

- **Sociocultural:** CLD students are able to make predictions that are based on the background knowledge they bring to the lesson. They are also given the opportunity to hear other student's predications about the meaning of the vocabulary, which can lead them to recall other associations with the word.
- **Linguistic:** Students at all levels of English proficiency have access to the vocabulary words. They are able to use linguistic or nonlinguistic representations to

express their predictions about the words/concepts.
- **Academic:** The information is made more comprehensible because it is divided into manageable and meaningful units.
- **Cognitive:** The Vocabulary Foldable strategy enables CLD students to record information about concepts and vocabulary in the form of a usable visual that is a hands-on representation of their understanding.

CONNECTION: The Broad & Narrow Strokes of Learning

Directions:

- **T** You may choose to list the vocabulary words on the board at the front of the class for students to refer to as they work in their small groups/individually. This provides multiple exposures to the written words.
- **I** Proceed with the lesson, and as you come across a vocabulary word or key concept during the lesson, have students individually record their new understandings in the column "What I learned/Examples of the word," along with the textbook page numbers on which they found examples/ideas related to the word. Students can also choose to do drawings for the examples they found.

- **S** As students work on their vocabulary foldables, at various points throughout the lesson allow them to do a turn-and-talk to discuss their new learnings about the vocabulary words/concepts with each other in their small groups.
- As students finish working on their foldables, allow them to discuss all the words with each other one more time to promote their English language acquisition and overall retention of the words/concepts.
  - Placing the students in a variety of small group settings during the lesson is highly encouraged, as

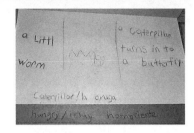

this regrouping allows them to benefit from hearing other students' perspectives and understandings related to the content being covered.
- **I** While information is being shared, encourage students to add new insights to their foldables.

Connecting to the "*i*+1"
How does this process move CLD students from the known to the unknown?

- **Sociocultural:** When using foldables in the Connection phase, CLD students are encouraged to work with peers to support their learning. In this environment, students are able to continue to build upon their existing vocabulary through learning the target words in context and through class discussions.
- **Linguistic:** Through the multiple exposures to the vocabulary, CLD students are expanding their conceptual connections and understanding of key content. Documenting the information related to the words as

they are encountered in the lesson/text also promotes acquisition of the terms in English.
- **Academic:** Foldables are concrete tools that allow the students to continually record and organize details and process the vocabulary/concepts covered in the lesson.
- **Cognitive:** CLD students are actively engaged in monitoring their learning throughout the process. This type of engagement leads to a higher level of understanding and greater retention of the vocabulary.

AFFIRMATION: A Gallery of Understanding

Directions:

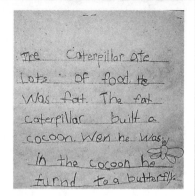

- **S** Ask each group of students to generate definitions of the words/concepts. Allow students some time to negotiate with each other to arrive at appropriate definitions for the terms.
- **I** After students have decided on definitions in their small groups, have them individually write the definitions on their foldables in the column "My definition."
- Next, have students use the back of the foldable to individually write a paragraph or a summary using the target words/concepts. Students

should focus on one or more of the following areas in their writing:
- ○ Setting, plot, and overall theme of the story.
- ○ Language conventions of sentences structure, mechanics, spelling, etc.
- ○ Persuasive or expository paragraph depending upon the topic.
- **P** You can also have students use the foldable to quiz a partner on the words/concepts.
- **T** When the unit or lesson is completed, revisit the foldable one more time and remind students to use it as a study tool.

Author Talk: Affirmation

Given the emphasis within the Common Core State Standards for English Language Arts (ELA) on the need to articulate rigorous grade-level expectations in the areas of speaking, listening, reading, and writing, hands-on strategies like Vocabulary Foldable are a wonderful way to ensure that CLD students meet the standards and are better prepared for college and career in the future (NGA & CCSSO, 2010). For CLD students, the way foldables specifically build on existing background knowledge is particularly critical. CLD students often have first language literacy knowledge and skills that boost their acquisition of language and literacy skills in English. The key for us as educators is to access this knowledge and then build upon it.

Highly effective teachers adapt the Vocabulary Foldable strategy to reflect the needs of their individual students. For example, they take into consideration their students' developmental level and need for native language support. For some students, teachers might require only a picture and a one-word description of the vocabulary word. Other students might be asked to provide a picture, a short definition, and a meaningful sentence for each term. Still others might also incorporate a full dictionary definition. In each case, the student is held accountable to demonstrate his or her understanding of the key vocabulary.

Affirming Student Ownership: *"I" Get It!*
How does this process celebrate CLD student learning?

- **Sociocultural:** Students will develop self-confidence in themselves as learners and in their understanding, as demonstrated through their construction of a personalized definition of each word.
- **Linguistic:** CLD students can continually revisit their foldable to solidify the grade-level vocabulary words and concepts they are learning in English.

- **Academic:** The final phase of the Vocabulary Foldable strategy holds the students accountable for documenting what was learned while integrating reading and writing.
- **Cognitive:** Students can use their foldable as a tool as they demonstrate their learning in written and oral formats.

SPOTLIGHT: Early Literacy Connection

"For children to learn to write, they must write" (Beaty & Pratt, 2007, p. 231). However, it is important to remember that young children's writing initially consists of drawing and scribbling. Foldables are a great way to document the evolution of young children's writing at home as it progresses from drawing and scribbling to more structured writing. To guide parents in the use of foldables at home, you can suggest using the following activity.

Let's Write!

Teachers can send blank foldables home with students and encourage parents to write culturally relevant "stories" with their children. To create these story foldables, parents can dictate the story to their children and have the children first draw a picture on each page. Then the children can listen as parents, sounding out the words in their native language, record one sentence for each page of the story. After the pictures and sentences have been completed, the parents can read the story again with their children, talking about the pictures and sentences together. The parents should should conduct this activity over several days so that their children will not be overwhelmed by having to do all of the pictures on the same day (unless, of course, the children want to).

For parents who might question the validity of creating the story in their native language rather than in English, emphasize the importance of the native language and cross-language transfer (Cummins, 2001). In addition, tell the parents that this helps their children build a solid literacy foundation that sets the stage for them to become proficient readers and writers.

Biography-Driven Response to Intervention

Foldables support students' understanding of the academic vocabulary words and promote their comprehension skills by providing a place to document initial connections, take notes, and record learning. This strategy enables students to organize their thinking about the content and provides a constant scaffold for language production within the core curriculum or as part of an intervention. Foldables also easily lend themselves to use as an extension toward tiered instruction after first being used during core instruction. Students can focus on the skills of predicting and summarizing as they work with the words.

One Classroom's Perspective

Activating:

Foldables are a tool that I use in my classroom regularly. My students enjoy constructing the foldables, and it has been proven to be effective for allowing my students to organize their thoughts in words. For this lesson, I was introducing a new story (*The Great Kapok Tree*) and I wanted to make sure my students understood the academic vocabulary associated with the rain- forest (i.e., rainforest, canopy, understory, underbrush, and ancestors). So I had the students each make a foldable and label each flap using the vocabulary terms I had identified before the lesson. Then I had students individually predict what they thought each word meant. After making their predictions, I had the students share them with each other.

One Classroom's Perspective (continued)

Connecting:

We then began to read the story as a whole group. To help students focus on the key vocabulary, I asked them to listen for each word on their foldable; when they heard one, they were to raise their hands to stop me. Each time we encountered a vocabulary word in the text, we discussed its meaning as a whole group. After agreeing as a class on the meaning of the word, students individually wrote the definitions into their foldable. Students also added a sentence or definition in their own words that would help them remember the meaning of the word.

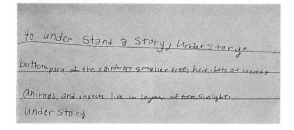

Affirming:

At the end of the lesson, students used the information from their foldable to write a summary of what they had learned about the rainforest. Students were encouraged to use specific vocabulary words from their foldable in their summaries. At the end of the lesson, I noticed that the Vocabulary Foldable activity not only helped my students have a better understanding of the story but it also increased their confidence. What I have learned about foldables is that a student at any level is capable of completing one, and students take ownership in their work when constructing a foldable.

Student Voices

It really helps me when I can write down the information and look at it again if I don't remember the answer.

—*ELL Student*
Speech Emergent

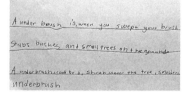

I like being able to use the foldable to take notes. It really helps me understand the vocabulary words a lot better—especially some of the words I never heard before but they kind of sounded like words I knew in Spanish.

—*ELL Student*
Intermediate Fluency

I really like being able to talk to my friends about the words! It helps me to write down what the word means. That way I can remember it better!

—*ELL Student*
Speech Emergent

INSTRUCTIONS: Creating Your Foldable

Materials: A single foldable will require four or five pieces of construction paper in different colors and a stapler.

Step 1:	Depending on the number of vocabulary words/objectives for the lesson, have students use four or five pieces of paper in different colors.
Step 2:	Layer the sheets of paper on top of each other with an inch of space between each color.
Step 3:	Fold the paper stack in half, stopping an inch below where the same color meets itself, so that there are two layers of the same color in the middle. Make a crisp crease.  
Step 4:	Staple at the crease. 
Step 5:	When finished, students should be able to flip and view both sides of each colored page. 

STRATEGY

Tic-Tac-Tell

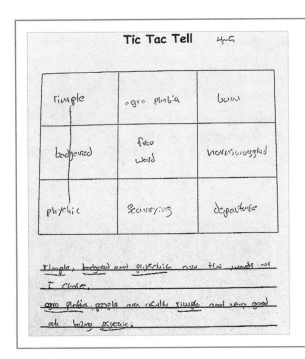

The strategy helped my students learn new vocabulary and information about the world around them. They will be able to build on this information/knowledge as steps to further knowledge. My students liked the strategy, especially when they got to draw the pictures and act out the different vocabulary words. Using more than one modality for learning really helps my students learn, retain, and generalize information, which is what I want.

—*Marcia Waite, K–5 Special Education Teacher*

Where Theory Meets Practice

Selection of vocabulary is paramount when approaching instruction. Yet the question that challenges many teachers, particularly those of CLD students is, What vocabulary is most important to teach? The answer to this question is not simple, but research by Beck et al. (2002) and Calderón (2007) has helped reinforce the importance of thinking about vocabulary in systematic and strategic ways. If we want our CLD students to have access to words that will accelerate their academic achievement and vocabulary comprehension, we need to focus on providing targeted vocabulary instruction.

Central to educators' success in selecting appropriate vocabulary to teach within the classroom is knowing the biographies of the students they are teaching (Herrera, 2010). Teachers who understand the backgrounds of their students know better the vocabulary that can be learned incidentally (through general discussion and out-of-school experiences) and the vocabulary that must be taught more intentionally (through explicit instruction). To set the conditions for academic vocabulary development—thus improving academic learning for CLD students—teachers need to select activities and strategies that

- Support students' construction of meaning with the new words
- Explore the relationship between the new words and what students already know
- Define the words by making cultural and linguistic links to student schemas (Herrera, 2010, p. 97)

Tic-Tac-Tell is a strategy that sets up these conditions by explicitly providing CLD students the opportunity to engage in the active construction of meaningful sentences as they define key vocabulary terms. A takeoff of the popular children's game Tic-Tac-Toe, this strategy begins with selecting nine key vocabulary words from the lesson and placing them in a Tic-Tac-Toe pattern (three across, three down). Each student is then asked to choose three words using the Tic-Tac-Toe approach of selecting three words "in a row." Once students have selected their words, they are asked to write meaningful sentences in which all three words are appropriately used.

Tic-Tac-Tell is a strategy that takes learners from a basic understanding of vocabulary words to a more sophisticated level. As noted by August and Collins (2005), although it may be tempting to keep vocabulary instruction for CLD students at the basic level, these students, like all others in the class, need and will benefit from rich instruction in sophisticated words and word understanding. As the strategy progresses through different layers of student-initiated and teacher-directed activity, it provides students with many opportunities to move to an advanced level of word understanding.

Materials Needed: Nine key vocabulary words (pre-selected) • colored construction paper or regular paper (one piece per student), sticky notes • a book to share with the whole class • pencils/pens

ACTIVATION: A Canvas of Opportunity

Directions:

- Identify nine key vocabulary words.
- **I** Post the words on chart paper or a white board, PowerPoint slide, or Smart Board at the front of the room where all students can see them. Pass out a piece of paper to each student and instruct them to fold their paper so they have nine boxes (in a 3 × 3 arrangement).
- Have students copy one word into each box. The arrangement of the words on the page is not important.
- Ask students to guess which game their paper looks like (i.e., a Tic-Tac-Toe grid).
- Tell them that by the end of the lesson, they are going to play a new game—Tic-Tac-Tell—with the vocabulary words.
- **P** To begin, have students search their permanent memory "folders" by quickly talking to a partner about what they know about each of the words on their Tic-Tac-Tell chart.
- **I** Next, instruct students to individually draw or write in English or their L1 one connection they

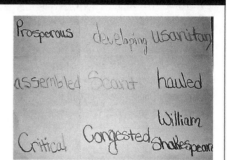

made for each word, under that word on their chart.
- Circulate around the room to observe students' connections.
- **P** Have students share their connections with their partner.

Activating the "*i*"

How does this process activate CLD students' existing knowledge?

- **Sociocultural:** Students are drawing from their background knowledge to make schematic connections to the vocabulary words.
- **Linguistic:** Peer interaction supports students in making meaningful connections to the vocabulary terms.

- **Academic:** Immersing students in the structured use of academic vocabulary promotes the achievement of grade-level skills and academic standards.
- **Cognitive:** The use of a game format to develop academic skills engages students in the learning process.

CONNECTION: The Broad & Narrow Strokes of Learning

Directions:

- **T** Conduct the lesson or the reading activity, with a focus on the vocabulary words.
- **I** As you encounter the vocabulary words in the lesson, discuss the meaning of each word and have students individually write a sentence using the vocabulary word on the back of their Tic-Tac-Tell chart in the box that corresponds to the word on the other side. *Tip:* Having students number the boxes on both sides of the Tic-Tac-Tell chart will help them correctly align the vocabulary terms and sentences.

- After the content has been covered, have your CLD students go back and write a definition for each vocabulary term in their own words. (***Note:*** For students with more limited skills in English, you can have them write the definition in their native language and/or draw a picture.)
- **P** **S** Next, have students share their definitions with a partner and/or small group.
- **P** Then have students work with a partner to select any three words (in any arrangement) from one

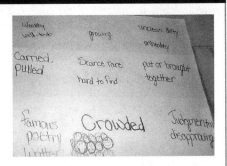

student's Tic-Tac-Tell grid and create a sentence using all three words.
- Circulate around the room and have each set of partners share their sentence with you. Provide additional modeling as needed.

Author Talk: Connection

Tic-Tac-Tell is a wonderful strategy for promoting the explicit and systematic instruction of key vocabulary. Not only does it support students' active construction of meaning but it also helps them make meaningful links between existing knowledge and new learning in a fun and interactive way. To truly understand the potential of this strategy, consider it through the eyes of Mrs. Clark, a 6th-grade reading teacher:

This strategy tied closely to my CLD students' background. They used their three chosen words that made the most sense to them. Building on their prior knowledge and background, it was easy for them to write their sentence. It is evident when CLD students struggle with meaning by the way they write, and it usually goes back to their upbringing in another language. One of my CLD students described a family celebration in her sentence. I was amazed at the ability she had to tie her three chosen words into a complete sentence that was perfectly written. It was very interesting reading their sentences and trying to clarify the picture in my mind of their family and home. The more insight I have into my students' biographies, the better I can provide proper education for

them. This was a fabulous way of continuing my own education about my students and their histories. I used this information to help them build/clarify their vocabulary and make it part of their permanent memory for future use.

As shared by Mrs. Clark, this strategy promotes individualized instruction. By allowing CLD students to select the vocabulary they are most comfortable with and use it to create meaningful sentences, you give them the autonomy to show what they know while still keeping their affective filters low.

Additional tips for promoting your CLD students' success with this strategy include

- Strategically pair CLD students so that they continually have the support of a peer with whom they can construct the meaning of the new words and make and share connections to what they already know.
- As students become proficient with this strategy, you can leave some squares on the grid blank and have students select words themselves.
- As you provide students with the vocabulary words, you can have them substitute antonyms or synonyms for words to demonstrate higher-level understandings.

Connecting to the "i+1"
How does this process move CLD students from the known to the unknown?

- **Sociocultural:** The collaborative construction of a meaningful sentence allows CLD students to work with peers to gain a deeper understanding of the content via discussion about each word and its meaning.
- **Linguistic:** Students are using all four domains—listening, speaking, reading, and writing—to create their meaningful sentences.

- **Academic:** Students are able to use their background knowledge and new learning to create content-based sentences that show their comprehension of the academic vocabulary.
- **Cognitive:** CLD students' thinking and learning is stretched to the i+1 as they incorporate all three academic terms together into one meaningful sentence.

AFFIRMATION: A Gallery of Understanding

Directions:

- Provide each student with a Tic-Tac-Tell grid that has the nine vocabulary words from the lesson prewritten in the boxes.
- Have students individually create sentences by using three vocabulary words from the Tic-Tac-Tell grid.
  - Explain to students that this time they are to create sentences in Tic-Tac-Toe fashion by choosing three words in a row (diagonally, vertically, or horizontally).

- Observe students' work to make sure the completed sentences make sense and demonstrate student learnings.
  - Initially, allow students with more limited skills in English to work in pairs or groups.
  - As students become proficient at the task, have them create sentences individually so you will be able to assess their personal understanding of the words/content.
- **P** **T** After students have created

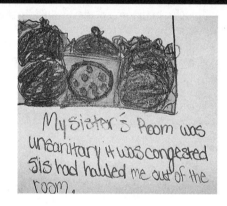

their sentences, ask them to explain the sentences to their peers and then finally to the whole group.

Affirming Student Ownership: "I" Get It!
How does this process celebrate CLD student learning?

- **Sociocultural:** This strategy builds on CLD students' individual biographies because they can use their own background knowledge and experiences as the starting point for sentence generation.
- **Linguistic:** Students have to use their knowledge of English syntax to successfully generate meaningful sentences.

- **Academic:** The Tic-Tac-Tell strategy empowers CLD students to actively transform text from words on a page to meaningful applications in their own lives.
- **Cognitive:** CLD students are cognitively engaged as they perform this activity, and they are pushed to demonstrate their understanding of key vocabulary in nontraditional ways.

SPOTLIGHT: Early Literacy Connection

For most native speakers of English, little to no thought is given as to how words are put together to form sentences. However, children must acquire two kinds of knowledge to successfully form sentences: "the order in which words are put together to form sentences and the relationship that exists among the different constituents, for in sentences, not all the words have the same magnitude of importance" (Piper, 2007, p. 42). Tic-Tac-Tell is a great strategy for promoting students' awareness of word order and word use within sentences.

Rebus Tic-Tac-Tell

A rebus text uses pictures or symbols to represent words in a sentence or story. This visual support is especially helpful for beginning readers who do not recognize many words by sight. The rebus cues enable students to follow along and "read" sentences of greater levels of difficulty. It is even more fun for students to create their own rebus sentences and eventually rebus stories.

To implement Rebus Tic-Tac-Tell with your students, follow these steps:

- Introduce your students to the idea of rebus stories by reading them examples such as Shirley Neitzel's (1989) *The Jacket I Wear in the Snow.*
- Have a class discussion about how this type of book is different from other books that have been read in the class. It is important that the students realize that the picture representations of the missing words are exactly the same each time they are used.
- Replace some of the words that might normally appear on the Tic-Tac-Tell grid with pictures.
- Model how to write a rebus sentence with the pictures and words from the grid.
- Have students create their own rebus sentences. (***Note:*** Some students may need additional assistance; if necessary, they can dictate their sentence explanations to an adult.)
- Next, have students share their sentences with a partner or small group of peers.
- Revoice some of the students' sentences for the whole class.

Biography-Driven Response to Intervention

The Tic-Tac-Tell strategy takes learners from a basic understanding of the vocabulary words to a more sophisticated understanding of each one, a critical aspect of literacy instruction for second language learners. During individual and group work, students progress through different layers of student-initiated and teacher-directed activities. Tic-Tac-Tell provides students with the support they need to move to an advanced level of word understanding. This strategy promotes word consciousness, which is critical for Tier 1 interventions.

One Classroom's Perspective

Activating:

I began the lesson by explaining to the students that Tic-Tac-Tell is a cognitive learning strategy that enables culturally and linguistically diverse (CLD) students (and *all* students) to articulate content-area learning, especially with vocabulary words. I then asked the students if they knew what a strategy was, and then what kinds of strategies they use to figure out new vocabulary words. I was amazed at the response I got. They identified strategies such as looking the word up in the dictionary, checking the glossary of the book, rereading the sentence that the word was in, and asking a friend or the teacher.

I shared with them that over this past year they have been learning strategies that specifically help students who speak another language (CLD students) and that these strategies are good strategies for all students as well. I then gave them a blank copy of a Tic-Tac-Tell chart with the preselected vocabulary at the top of the chart. I also gave each student a 3 × 5 index card. We talked about vocabulary words in the story and how we go about giving each word a visual image in our mind. We took time as a class to fill in the Tic-Tac-Tell chart with nine vocabulary words of their choosing.

Connecting:

Taking time to play a short game of Bingo allowed the students to focus on each word as I pronounced the words randomly. Once they had three in a row they had to repeat those words back to me and then provide a sentence with one or more of the vocabulary words. This provided the extra practice of hearing the word pronounced correctly and locating the word in written form as well. Next, students had to choose two of those words to illustrate. Students paired up with a person in their

team to share their pictures and explain why they the illustrated the words that way. I moved around the room, providing students time to express their words and share them with their partners. This also allowed me to see who was having difficulty and to determine if they truly understood what a word meant by having them explain their drawing to me.

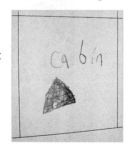

One Classroom's Perspective (*continued*)

Affirming:

Finally, the students used their 3 × 5 index card to create a sentence using three of their vocabulary words. This allowed for higher-level application in using the words in a sentence. In pairs, the students read their sentences to each other for peer review/edit. This took the failure option out of the task and allowed the students to accept ways to fix the sentence if it didn't make sense or if a word was not used correctly. At the end of the class time, I gathered all the index cards and read each one aloud without telling the class who created that sentence. After each sentence was read, we gave a Kagan (round of applause) or thumbs up for what a great job the student did. What I learned by doing this strategy with the 3rd-graders was that each student was eager to learn a new way to deal with familiar and unfamiliar words. It took the fear out of learning, and the affective filters were very low because they had many opportunities to be a participant and to be successful at the tasks given to them.

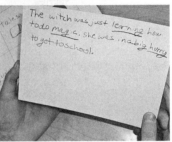

Student Voices

The grid helped because the definitions we wrote in our own words were really close to look at.
—*ELL Student*
Intermediate Fluency

Reading my sentence at the end helped me know what I know about the words we learned.
—*ELL Student*
Intermediate Fluency

I did not know the words when we started. Now I know them better.
—*ELL Student*
Advanced Fluency

TEMPLATE: Tic-Tac-Tell

Tic-Tac-Tell

Write a vocabulary word in each box.

STRATEGY

Vocabulary Quilt

Vocabulary quilts are an unlimited way to get children to start thinking about a new topic or story. Vocabulary quilts allow students to tap into their prior knowledge through not only words but also pictures and discussion with peers. I think the most noticeable impact of this strategy is the fact that the students remember these words throughout the story and even after, when we see them in other content areas.

—*Mikki Rouse, 2nd-Grade Teacher*

Where Theory Meets Practice

When provided with numerous opportunities to discuss and reflect on relationships among concepts, as well as connections between lesson content and their own background knowledge, students are able to deepen their understanding of the target vocabulary during the lesson. These meaningful interactions with the new vocabulary in the context of the lesson promote student transfer of vocabulary from their working memory to their permanent memory (Sousa, 2006; Willis, 2006). For educators, the goal of vocabulary instruction is to have students store the meanings of vocabulary words in their permanent memory to be accessed, consciously or unconsciously, whenever needed (Stahl, 1999). The more connections that are made to known information in the permanent memory, the easier it is for students to retain and access the new content at a later time.

The Vocabulary Quilt strategy extends from literature and research indicating that the brain continually strives to create connections between preexisting, known information and new, unknown information (Donovan & Bransford, 2005; Wessels, 2008; Wolfe & Brandt, 1998). Students record thoughts and images that they immediately associate with the target words in a process that prompts them to draw from their background knowledge. For CLD students, this strategy is particularly effective because it allows them to document what they know by using nonlinguistic representations (illustrations), their native language, or individual words or phases in English.

The ongoing use of the vocabulary quilt throughout the lesson enables teachers to encourage and guide CLD students to make connections from the known to the unknown, clarify misconceptions, and add to their understanding of the academic vocabulary. Because ELL students cannot always rely on their existing language skills to learn and retain knowledge in English, nonlinguistic supports such as those used in the Vocabulary Quilt strategy have been found to be particularly important (Gregory & Burkman, 2012; Hill & Flynn, 2006).

A video clip illustrating implementation of this strategy appears on the DVD included with this book and is available for viewing online at:

www.tcpress.com/AcceleratingLiteracyVideos.html

Materials Needed: Chart paper • sticky notes • textbook or other books • markers/colored pencils • pencils/pens • paper

96

ACTIVATION: A Canvas of Opportunity

Directions:

- Choose eight vocabulary words based on their relevance to the lesson.
- To make the vocabulary quilt, create eight boxes on chart paper (or any other kind of paper) by folding it vertically twice and horizontally once.
- Write the preselected vocabulary words in the squares (one word per square).
- **T** Share with the class the topic of the lesson.
- **S** Divide students into groups of four or five and give each group a vocabulary quilt.
- Explain to the students that they are going to write (in English or their native language) and/or draw whatever comes to mind when they read each of the vocabulary words in the boxes.
  - Make sure to stress that students should reach into their permanent memory to look for connections to the words on the paper.

- If a student does not have an association with the new vocabulary word, he or she can simply rewrite the word in the quilt square. This allows the the individual to continue to be engaged in the vocabulary strategy and lets the teacher know that the he or she needs more direct instruction with the word.
- **I** Give students 3–5 minutes to individually write something in the box for each word. To enhance your ability to determine what individual students know, have each student in a group use a marker of a different color.
- **S** After the students have written/drawn their associations, provide them with the opportunity to discuss in their group the rationales behind their connections.
- You can also have students look for similar words on the quilts and circle/highlight these words to show the similarities among students' thoughts.

Author Talk: Activation

When implementing the Vocabulary Quilt strategy in the primary grades, you might want to limit the number of vocabulary words to four. It is also helpful to remember that the vocabulary words should focus on a central theme. This theme should allow for conceptual growth around a topic. When selecting vocabulary words, a good question to ask is, What vocabulary words are my students going to need to use to develop oral language and listening comprehension? To reinforce the development of these vocabulary words, use authentic literature to maximize children's vocabulary growth. Additional activities such as word sorts and word associations can be used to help students continue to learn the words.

For students in upper elementary grades, you may want to have them develop their own individual vocabulary quilt to revise and confirm their understanding of the vocabulary as the lesson develops. The new vocabulary quilt can then be compared with the first one as a baseline for vocabulary learning (i.e., an informal pre/postassessment).

Activating the "*i*"

How does this process activate CLD students' existing knowledge?

- **Sociocultural:** Students benefit from hearing their peers' personal associations with the vocabulary words, which can lead to a new level of understanding about the words.
- **Linguistic:** All students are actively engaged in the learning process. Linguistic representations (words or phrases) can be done in English or their native language. In addition, the students can use nonlin-

guistic representations (pictures) to express their associations.
- **Academic:** This strategy allows *each* student to show what academic knowledge he or she brings to the lesson before formal instruction by the teacher.
- **Cognitive:** When students provide rationales for their connections, they more fully explore the depths of their existing knowledge of the words.

 CONNECTION: The Broad & Narrow Strokes of Learning

Directions:

- When the students have finished with the words (i.e., after the Activation phase), post the vocabulary quilts to make "interactive word walls" that students can revisit as the lesson proceeds.
- **T** As you read the text with the students, give them sticky notes they can use to write down additional information about the key vocabulary words as they encounter them in the text.
- **I** When a vocabulary word is found in context, students individually can write the meaning of the word on a sticky note.

- Have students add their sticky notes to their vocabulary quilts.
- **S** At pertinent points in the reading, you can have students adjourn to small groups to discuss specific details about the immediate topic of concern. They can add to their quilts additional information gleaned from these group discussions.
- Working as a facilitator, refer to students' vocabulary quilts and revoice the connections between students' initial associations and added text-related knowledge.

Connecting to the "*i*+1"

How does this process move CLD students from the known to the unknown?

- **Sociocultural:** The vocabulary quilt is a concrete tool that students can continually refer back to as they connect with the activated existing knowledge they recorded in the initial stage of vocabulary instruction.
- **Linguistic:** Having students add to the quilt key words from the text supports their academic vocabulary development in English.

- **Academic:** Through multiple exposures to the vocabulary words, students expand their conceptual understandings of the terms.
- **Cognitive:** After discovering the vocabulary word in context, the students are able to revisit their initial associations with the words on the vocabulary quilt to revise or confirm their original understandings.

AFFIRMATION: A Gallery of Understanding

Directions:

- **S** Assign each group two or three vocabulary words. Have students work to generate a definition for each word.
- **T** Once groups are finished with their definitions, they can share them with the whole class.
- **I** Then have students individually or in pairs write a paragraph summarizing what was learned. Remind them to use the vocabulary words on the quilt and the student-generated definitions.

- For students with limited abilities in English, the following adaptations can be made in the writing activity:
  - Have students dictate the sentences to a teacher, paraprofessional, or peer who can write them.
  - Allow students to write in their native language.
  - Pair the students with more proficient peers who can help them write the paragraph/journal entry in English.

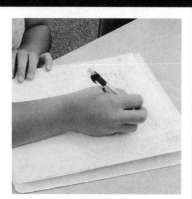

Affirming Student Ownership: *"I"* Get It!
How does this process celebrate CLD student learning?

- **Sociocultural:** Students have the opportunity to interact with peers as they generate meaningful definitions of the vocabulary terms.
- **Linguistic:** Students at all levels of language proficiency are able to use the vocabulary quilt as a resource to support them in documenting their learnings.

- **Academic:** Vocabulary quilts are a great way to independently assess learning via the student-generated paragraphs, which incorporate the academic vocabulary with an emphasis on conceptual understanding.
- **Cognitive:** Revisiting the original vocabulary quilt to write their summary allows students to evaluate their deepened level of understanding of the vocabulary.

SPOTLIGHT: Early Literacy Connection

Because vocabulary development is a key ingredient in the learning-to-read process and is a predictor of success with future reading skills, children must be given more opportunities in the early grades to increase their vocabulary (Bortnem, 2008). The Vocabulary Quilt strategy allows students to interact with vocabulary words before hearing them in a story or upcoming lesson in order to make concrete connections between their existing knowledge and the newly introduced vocabulary. This foundational knowledge can then be used to build new understandings of the vocabulary.

Post What We Know

When implementing the Vocabulary Quilt strategy with young learners, consider the following adaptation:

- Start with a poster-sized vocabulary quilt with six to eight folded rectangles (depending on the number of vocabulary words). One vocabulary word should be written in the center of each rectangle. In addition to the poster-sized quilt, write each vocabulary word on a blank sheet of paper.
- Gather the students in a whole-group area and explain the class vocabulary quilt. Read and point to each word to make sure all the students can see and hear the word being read aloud.
- Model activating your background knowledge with one of the words from the quilt. Write words and draw your associations with the vocabulary word.

- Next, ask students to volunteer their associations with the word you chose. Add those to the quilt.
- Place the students in small groups; there should be enough groups for each group to take one of the remaining vocabulary words. Make sure that every student in the group has a writing implement of a different color. This allows you to make a quick assessment of the students' background knowledge and engagement in the task.
- Explain that they are to write or draw whatever comes to mind when they hear or read their group's vocabulary word. Remind students that if they have no associations with the words, they can simply rewrite that word on the paper.
- After each group has finished, bring the students back together as a whole group.
- Revisit the whole-class vocabulary quilt, and as you read each word, have the group with that particular word share their associations.
- As the group is sharing, rewrite their thoughts on the whole-class quilt. Then ask the whole group if they have additional associations with the word that need to be added. Continue this process until all the vocabulary words have been discussed.
- Throughout the story or lesson, continually refer back to the whole-class quilt and make necessary changes to capture the accurate meanings of the vocabulary words.

Biography-Driven Response to Intervention

The Vocabulary Quilt is a strategy that can expose students to vocabulary at many levels. The linguistic and pictorial representations generated by each student and his or her peers help learners of all levels of English language skill to grasp the meaning of the target vocabulary. This is a great tool for supporting students as they extend upon their existing word knowledge and oral language skills to record and discuss initial impressions of the vocabulary words. Students further solidify their understanding of the words as they collaborate to define them. When students use the same quilt during tiered instruction, they are able to focus on multiple perspectives on the words, thereby strengthening their understanding of the vocabulary they encountered in the core curriculum.

Vocabulary Quilt: Scaffolding for CLD Students' Success

SOCIOCULTURAL BENEFITS	LINGUISTIC BENEFITS
• Helps enhance students' social interactions. • Allows for students' experiential background to be used in responding. **Classroom Tips** • As you ask your students to define the words, allow students to describe the words in their native language. • Have students discuss the words to share their experiential knowledge as they are done.	• Allows for students to describe the words using linguistic and nonlinguistic representations. • Works as a language development tool. **Classroom Tips** • Students can classify the words by looking at the origin, word parts, root words, cognates, etc. • Post the completed quilts on the wall to serve as a reference tool for language development.
ACADEMIC BENEFITS	**COGNITIVE BENEFITS**
• Important concepts are clearly defined. • Vocabulary is explicitly identified and connected to the critical concepts. **Classroom Tips** • As the quilts are completed, have students use the words from the quilt to write sentences. • Have students explain a specific concept using words from the quilt. If you plan to do this, make sure that the words relate to the specific concept.	• Allows students to access their prior knowledge and schema. • Students make experiential and academic conceptual connections through vocabulary words. **Classroom Tips** • Have students explain their schema and the thought process regarding the words to gain an access into students' thought processes. • Quilts can work as a pre-assessment tool for you to gauge your students' understanding of a concept.

One Classroom's Perspective

Activating:

The Vocabulary Quilt is a strategy I enjoy using, and it is frequently requested by students. As we begin the activity, we discuss how to think about the words—and not just guessing, but using decoding skills taught throughout the year. As I introduce the words, discussion occurs about the story and how the particular word might relate to the context. I choose this strategy because all students are engaged at once. Each student has a section to write in at the same time. All students are the leader (first to write about a word) as well as get the opportunity to take less of a risk by seeing what others have written. Before I let the students begin writing, we read the words aloud to make sure students know pronunciation. This also gives the students a little thinking time.

Since we have done this many times, students each have their assigned colors in their groups. At the beginning of the activity, I remind the students they have 3 minutes to write or sketch what they think the word means. When the timer goes off, they need to move to the next word, finished or not. As students are looking through what others have written, I encourage students to add or expand on what others have written. When students do not have any idea about the word or someone has already written what they believe to be the correct idea, they are to find a different way to represent the word (sketch/drawing/sentence using context clues/real world example). Since each student has 3 minutes, there is little time for off-task behavior. With

each student having different colors, it is easy to see what each one has done. When all words have been worked through, we hang the pages at the front of the room.

One Classroom's Perspective

Connecting:

Each group has sticky notes. We begin reading the story, stopping each time one of the vocabulary words is read. Discussion occurs about whether what was written on the vocabulary quilts is accurate. Using the context clues, students write the correct definition on the sticky note and stick it to the chart. Depending on the length of text, this process can take two days.

Affirming:

When we have finished all the words, students take their charts back to their groups. The students write the correct definitions from the sticky notes in their vocabulary journals. Again, this part of the activity engages all the students. When the words are entered in their journals, students write either sentences using the words correctly or use the words in a story with correct context. Depending on the writing skill we are using, I try to integrate skills with vocabulary. One particular instance was when we were working on dialogue. Students were to use the vocabulary in a dialogue amongst characters.

As groups, students present their sentences to the other class members. I have found that my students are tougher on each other than I am. As they are reading, positive suggestions are given to make sentences more accurate or stronger.

Student Voices

I liked working with my friends because if I didn't understand something someone else could help me.

—*ELL Student*
Intermediate Fluency

I like drawing the pictures because I did not know how to spell the words.

—*ELL Student*
Speech Emergent

That seemed like a lot of extra work but now I see that it was cool 'cause I got to use pictures.

—*ELL Student*
Intermediate Fluency

TEMPLATE: Vocabulary Quilt

Vocabulary Quilt

Write a vocabulary word in the center of each box.

STRATEGY

Thumb Challenge

I loved to see them interact with each other on a personal level and try out their English. Students interacted by listening, speaking, and responding to a partner while giving the definition and an example word. The background knowledge came into play with the example they were to come up with. I could see them open up to each other, and it was a nice way to see them try out their listening and speaking skills in a safe environment. Because of the way it is set up, I walk around the room and can listen to the discussions and questions my students ask each other. Students were very excited to use something new to help them learn.

—*Anne Abell, 1st-Grade Teacher*

Where Theory Meets Practice

Research by Jensen (2000a, 2000b) has found that learning is best when focused, diffused, and then focused again. The Thumb Challenge strategy provides students with this opportunity for learning that is focused, diffused through conversation, and then focused again as it is connected back to the text. By allowing students to engage in student talk, where they are able to practice and apply their language/vocabulary in a safe environment, we provide them with the "brain break" they need to absorb the vocabulary.

Student talk is further enhanced when learners have opportunities to practice language with peers who have more advanced language skills. The more opportunities we provide for students to work together to negotiate meanings of academic terms, the more chances they have to extend upon their own learning. Because students are both

orally and physically involved in the activity, this strategy also speaks to the multiple learning styles present in our classrooms.

Finally, repeated, meaningful exposure to vocabulary terms throughout the lesson is essential for CLD students to internalize new words and make them part of their permanent vocabulary. Thumb Challenge allows learners to practice their vocabulary repeatedly during interaction with peers. Through this strategy, students summarize the most salient information about each word in order to define it for their partner in a concrete way. Such summarization, according to research by Marzano et al. (2001), is a learned process and is a critical skill for all students.

Materials Needed: Six to eight key vocabulary terms • Thumb Challenge strips • sticky notes • textbook/story • pencils/pens

ACTIVATION: A Canvas of Opportunity

Directions:

- **T** Explain the activity to the whole class, and introduce the six to eight vocabulary words for the lesson.
- **P** Place students in pairs. Consider pairing students who share the same native language and are at slightly different levels of English language proficiency.
- Give each pair a Thumb Challenge strip with the vocabulary words already written on it. Make sure the same words appear in the same order on both sides of the strip (see example below).
- Tell students that they will be using the strips throughout the lesson.
- Have students discuss the words on the strip. They can use both English and their native language if they wish.
- As students discuss the words, give each student a sticky note for each word on the strip.

- **I** Have students individually record on a sticky note what they know about each word based on the conversation they had with their partner. They may choose to draw what they know or write in the language of their choice. Then have them put their sticky notes below the words on the Thumb Challenge strip. (**Note:** You may choose to have both students in each pair do all the words, or you can divide the words equally among students.)
- Circulate around the room to silently observe students as they are working and note connections that you can revoice for the whole group.
- **P** Have partners work together to make a prediction about what the lesson/text will be about.
- Have each pair share their prediction with another pair.

Front of the Sentence Strip

| plantation | wharf | customs | suspiciously | confronted | detain |

Activating the "i"

How does this process activate CLD students' existing knowledge?

- **Sociocultural:** By accessing the personal memories and experiences each student brings to each word, the Activation phase provides a great opportunity to create a community of learners in which each member's prior knowledge is valued.
- **Linguistic:** Initially placing students in pairs provides them with a safe environment to orally share their ideas with a partner. The pairings are further enhanced when native language support is provided and stu-

dents are allowed to discuss key vocabulary terms in the L1.
- **Academic:** The connections discussed and recorded by students in this phase of the lesson allow teachers to tap into students' prior academic experiences with the vocabulary words.
- **Cognitive:** Students are more likely to take ownership over learning when they know a given strategy will be used through the entire lesson.

CONNECTION: The Broad & Narrow Strokes of Learning

Directions:

- **T** After students have finished sharing, bring the class together and proceed with the lesson.
- **P** As you come across the vocabulary words in the content portions of the lesson, make sure to allow partners to discuss the words again

to build their contextual understanding of the words. Encourage them to compare their new understandings with their original thoughts about the words.

- Once students have discussed a specific word, have each student in

the pair write the definition of the word on the back of the strip, along with the textbook page number on which the definition was found.

- Have students remove their sticky notes from the front of the sentence strip.

Plantation | Wharf | customs | Suspiciously | confrunted | detain
A large farm used to grow cotton, tabacco, or sugar can worked. p. 31 | a dock used to let passengers board on d. steamboat a shop. P. 33 | People that check the passengers or luggage for safety or illegal items, p.34 | behavior causing another to mistrust. p. 37 | to come face to face with in aggression, p.39 | to keep from going on "today" p. 41

Author Talk: Connection

As students work together to discuss and define the vocabulary terms, the teacher is able to circulate around the classroom and informally assess student comprehension and language use. One teacher noted that she found this aspect of the Thumb Challenge strategy particularly beneficial:

I liked to listen to the CLD students' groups in the Thumb Challenge. This gave me an opportunity to discover the CLD students' ability to use their CALP [cognitive academic language proficiency] language in a social, less stressful setting. This really helped me know the starting point of one of my newer CLD students' CALP language development.

Promoting the use of the CALP language is a natural outcome of the Thumb Challenge as students are using the academic vocabulary to complete the strategy. However, what makes this strategy meaningful for the CLD student is the explicit activation of existing background knowledge and its connection to new learning in context. One teacher noted that it was during these discussions that he could see the connections students were making between the L1 and the L2 via cognates. For example, he overheard one student tell his partner, "You know, it's like *musica*, music." The student talk promoted throughout the phases of this strategy provides the teacher with ample opportunities to observe and document learning and gather information that can be used to make the lesson more meaningful and comprehensible to all students.

Connecting to the "*i*+1"
How does this process move CLD students from the known to the unknown?

- **Sociocultural:** Making links between what they initially thought about the vocabulary words and the actual meaning of the terms in context allows students to revise their schemas about each word.
- **Linguistic:** Students' repeated articulation and refinement of the meaning of the words supports their acquisition of the academic language.

- **Academic:** Constant reinforcement and use of the vocabulary words allows learners to take ownership of the vocabulary terms and solidifies the transfer of the words into their permanent memory.
- **Cognitive:** Encountering the key terms in context and discussing them in a meaningful way supports students in examining their understanding of the words.

AFFIRMATION: A Gallery of Understanding

Directions:

-  Have each pair engage in a Thumb Challenge. To begin, have the students in each pair sit facing each other, with the Thumb Challenge strip between them.
- Ask both students to hold the strip by putting a thumb on the first word on the side facing them.
- Have one student start by reading the first word and then stating its definition.
- If the student who began first struggles or does not know a word, the other student starts sharing from the very first word. As this student shares his or her definition, the first student's comprehension is stretched to the next level.
- Be sure to tell students that if at any point they are both unable to figure out a word, they can flip the strip over to find the correct answer.
- As students are sharing, circulate around the room and listen to them to check for understanding.
- ◼ To move toward individual accountability for students:
  - ○ Have students choose words from the strip and write sentences that summarize their understanding of the words.
  - ○ Have students use words from the strip to write a summary of the main topic/concept of the story/lesson.

Affirming Student Ownership: *"I" Get It!*
How does this process celebrate CLD student learning?

- **Sociocultural:** The Affirmation phase allows the CLD student to articulate his or her complete understanding of the vocabulary term. This understanding reflects not only what was learned in the text but also the wealth of background knowledge he or she brought to the term, along with that which was learned from peers.
- **Linguistic:** CLD students are able to demonstrate their learning both orally and in writing.

- **Academic:** The Thumb Challenge strategy allows students to participate in a process-oriented activity for practice and application of the key vocabulary that also allows for authentic assessment of learning.
- **Cognitive:** Students can challenge each other at any point during the Thumb Challenge. When responding, they are stretched to a higher cognitive level as they justify their responses.

 SPOTLIGHT: Early Literacy Connection

The Thumb Challenge can be used to promote language development in young children by using visual cues such as those modeled on the strip below. As in the word challenge, pictures should be mirrored on both sides of the strip.

What Do You See?

This is a great activity for the classroom or home. Create a Thumb Challenge strip with visual cues, such as the one pictured here, and have two students or a parent and child play together. Select one person to begin by pointing to the first clue on his or her side of the strip. Instruct this person to identify the object and/or describe it (e.g., What shape is it? What color is it?). If the person gets it right, he or she continues until he or she gets one incorrect. Then it is the next person's turn. The game is over when someone gets to the end of the strip without stopping!

Biography-Driven Response to Intervention

The Thumb Challenge strategy helps students focus on the cognitively challenging skills of explaining, comparing, and finally synthesizing their understanding of the vocabulary words. The nonthreatening nature of the activities helps students express their level of word knowledge and use their language skills to agree or disagree with peers. Thus, this strategy is ideal for Tier 1 interventions. As part of the core curriculum, the strategy can be used as a screener to determine which areas of word understanding and pronunciation students might struggle with. The Thumb Challenge can further be used for planning specific intervention services.

One Classroom's Perspective

Activating:

I considered the biographies of my CLD/ELL students by looking at the prism model as I planned and introduced the strategy. I paired the students with partners that created positive relationships. This is important in the first dimension of the prism model (sociocultural) to help the students not feel anxious. Their partners also help in guiding their learning,

making sure they understand so that frustration does not occur. Before the lesson, the students were assessed with play-based assessment (using the Thumb Challenge) on knowing the definitions of the six terms (schema, mental images, making connections, inferring, questioning, and finding the big idea). I noted the students who struggled.

Make connections | Mental Images | Infer | Question | Schema | Big Idea

Make connections | Mental Images | Infer | Question | Schema | Big Idea

Connecting:

I used the strategy to reinforce key content and/or academic vocabulary development *throughout* the lesson and used multiple grouping configurations (TPSI). The total class listened to the story. Students wrote their thinking in their reading journals as I read the story. At the end of the lesson, they reflected on their learning and shared this with the entire class. The Thumb Challenge is a partner game played with their "thinking partners." Students have the same partner for the entire year. This allows a positive relationship to form, and

partners are used to working with one another. The students then worked in small groups. They were asked to discuss what they had learned about the six terms we had

been studying. Last, individually, the students were asked to read their books and place sticky notes in their book with examples of the six terms.

One Classroom's Perspective (*continued*)

Affirming:

I used the strategy to support me in authentically assessing my students' understanding of the lesson, as evidenced by my anecdotal notes. Students were then assessed again with the Thumb Challenge at the end of the lesson to see if they could apply the terms. This allowed me to see if they had mastered the terms. Applying the knowledge requires a much higher level of thinking. Again, as students did this, I walked around talking to each group and noting areas of struggle.

Student Voices

I like working with a partner; it makes me feel more comfortable.
—*ELL Student*
Speech Emergent

I like telling my answers to questions instead of writing it.
—*ELL Student*
Intermediate Fluency

I like this challenge because before I learned all of the stuff I didn't know so much and couldn't do the challenge so good, but afterward you can answer all of the questions and make sentences with all of the words.

—*ELL Student*
Advanced Fluency

STRATEGY

Magic Book

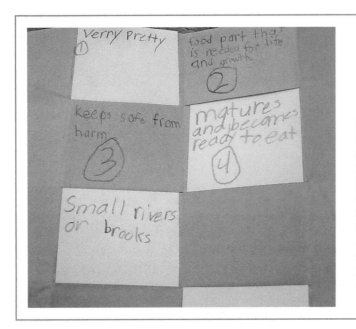

I enjoyed doing the strategy of Magic Book with my students. They remained engaged throughout the class and kept the focus on the vocabulary words. I heard extremely in-depth conversations and dialogues regarding the concept that we were working on. The groupings also helped my students move the strategy forward, and the best part was my students were able to use their Magic Books throughout the lesson regardless of their language levels.

—*Lindsay Blanchard, 2nd-Grade Teacher*

Where Theory Meets Practice

Exploring promising practices for English language learners and the link between literacy instruction and language development, researchers such as Wong Fillmore and Valadez (1986), Anderson and Roit (1994), and the members of The Education Alliance (Coady et al., 2003) emphasize a cognitive strategies approach to integrating reading and writing instruction. Research has also shown that learning is more effective when students give input into the vocabulary they need to learn (Echevarría et al., 2010). Drawing on both areas of research, Magic Book is a cognitive strategy that allows students to take control over their own vocabulary learning.

Magic Book provides CLD students with a note-taking strategy that actively involves them in the learning process. Not only does the strategy provide students with a concrete note-taking tool that can be used throughout the lesson, but it is also a very fun and interactive way to get students involved in learning. According to research by Willis (2006), there is a direct correlation between increased student attention/engagement and the retention of information taught during the lesson. This is due in large part to the fact that engagement differs from participation in the level of thinking that is taking place on the part of the student.

In addition, the Magic Book strategy encourages students to use this note-taking tool to record summary statements of what they have learned. They then share with or quiz a partner based on this information. The completed Magic Book provides the perfect support for students' review of lesson material both at the end of the lesson and before summative or high-stakes assessments. This strategy helps educators ensure that all students are cognitively engaged as they manipulate the content, and the hands-on tool allows learners to make "magic" happen throughout the lesson!

Materials Needed: Colored construction paper (two pieces per student) • scissors • curricular materials • pencils/pens

ACTIVATION: A Canvas of Opportunity

Directions:

- Following the instructions at the end of this strategy description (pages 116–117), either make the Magic Books for the class ahead of time or provide students with the materials and guide them through the process of constructing their own Magic Books.
- **S** Place students in small groups, with three or four students per group.
- **T** Begin the activity by sharing with students the academic vocabulary of the lesson. (When selecting the academic vocabulary, think of the six to eight most important words that will illustrate the topic for the students.)

- For primary students, the strategy can also be used to teach phonics rules. Simply choose six to eight words based on skills involving blends, ending sounds, prefixes, etc.
- **I** Have the students individually write the words in the boxes on the checkered mat (see image).
- Next, have students splash some of their own words and ideas associated with the vocabulary around each of the words (or, in the case of primary students, have them discuss the words with each other). Encourage students to draw visuals related to the words or write in their native language.

- **P** Have students briefly share their ideas with a partner, and encourage them to add their "partner words" to the boxes as desired.
- As students are sharing, circulate around the room to gather ideas that you can revoice for the class.

Activating the "*i*"

How does this process activate CLD students' existing knowledge?

- **Sociocultural:** Drawing visuals and writing in their native language helps students reflect upon their own personal experiences and look for meaningful associations with the words.
- **Linguistic:** When students write and discuss the words, they gain valuable practice with the academic vocabulary of the lesson.

- **Academic:** Students' initial encounter with the vocabulary words is at their individual baseline (*i*) level. Subsequent exposures promote exploration of the vocabulary at the *i*+1 level.
- **Cognitive:** The Activation phase allows students to compare their own associations with the target words to those of a peer.

CONNECTION: The Broad & Narrow Strokes of Learning

Directions:

- **S** As you proceed with the lesson and/or read the text aloud, stop at several points for the students to discuss the content in their small groups.
  - You may choose to pose some guided questions at this time or simply ask the students to discuss their understandings of the text based on what they have heard.
  - Encourage students to use as many of the vocabulary words as possible when they discuss the content of the lesson.
- **T** At relevant points, stop and discuss the vocabulary words with students as a class.
- **I** During discussions of the vocabulary, have students individually crack open their Magic Book and write the description of each word along with the associated page number from the textbook.
  - In the case of a phonics-based activity, you can have students write the meaning of the word or the associated root word.
- After the content of the lesson has been covered, have students individually revisit the words and images they initially recorded for each vocabulary word. Ask them to cross out words and images that do not apply.
- Next, have students write on the left flap of the Magic Book some of their new understandings related to the vocabulary words. Encourage them to include visuals to help them remember difficult words.
  - In the case of a phonics-based activity, you can have students write different words (or have them draw a visual representing the words) that incorporate a particular sound, blend, prefix, etc.
- **P** Have students share what they learned with a partner.

Connecting to the "*i*+1"
How does this process move CLD students from the known to the unknown?

- **Sociocultural:** The numerous opportunities to discuss the lesson/text with peers allow students to feel valued in the learning process and engaged in the lesson.
- **Linguistic:** The language on the Magic Book serves as a scaffold that students can use to express their learning with peers.

- **Academic:** Students' multiple exposures to the new vocabulary words via reading, writing, and discussion promote their retention of the words.
- **Cognitive:** The students' metacognitive processes are supported as they are asked to confirm/disconfirm their initial associations with the vocabulary words in light of their new understandings.

AFFIRMATION: A Gallery of Understanding

Directions:

- **I** When students have finished sharing their ideas regarding the words, have them individually summarize the key ideas specific to the topic on the right flap of the Magic Book. Challenge them to incorporate as many vocabulary words as they can.
  - Primary students can be given a cloze paragraph in which they simply write the vocabulary words in the blanks. This paragraph can then be glued to the flap.

- In the case of a phonics-based activity, you can have students create sentences to show their understanding of the words and to provide an authentic context for application of the targeted skills.
- **S** Next, have students share their ideas/answers with the members of their small group.
- **P** As an extension activity, have students use their Magic Book to quiz a partner on the vocabulary words.

- **I** Have students keep their Magic Book for future use as a study tool.

Author Talk: Affirmation

We know that words are powerful and can provide students with a means of expressing themselves. Yet, at the same time, words become one of the biggest stressors when it comes to comprehension and expression for many CLD students. The Common Core State Standards emphasize the importance of "determining the meaning of words and phrases in context" (NGA & CCSSO, 2010, p. 2). Thus, as educators we need to continually provide students with multiple ways to connect to words. Magic Book is one tool that can support our efforts to help students make personal connections to, and expand upon, their vocabulary. The Magic Book becomes a "tool in their hand" that they can use both to activate their existing ideas about the words and to manipulate the words throughout the progression of the lesson.

Teachers who have used the Magic Book strategy as a way to expand their students' vocabulary have shared the following tips:

- Place students in pairs (e.g., students with same native language—one with more advanced English proficiency and one at an earlier stage of second language acquisition) and have them work together using one Magic Book. Allow the pairs to discuss the words from the very beginning and continue working with them as they progress through the lesson.
- After students have finished their Magic Books, display them on the wall of the classroom so the students can refer to their own understandings of the words as they complete subsequent tasks.
- Keep students' Magic Books on various topics in separate containers (e.g., shoeboxes) so that they can be used later as study tools for standardized tests.

Affirming Student Ownership: "I" Get It!
How does this process celebrate CLD student learning?

- **Sociocultural:** Because students have had numerous opportunities to develop and articulate their understanding of the target vocabulary, a low-risk environment is maintained as students quiz each other using their Magic Books.
- **Linguistic:** The continuous nature of the activity and the additional opportunities for peer discussion and collaboration allow students to gain proficiency with

high-frequency words as well as the academic vocabulary of the lesson.
- **Academic:** The Magic Book becomes a personal learning tool that students can use during the lesson and in the future to interact with the content.
- **Cognitive:** Students are able to evaluate and add to their understanding of the content as they hear their peers' diverse perspectives.

SPOTLIGHT: Early Literacy Connection

Magic Book is a strategy that can be especially meaningful for students at the early literacy level who are working to understand sound–symbol associations. Young students may need help with creating the Magic Books; however, once they have been put together, students can also take them home to work with their parents on literacy skills. The Magic Book serves as an excellent tool for activities such as shared reading and shared writing. Some early childhood teachers have shared with us the following ideas:

Show and Tell. Place students in pairs and give each pair a Magic Book. Student A from the pair writes a letter or a word (depending upon the language level) on one side of the Magic Book. Student B then shares/draws a picture that represents that letter or word on the other side of the Magic Book. Students A and B together read the letter or the word and think of two or three things that begin with the same letter and write the words on the side flap in their native language or draw pictures that represent the words/letters.

Spell It. This activity helps students focus on each word as a whole and provides an opportunity for assessing how well students understand the letters within a word. Choose five or six words and give each student a Magic Book. Instead of saying each word as a whole, say just the spelling of the word, and have students write the letters on one side of the Magic Book. After students have written the letters, have them talk to a partner about what word the letters might represent. After this discussion, have students share their thoughts with the whole group. This allows you to make sure that everyone has associated the correct word with the letters. After the word has been identified, have students spell it out loud. Continue this process with all the words. Next, have students draw a picture representing the word on the other side of the Magic Book.

Biography-Driven Response to Intervention

Magic Book is a strategy that can help students connect to the vocabulary words through a focus on their background knowledge and prior experiences. In addition, this strategy provides learners with a study tool that lists the words on one side and their definitions on the other. This study tool can be used with core instruction and as part of tiered learning. For intensive instruction, the strategy can be tailored for individual student needs by giving each student a chance to interact with the words at his or her academic and linguistic level.

One Classroom's Perspective

Activating:

Today was the first day we were working on the strategy of Magic Book. I have several ELL students that range from early production to intermediate fluency. Since the topic of our lesson was nutrition, I knew I needed to do something that would be hands-on and catch my students' attention.

Magic Book worked great with my students in writing the six vocabulary words that we chose. I preferred to keep the vocabulary at six words and not eight, since the students were working on this topic for the first time. The first thing I did with the students was to share with them how the Magic Book

worked. They were quite fascinated by the way they could use their Magic Books on both sides. I brought all my students onto the carpet and modeled how they were going to write the words on the Magic Book. Next I divided them into pairs (based on their language proficiencies) and gave them one Magic Book per pair. To begin the activity, I had the students talk to their partners about the words on the Magic Book as one partner wrote all the vocabulary words. This phase of the lesson really helped my learners extend their ideas about the words.

Connecting:

Next, I shared the PowerPoint presentation with the students. On the Power-Point we had pictures of the words embedded on the slides. That gave my students an idea as to how a word worked within the context of the lesson. So, as I shared the PowerPoint with my students, I stopped at each slide and had students talk about the words again with each other. This constant sharing of ideas in pairs and small groups really allowed my learners to gain multiple perspectives on the words. As students shared the words this time, I had them turn the Magic Book over

and write the definitions on the other side. As the students talked in pairs and wrote the definitions, I also allowed them to draw pictures relating to the words along with the definitions. Since 2nd-graders tend to respond more to the pictures, this really helped my students. Also, the visuals really supported to the multiple linguistic levels of my students.

As my students worked on the pictures and the meanings of the words on the other side of the Magic Book, I circulated around the room to listen to some

of their conversations. This really gave me an idea as to who was able to follow the words and who needed some more help with them.

Affirming:

To bring the lesson together, I had my students write their own sentences about the words on the side flaps of their Magic Books. My students were

just amazed at how they could use the strategy of Magic Book in working throughout the lesson.

Student Voices

I loved the activity of Magic Book especially since it has so many colors and I can write the words or draw my ideas. I was also able to talk to my partner, and it gave me more ideas on what to write about the words.

—*ELL Student*
Speech Emergent

This book really does work like magic since I can work on both the sides. I wrote in Tamil on one side and English on the other, and the other ideas that I had about the words I also wrote them on the side. I get to take it home to show my mom.

—*ELL Student*
Early Production

I like to work with a partner since some of the words were hard and we talked to each other and looked around the room to find some ideas. I wrote the definitions about the words through my memory and I still remember them.

—*ELL Student*
Intermediate Fluency

INSTRUCTIONS: Creating Your Magic Book

Materials: A single Magic Book will require two pieces of construction paper in different colors and a pair of scissors.

Step 1:	Take a piece of the construction paper, make sure it is in landscape orientation, and fold it in half from left to right, making a sharp crease.
Step 2:	Once again, fold it in half from left to right, making another sharp crease.
Step 3:	Fold the paper in half again, but this time fold from the bottom of the paper up. Make another sharp crease. Repeat this step a second time.

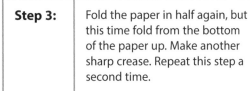

When the paper is unfolded you should have 16 squares.

INSTRUCTIONS: Creating Your Magic Book (*continued*)

Step 4:	Then take a pair of scissors and *on the fold side* cut along the three folds, making sure you cut only to the middle fold of the paper. When you open the paper, you should have three horizontal slits in the middle of your paper.			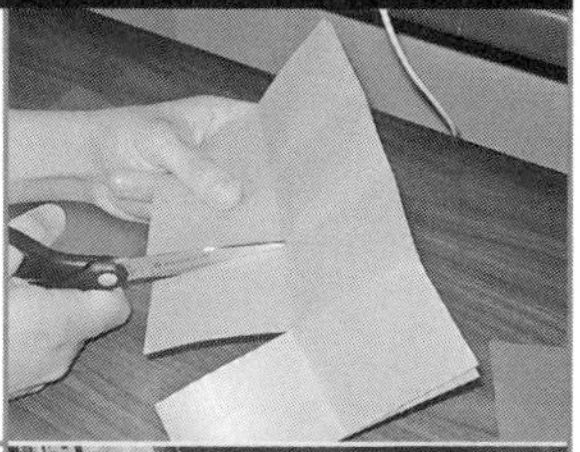
Step 5:	Using the second piece of construction paper (a different color than the first piece) repeat Steps 1 and 2. Then open the paper and cut along the fold lines. You will end up with four strips of paper, but each student will need only two of the strips. (You could have two students share the second piece of construction paper. Each student should end up with two strips.)			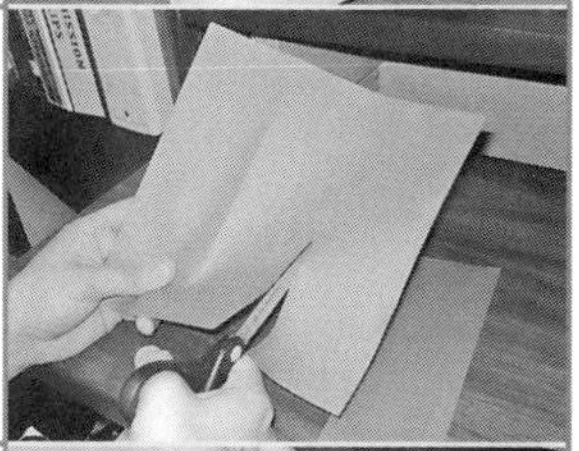
Step 6:	Take one of the strips of paper and weave it under the bottom slit in the first piece of construction paper, up through the middle slit, and then back under the top slit.	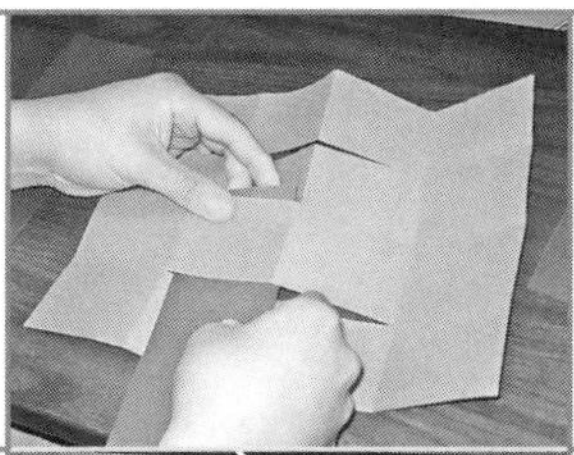	Your Magic Book should now look like this:	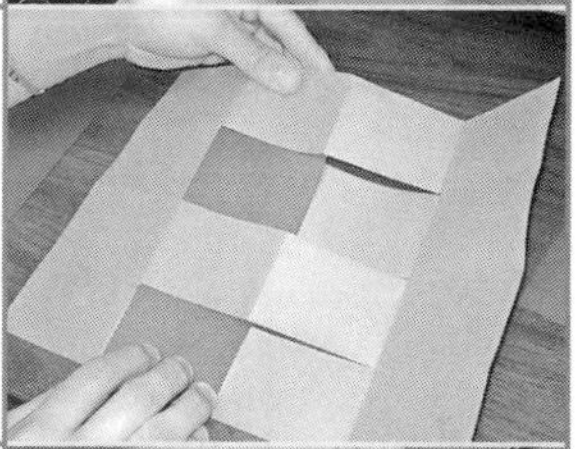
Step 7:	Take the other strip of paper and weave it up through the bottom slit in the first piece of construction paper, under the middle slit, and up through the top slit.	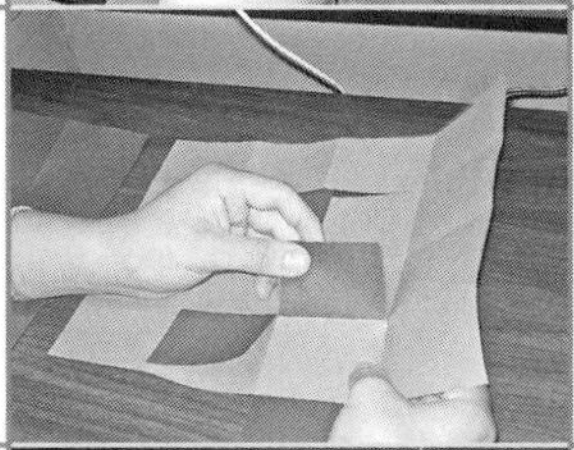	Your Magic Book should now look like this:	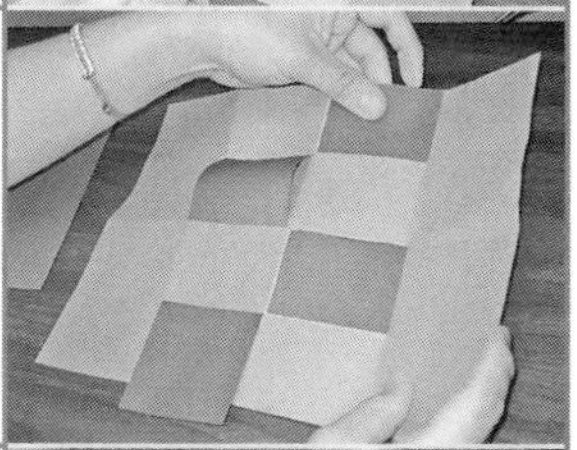
Step 8:	Fold each outside flap toward the middle.	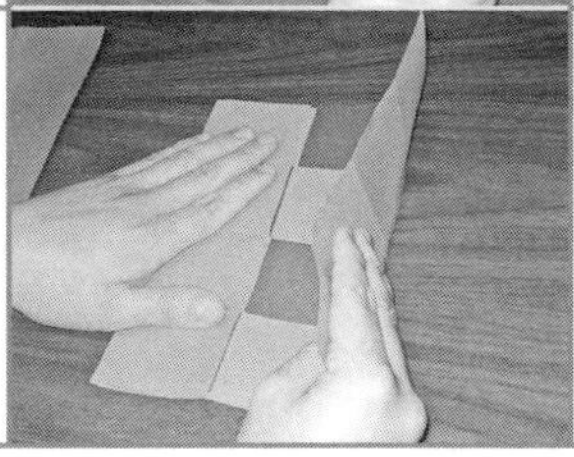	When you hold the Magic Book up, you should have a **W**.	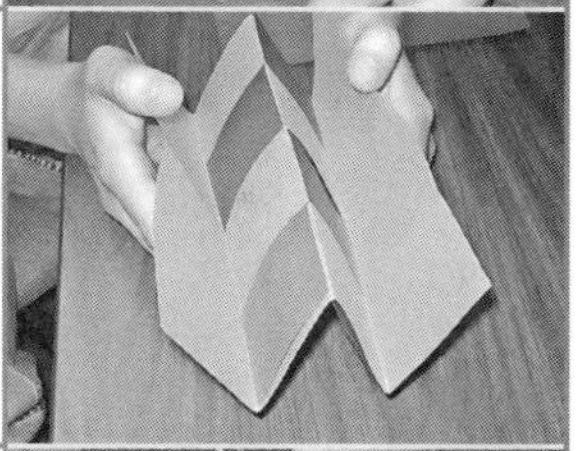
Step 9:	To crack open your Magic Book, fold it loosely (see picture at right) and place each thumb into the center fold. Open the crease by pulling the woven sections apart.			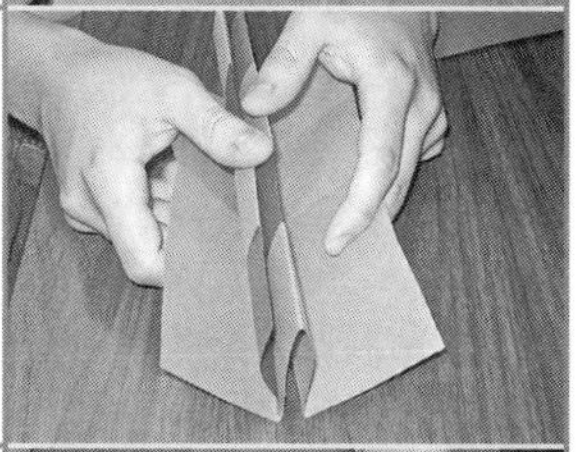
	Voila! You have cracked open your Magic Book and created endless possibilities for students' information learning and retention! To return to the starting point, simply pull on the outside flaps that are now tucked under the checkered part pictured here.			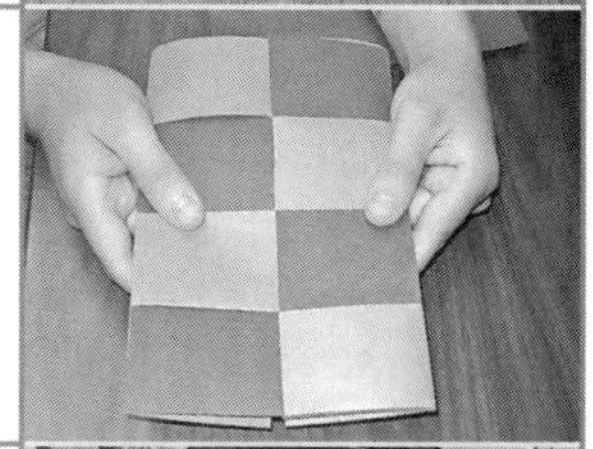
Step 10:	The magical thing is that you can turn your Magic Book over (so that it looks like an **M**) and then repeat Steps 8 and 9 to crack it open on this side as well!			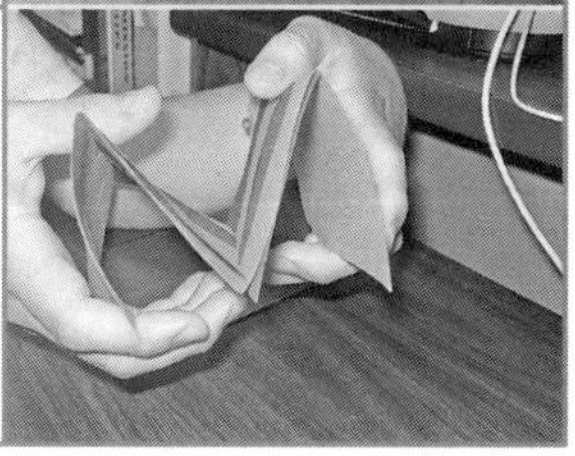

STRATEGY

IDEA

I gnite
D iscover
E xtend
A ffirm

The implementation of this assessment strategy provided me with the insight that many of my CLD students use the context to figure out the meaning of new vocabulary words. Students were able to successfully give definitions and use the vocabulary words correctly in context. The students were excited and engaged throughout the activity. My CLD students, especially the ones identified as special education students, used pictures to show their background knowledge.

—*Amanda Donahey, 2nd-Grade Teacher*

Where Theory Meets Practice

As teachers responsible for enhancing our students' literacy skills, we often ask ourselves, "How can we provide a balanced literacy approach to our students?" In reality, if we think about a balanced literacy approach, we may not be able to find one concrete answer, given the changes we are seeing in society. Our student population has changed drastically and so have the academic, linguistic, sociocultural, and cognitive needs that our students exhibit. Even though we may have diverse perspectives on literacy development, we will all agree that there are certain literacy skills that all of our students need to be successful. Oral language skills are one example. Often for our ELL students, an inability to communicate fluently goes hand in hand with a lack of vocabulary understanding. One of the most prominent measures of oral language proficiency/linguistic knowledge is

vocabulary knowledge (Geva & Yaghoub Zadeh, 2006; Proctor, Carlo, August, & Snow, 2005).

IDEA is one strategy that helps teachers work with students on the enhancement of both oral language skills and vocabulary development. Spycher (2009) found that ELL students and English proficient students in early stages of language development benefited equally from intentional and explicit vocabulary instruction that was a part of rich content instruction that combined multiple readings of narrative and expository texts with scaffolded opportunities to engage in academic talk with the words and concepts students were learning. This is exactly the type of instruction that IDEA promotes.

The "**I**" in IDEA stands for "*ignite*." As Swan (2003) reminds us, cooperative learning groups are especially helpful for creating classroom cultures that support students' thinking, strategy use, connections to background knowledge, and engagement with text and vocabulary words. As students work in their small groups to create their first impression of the vocabulary words, they are able to tap into their background knowledge systems (Herrera, 2010).

The "**D**" of the strategy symbolizes "*discover*," allowing students to focus on the vocabulary words through a context-based approach to the text. During this portion of the lesson, students are able to use their own words to describe new information gained from texts. Students' sharing of ideas in their small groups provides the teacher with multiple opportunities to help enhance their oral language skills and vocabulary. As students continue working in their small groups and pairs, they are able to initiate dialogue and discover the meaning and the context of new vocabulary.

The "**E**" of this strategy refers to the "*extend*" portion of the lesson. During this part, students extend upon their new understanding of the vocabulary words by creating links between the words. Students' language abilities are further strengthened as they connect the vocabulary words in oral or written form. Students work with peers to recall critical information from the text and retell the connections that exist between the words.

The "**A**" of IDEA reminds us as teachers to take time to "*affirm*" students' learning. Given that teachers cannot frequently meet one-on-one with each student, classroom practices must allow for students to display their thinking so the teacher will be aware of it (Darling-Hammond & Bransford, 2005). At the end of the lesson, the teacher listens to each group share their learning, affirms the efforts of the group, and provides feedback.

Materials Needed: Five to seven key vocabulary words • visuals for the vocabulary words • chart paper/paper with key vocabulary words (one for each group of students) • markers/colored pencils • book/text • sticky notes • paper • pencils/pens

---

ACTIVATION: A Canvas of Opportunity

Directions:

- **T** Select five to seven key vocabulary words that are related to the same concept. Explain to students that they will be doing a "word carousel." To do this:
  - **S** Place students in small groups of three or four students.
  - Write the vocabulary words on poster paper (one word per paper) and place one poster at each table.
  - Explain that groups will move from one table to the next, and each group member will record his or her individual thoughts about the word.
  - **I** To help students *ignite* their understandings, encourage them to both write and draw. After recording their own ideas, they should also read what others students have already written about the word on the poster.
  - You can also show students visuals of the words to further ignite their thinking.
- As students work on the posters, circulate around the room to make note of the kinds of things students are recording.
- **T** After the groups have finished with all of the posters, bring the class back together. Place the word posters on a wall where the entire class can see them. Go over the words and revoice some of the associations that students provided for the words.
- Next, explain to students that these initial connections to the words are

based on their background knowledge and past experiences. As they read the text, they will see whether or not the way each vocabulary word is used in the text matches the way they initially used/understood it.

Activating the "*i*"

How does this process activate CLD students' existing knowledge?

- **Sociocultural:** Revoicing students' associations with the words for the entire class allows all learners to hear multiple perspectives on the words.
- **Linguistic:** Students have multiple opportunities to write about their initial understandings of the target vocabulary words.

- **Academic:** Students are exposed to academic content vocabulary along with their monolingual English-speaking peers and are provided support through visuals to make meaningful connections to the words.
- **Cognitive:** Students are able to make comparisons between their initial associations to the vocabulary words and those of their peers.

 CONNECTION: The Broad & Narrow Strokes of Learning

Directions:

- Keep the word posters displayed in the room so that students can connect to them during the lesson.
- **T** Support students during the lesson as they *discover* the meaning of the words in context by:
  - Talking about the words within the context of the lesson.
  - Reading a text/story in which the words appear.
  - Having students generate and write definitions of the words that reflect their use within the context of the lesson.
- In this phase, be sure to have students make connections back to their initial ideas discussed

during the Activation phase. To do this:
- **I** Have students individually write each vocabulary word on a sticky note.
- Direct students to record any new discoveries they make about the word during the lesson (i.e., during the course of the read-aloud, individual reading of the text, and/or discussion of the text).
- **P** Have students share their new discoveries with a partner.
- **S** After the content has been covered, have students add their new connections to the group

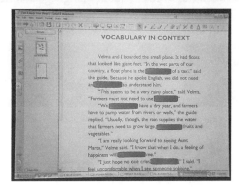

posters they completed during the Activation phase.
- Have students circle the original associations on the posters that came closest to the contextually correct use of the vocabulary words.

Connecting to the "*i+1*"

How does this process move CLD students from the known to the unknown?

- **Sociocultural:** As students work within the context of the lesson to gain new understandings, they continually reflect back on their own background experiences.
- **Linguistic:** CLD students practice writing academic language as they document new discoveries/learnings during the lesson.
- **Academic:** Having students share their new learnings with a partner before bringing them to the larger group

allows them to "test" their learning and clear up any confusion.
- **Cognitive:** As students confirm/disconfirm their original associations with the words, they are able to modify their schemas, as needed, to reflect their more thorough understanding of the words in the context of the lesson.

AFFIRMATION: A Gallery of Understanding

Directions:

- Once the students have finished working with the words and posters, bring the class back together.
- **S** Have students *extend* upon their learning by creating a word chain. To do this:
  - Assign one person from each group to write all of the vocabulary words on index cards. Alternatively, give each group a set of index cards with the words on them. Students at primary levels can use index cards with pictures on them.
  - Explain to the groups that their task is to connect the words/pictures with each other to show the relationships that exist between the words.
- Have students take turns articulating for one another the connections between the words in their word chain, as based on the story or topic the class just covered.
- After students have had a few minutes to practice, circulate to each group so they can share their word chain with you and you can *affirm* their understandings.
- **T** Next, have each group share their word chain with the rest of the class.
- **I** To get an individual assessment of students' understanding, have each student independently write a paragraph using all the vocabulary words.

- *Tip:* If you do this type of assessment, allow CLD students in the preproduction or early production phase of second language acquisition to draw and label their connections in English or write them in their native language.

Author Talk: Affirmation

In talking one day with Ms. Johnson about the language development of some students in her 5th-grade class, we kept coming back to the importance of CLD students' oral language development. Students' reading comprehension skills are highly dependent upon their oral proficiency in English. As teachers, we need to provide students with contexts and situations that allow them to continually build their language skills. The IDEA strategy is a great tool for helping students develop their oral language skills, which are most strengthened during the Affirmation phase when students link the vocabulary words and verbally articulate

the connections for their classmates. Ideas that teachers have shared to promote language development include

- Pair students with high and low proficiencies as they work on the strategy. Doing this allows students with limited English proficiency to observe how the language works.
- As you introduce the vocabulary words, show visuals associated with them and have students first share their ideas about the words with a partner before moving to the word posters.
- As students work together to create the word chains, have them also write their word chain associations.

Affirming Student Ownership: *"I"* Get It!
How does this process celebrate CLD student learning?

- **Sociocultural:** Students' negotiation of links between the words with peers demonstrates cooperative learning in action.
- **Linguistic:** CLD students use all four language domains—listening, speaking, reading, and writing—to demonstrate their understanding of the content.
- **Academic:** As students discuss the relationships

among the vocabulary words with peers, they strengthen their overall understanding of the terms and larger concepts.
- **Cognitive:** Students are able to evaluate their understanding of the vocabulary as they hear other groups' alternative arrangements of the words and associated relationships between the terms.

SPOTLIGHT: Early Literacy Connection

Researchers have found that emergent reading, like emergent writing, begins with pictures that help children establish the meaning of the words that make up the stories they will eventually be able to read (Beaty & Pratt, 2007; Neuman & Roskos, 1993). For young children, the majority of the books they are reading (or that are being read to them) are picture books. When children are being read to, the reader significantly influences how the children interpret the texts. When the child becomes the reader of the text, he or she takes on the role of "author" and gets to interpret the meaning of the pictures through his or her own voice and understanding. The IDEA strategy can be adapted for use in early literacy classrooms for just this purpose with the "Picture Me a Story" variant described below.

Picture Me a Story

To implement this version of the IDEA strategy, select six pictures from a picture book with which your students are familiar. Make enough copies of the pictures so that when you pair your students, each pair has a copy of each picture. Explain to the students they are going to be the "authors" of their very own story by working together to put the pictures in order and then tell the class their story using the pictures. Next, give the students time to organize their pictures. After they have finished, circulate around the room to each pair and listen to their story. After all the stories have been told to the class as a whole, talk with your students about what was the same and different about the stories. Emphasize the similarities as well as the differences, reminding students that all authors have different points of view.

Extension. This is also a great activity you can encourage the parents of your children to do at home with pictures from a story or magazine, or even pictures the students draw on their own. The key is to get the students engaged in the act of telling/retelling stories!

Biography-Driven Response to Intervention

IDEA is a strategy that helps students use their background knowledge and newly acquired academic knowledge of the vocabulary words to support their comprehension of the text and the larger lesson. When implemented as part of core instruction, the strategy supports students' connections between themselves and the words and among the words with other words. These connections then give students a foundation to connect their own multiple thoughts and ideas, which is an important skill for summarizing. This strategy can also be used effectively as an extension of core instruction. In tiered instruction, students can work with the same words and further develop their understanding of them in relation to the topic.

One Classroom's Perspective

Activating:

I really like the strategy of IDEA, since it helps me work on the vocabulary words with my students and also allows for me to extend their learning about the words to a much deeper level. The many stages of the strategy are really helpful in providing me with an opportunity to construct meaning with my learners. To ignite my students' understanding of the words, I started the activity with a variation of the Vocabulary Quilt (see page 96 of this volume). In order to do this, I put six vocabulary words on each table and then placed my students in groups of two or three. I grouped my students based on their language and academic proficiencies, considering this was the first time my students were seeing the words. We started the activity by having the groups go to each of the words and spend about a minute writing or drawing their initial thoughts about the words. By doing this, my students were able to be exposed to all of the vocabulary words in the chapter.

Once the groups were finished working on the words, I gathered the vocabulary words from the tables and had all of the students join me at the carpet. The first thing I did with my students was show them the words one by one, and I read some of the thoughts that they had put on the papers. As I read some of their initial ideas, I also had my students talk to each other

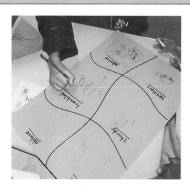

regarding how the initial thoughts on the papers connected with the words. I did not give them any correct definitions at this time, since I just wanted to review some of the ideas that my students had put on the paper.

Connecting:

We then gathered in front of the smart board and I pulled up the words on a PowerPoint slide. I had students come up and add pictures from their posters to make connections to what they already knew. Next, I sent my students back to their desks and had them cut apart the words of their Vocabulary Quilt. I told them I was going to read them a short paragraph from the story, and it was their job to fill in the words that were missing from the paragraph with their vocabulary words. (I covered the words as they appeared in the pas-

sage, since I wanted my students to see how the words worked in context.) I read a little bit of the passage, and when I came to the point of the word within the passage, I had my students guess which one of their vocabulary words would fit. I gave students some time to think about this, and they wrote the answers on their white boards. This activity served as a great informal assessment for me, since I was able to see if my students were able to understand the idea of context. We went through the entire passage and I asked

the students to follow the same procedure. By the end, students were able to see all the vocabulary words written on the screen within a context.

Affirming:

Now that my students had been through many stages of vocabulary development, I wanted them to use the words without a context in front of them. So I asked them to go back to their original groups for this Affirmation phase. To challenge the groups and see what they truly understood about the vocabulary, I gave each

group all six words on the original Vocabulary Quilts. I told them that they now had to connect the words to each other in a meaningful way to show a relationship between the words. As students put the words together, I walked around to listen to their connections. As a further exten-

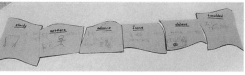

sion to the activity and as part of their assessment, I also had my students individually create summaries using all six vocabulary words.

Student Voices

I learned my words because I can draw pictures and I got to write sentences.

—ELL Student
Intermediate Fluency

I kinda like it a lot. I like writing my ideas.

—ELL Student
Speech Emergent

I liked it because it gave me more interest. I liked reading the story to find out words.

—ELL Student
Advanced Fluency

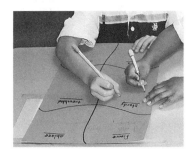

CHAPTER 3

From Word Knowledge to Comprehension

DURING A LESSON, students are inundated with a wealth of new information, from academic vocabulary to content concepts. To assimilate this information, they must be able to decode the words they are reading (phonemic awareness and phonics), understand them (vocabulary), and read them accurately and with the proper rate and expression (fluency); finally, they must grasp the overall message of the text (comprehension). Consider how you use all of these skills as you read the following passage:

> Han was very excited about Tết. Because it was January, she was getting ready for the annual Tết celebration with her family and friends, just like her family used to celebrate it in Việt Nam. Han especially liked eating mung bean rice cakes and bong mai—the plum blossoms. The câu dôi were her favorite of all, though. These poems written about yearning for home and family were really important to her because she and her family now lived in the United States and they missed family members back in Việt Nam.

Take a moment to reflect on the passage you just read. Were there words with which you were unfamiliar? How did you use your phonemic awareness/phonics skills to help you decipher these words? In what ways did you use context clues to help you determine the meaning of unfamiliar vocabulary (e.g., Tết, bong mai, câu dôi)? Even though some of the vocabulary might have been unfamiliar to you, were you still able to read the passage fluently? Based on what you read, what celebration do you think Han was preparing for? Your answers to these questions illustrate how you use all of your linguistic knowledge and skills to comprehend what you read.

Comprehension: Getting to the Heart of Meaning

Reading comprehension research has been profoundly influenced by schema theory, a hypothesis that explains how information we have stored in our minds helps us gain new knowledge (Reutzel & Cooter, 2012). Schemas (or schemata) can be thought of as a filing cabinet system in our brains, with different drawers and file folders containing different information about concepts (tables, monkeys, cars), events (birthday, school day, haircut), emotions (happiness, anger, sadness, pleasure), and roles (sibling, parent, teacher) based on our life experiences (Anderson & Pearson, 1984; Rumelhart, 1980). Each person has distinct schemas based on his or her individual life experiences.

Research has shown that "if the schemata for a particular topic are well developed and personally meaningful, new information is easier to retain and recall, and proficient learners initiate and activate their associations between old and new learning" (Echevarría et al., 2010, p. 97). For CLD students, the identification of existing schemas is particularly vital, as their culturally influenced schemas may be different from those of a text's intended audience. When we focus first on what it is our students understand and bring to the lesson, we are able to provide instruction from a *biography-driven perspective* (Herrera et al., 2011). Biography-driven instruction allows us to get to the heart of who our students are and use what matters most to them as a vehicle for helping them learn new material.

The strategies described in this chapter not only support teachers in determining what their CLD students already know about an academic topic, key vocabulary, and critical concepts, they also teach students how to monitor their own comprehension and learning throughout the lesson. These strategies help CLD students develop the metacognitive skills they need to successfully overcome difficulties they might encounter when reading text. To understand how strategies can be used to accomplish such a task, let us first define what we mean by metacognition.

Metacognition: More Than Thinking About Your Thinking!

Metacognition was first defined by Flavell (1976) as "one's knowledge concerning one's own cognitive processes and outcomes or anything related to them" (p. 232). Metacognition is often described more simply as the ability to think about your own thinking. This definition, however, tends to downplay the many skills involved in using metacognition for learning. What makes metacognition so powerful when it comes to reading comprehension, for example, is that readers who are metacognitively aware know what to do when they encounter difficulties in text. As Anderson (2002) notes, "the use of metacognitive strategies ignite[s] one's thinking and can lead to more profound learning and improved performance" (p. 1). Metacognition supports the reader's ability to identify and apply strategies to resolve problems that might occur during reading.

According to research by Rea and Mercuri (2006), teachers can encourage schema building and metacognition by:

- Helping students build background knowledge and understanding
- Helping students access the background knowledge they have and use it as a bridge to new learning
- Helping students become consciously aware of their thinking processes and the strategies they use to accomplish tasks (p. 47)

This blending of attention to schemas and to metacognition supports CLD students' ability to make conscious decisions when reading text.

To help teach metacognitive skills, Anderson (2002) proposes a model of metacognition that involves

- Preparing and planning for learning
- Selecting and using learning strategies
- Monitoring strategy use
- Orchestrating various strategies
- Evaluating strategy use and learning (pp. 1–2)

In preparing and planning, students are taught how to think about the overall goal and about what they need or want to accomplish from the reading. For selecting and using learning strategies, students need to be taught how to identify and implement specific strategies based on the text and the purpose of the reading. Monitoring of strategy use involves explicitly teaching students how to strategically monitor their application of learning strategies to make sure they are meeting their overall learning goals. Knowing how to orchestrate and use more than one strategy at a time requires that students have opportunities to practice implementing metacognitive strategies. Finally, students are taught to evaluate the effectiveness of their individual strategy implementation.

Rea and Mercuri (2006) emphasize that for metacognitive strategies to be effective, students must (a) understand the strategy, (b) understand why they need to know it and why it will benefit them, (c) be able to think through the strategy process aloud or voice the strategy in their mind, (d) see examples of the strategy in use, (e) know when and where it is appropriate to use the strategy, and (f) be able to monitor themselves (Is the strategy working? What should be done if it does not work?). CLD students need more than cursory exposure to various learning strategies; they need explicit opportunities to learn and apply strategies in ways that support their reading and learning. The goal of metacognition is reached when a student "mobilizes his/her resources to interact with the text to create meaning" (Simonsen & Singer, 1992, p. 202).

Using Peer Support to Enhance Strategy Use

For many CLD students, some of the most valuable resources in the classroom are their peers, particularly their bilingual peers. Peers are the ones who can translate information for CLD students when they do not understand what is being said. Peers can often connect with them on a cultural level when many of their other classmates cannot. And peers can often provide that sense of "comfort" and "home" when CLD students are feeling lost and overwhelmed in the classroom. Thus, CLD students should be explicitly taught to work collaboratively to help create positive learning situations. If we strategically build upon the assets of our CLD students and actively create an environment in which they can learn from one another, we can accelerate not only their comprehension but also their effective application of learning strategies in practice.

In conclusion, the primary questions to remember when selecting strategies are

- What strategy would best help the students meet the objective of the lesson?
- What are the biography-driven needs of the students?
- Which grouping configurations would best address the needs of the students and enhance their application of the selected strategy?

Strategies in Practice

In this chapter you will find descriptions of the following six strategies, which you can use before, during, and after lesson delivery to increase CLD students' motivation, engagement, comprehension, and academic achievement:

- U-C-ME
- Extension Wheel
- Hearts Activity
- Active Bookmarks
- Mini Novela
- Word Drop

STRATEGY

U-C-ME

U ncover ideas
C oncentrate on the topic
M onitor understanding
E valuate learning

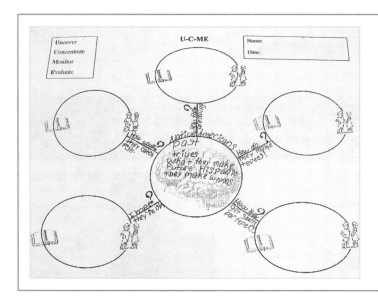

I thought the strategy was great! I was able to ascertain what the students knew successfully and was able to plan a good lesson with a starting point that the students could relate to. The students reacted well and were able to remember a lot of the content and vocabulary from the lesson.

—*Timothy Brenkman, 4th-Grade Teacher*

Where Theory Meets Practice

To support CLD students' comprehension of content concepts and academic vocabulary, it is important to help them make connections from the known (knowledge they already bring to the lesson) to the unknown (new academic content). According to research by Hill and Flynn (2006), one of the ways teachers can do this is by using specific cues and questions at the beginning of the lesson. This structured approach helps to make public students' connections to their prior knowledge, which also helps the teacher understand how they are processing and applying the information being taught. Questioning that facilitates student talk, therefore, is key to understanding how best to support them in reaching the goals of the lesson.

The U-C-ME strategy was specifically designed to promote student questioning and academic talk. The "**U**" of U-C-ME first has students **uncover** existing connections based on what they already know about the topic of the lesson and consider how their knowledge might be related to the lesson content. Research has shown that "the ability to recognize and construct patterns that identify the familiar or not familiar relies on schemas formed by prior knowledge and experiences" (Gregory & Burkman, 2012, p. 38). Students first have an opportunity to uncover and record existing connections and associations with the topic. These meaningful connections to the content will later empower students to take ownership of the material and transfer their new learning to long-term memory (Blachowicz & Fisher, 2000; Jensen, 2006).

Students are then asked to think of specific questions they have about the topic. The "**C**" of U-C-ME moves students toward metacognitive strategy use by asking them to **concentrate** on critical concepts during the lesson. The key in this portion of the lesson is to guide students by "challenging them to link to the past, think beyond, and use questions to discover and uncover new learning" (Herrera, 2010, p. 131). According to Kinsella and Feldman (2003), questioning has the potential to engage students in academic talk that allows for:

- Clarification and elaboration of learning
- Review of information as it is taught
- Rehearsal of responses before they are shared with the learning community
- Multiple opportunities for retrieval of information

Keeping all of these things in mind, it is important to provide CLD students with the opportunity to practice posing and answering questions.

The "**M**" of U-C-ME represents the *monitoring* performed by students when they place answers to their questions on the U-C-ME chart and reflect on the degree to which they understand the related content and vocabulary. Students are also given the opportunity to share and nego-

tiate their answers with their small-group members. As Herrera (2010) notes, this type of structured release to a small group increases the chances that an "*i*+1 response will become part of the group answer" (p. 132). The "**E**," or final *evaluation* of student understanding, takes place at the end of the lesson as students summarize their key learnings.

A video clip illustrating implementation of this strategy appears on the DVD included with this book and is available for viewing online at:

www.tcpress.com/AcceleratingLiteracyVideos.html

Materials Needed: U-C-ME template (one per student) • poster paper • picture for key vocabulary words • markers/colored pencils • curricular materials • paper • pencils/pens

---

 ## ACTIVATION: A Canvas of Opportunity

Directions:

- Give each student a blank U-C-ME template before the lesson.
- Have students write the name of the topic/concept that is the focus of the lesson around the outside of the template's center oval (toward the top of the oval).
- **S** Place students in small groups and have each group orally share what they already know about the topic.
- **I** Have each group member choose at least two or three schematic con-

nections he or she made to the topic as a result of this oral sharing and record them individually on the back of the U-C-ME chart in writing and/or with drawings.
- Once students have finished recording their ideas on paper, share with the class six to eight academic vocabulary words essential to their understanding of the topic.
- **S** Ask each small group to select, from their combined collection, up to four words/ideas that they think are

most relevant, given the topic and the academic vocabulary for the lesson.
- Have students transfer the selected ideas to the center oval on their individual templates.

Activating the "*i*"

How does this process activate CLD students' existing knowledge?

- **Sociocultural:** This phase of the strategy helps students uncover their existing knowledge about the topic and make schematic connections to the lesson.
- **Linguistic:** By having students first share what they know orally, they have a chance to verbalize their understandings as well as share information informally with one another in a low-stress environment.

- **Academic:** Students are guided to attend to key information from the onset of the lesson as they select and record the schematic connections they predict are most relevant to the lesson.
- **Cognitive:** The U-C-ME chart provides CLD students with a concrete "tool in their hand" to support them in organizing their thoughts and guiding their metacognitive processes.

CONNECTION: The Broad & Narrow Strokes of Learning

Directions:

- **S** Have students work in their small groups to generate questions they have about the topic and record one question for each spoke of the U-C-ME template.
  - Model this step for students by posing sample questions for one of the spokes.
  - Steer students in the direction of questions that require higher-order thinking skills.
  - Explain to students that these questions will become a guide for their learning and monitoring of their lesson comprehension and understanding of the text.
- **T** Circulate around the room and note the questions students are recording on their spokes.

- Using the questions as a guide, proceed with the lesson.
- During instruction, make sure to stop periodically to provide students with time to individually monitor their comprehension and use the new information to answer the questions.
- Direct students to write the answers to their questions in the corresponding oval at the end of each spoke.
- **S** Toward the end of the lesson (or after students have completed the reading), have group members share and discuss their individual answers with the group. Encourage them to refer back to the lesson materials/text to evaluate the validity of their answers.

- Have each group confirm/disconfirm their predictions regarding the topic-related words/ideas they placed in the center oval of their templates. Have students cross out any words/ideas that did not pertain to the topic.

Author Talk: Connection

As teachers plan lesson delivery, one of the questions they often ask is, How do I make sure my CLD students are getting the main points of the lesson? For many teachers, this is the $100 question! We have found that one of the best ways to support CLD students is through the use of strategies such as U-C-ME. This strategy provides students with a metacognitive tool they can use to monitor their own learning throughout the lesson. By providing students with guiding questions at the onset of the lesson, teachers steer learners toward the main ideas of the lesson and provide a path for them to follow. In addition, when teachers allow students to come up with some of the questions themselves, the students take ownership of the learning process.

As we watched this strategy being implemented in one 3rd-grade classroom, we were impressed with the level of interaction and engagement we saw among the students. The talk was very loud, but very much on task and centered on the topic. The questions the students generated were also very impressive. In fact, some of them were at a much higher level than we would have anticipated. After the lesson, in discussing the students' questions with the teacher, she too commented that she was impressed by the depth and level of reflection in which her students had engaged.

Connecting to the "*i*+1"

How does this process move CLD students from the known to the unknown?

- **Sociocultural:** The collaborative nature of this phase of the U-C-ME strategy enhances the students' ability to generate meaningful questions as they build off one another's background knowledge.
- **Linguistic:** Students engage in academic talk and the use of key content vocabulary as they generate and subsequently share answers to their questions.

- **Academic:** Students are challenged to evaluate their predictions about the content by using the lesson material to confirm/disconfirm their initial ideas.
- **Cognitive:** Students are stretched to come up with questions that require higher-order thinking as they fill out their individual U-C-ME charts.

AFFIRMATION: A Gallery of Understanding

Directions:

- **S** **P** Have students use what they wrote in the ovals to summarize what they learned about the topic or concept. Students can complete this task by doing one or more of the following:
  - Discuss what was learned with a peer.
  - Work as groups to use the information recorded in the ovals to create a final class quiz or end-of-chapter test.

- Work individually or in pairs to write a persuasive or narrative paragraph.
- Additionally, students can do a "connected talk" at the end of the lesson to discuss the things they learned. To do this:
  - Have one student start the connected talk by sharing one thing he or she learned about the topic.
  - Then have each additional student

connect his or her idea to what the previous student shared.

Affirming Student Ownership: *"I" Get It!*
How does this process celebrate CLD student learning?

- **Sociocultural:** Opportunities to collaborate allow students to celebrate both individual and class learning.
- **Linguistic:** Providing multiple ways for the students to respond/demonstrate what they have learned meets the needs of students at different levels of language proficiency.

- **Academic:** The completed U-C-ME chart provides students with a concrete study tool for reviewing key learnings from the lesson/unit.
- **Cognitive:** The connected talk activity requires students to use creative and critical thinking to make appropriate connections among topic-related ideas.

SPOTLIGHT: Early Literacy Connection

Research has shown that questions "are at the heart of classroom practice" (Marzano et al., 2001, p. 113). In fact, questioning can account for as much as 80% of what occurs in a classroom on any given day (Marzano et al.). Thus, young CLD students should be asked a variety of questions that are appropriate for their age and language proficiency level. The U-C-ME strategy is a great way to model the question and answer process while addressing both of these levels.

U-C-ME in Pictures!

When initially using the U-C-ME strategy with younger CLD students, use one U-C-ME template with the whole class. This allows you as the teacher to model use of the strategy through each phase of instruction. When describing each phase on the U-C-ME template, use a writing utensil of a different color. This allows the students to better understand and remember each distinct stage.

Initially, you can simply ask questions related to the content and have the students find the information in the text. The students can then draw a picture to represent the answer for the appropriate bubble. As students get comfortable with generating and asking questions, they can begin to ask their own questions about the vocabulary and content and look for the related information in the text or other resources.

> **Biography-Driven Response to Intervention**
>
> One of the goals of core instruction is to provide learners with opportunities for meaningful repetition of the content. The U-C-ME strategy ensures that learners have meaningful repetition of the tasks and concepts of the lesson as they first dig into their own schemas and then revisit the ideas through the questions they generate and answer. The strategy provides a tool that can be first used during core instruction and then extended upon during tiered instruction. By starting with overarching ideas about the topic and moving toward the specifics of the content, this strategy provides students with a systematic plan for comprehending the lesson.

One Classroom's Perspective

Activating:

I considered the biographies of my CLD/ELL students as I planned and introduced the strategy by modeling how a U-C-ME graphic organizer is done, which we worked on together as a whole class. I chose this in order to activate the students' prior knowledge concerning Native Americans and their culture. I thought this would be able to tell me exactly what the students knew about Native Americans. With this information, I was able to plan my lesson accordingly. Using this information and a good understanding of the CLD students' biographies, I decided to teach them where Native Americans came from and how they migrated to North America across the Bering Strait. I also decided to include their migration all the way down into Mexico. I hoped the CLD students would be able to relate to this. In addition, I wanted the ELL students to be able to see another culture and how it developed, and where it is today compared to their own. I hoped they would relate and really be engaged in the lesson since it involved drawing.

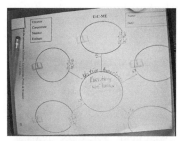

Connecting:

My groups were arranged with four students per table. At each table, a range of academic proficiency levels and a mix of ethnic groups were represented. I taught using a lesson on the Internet that had good graphics and simple explanations of how Native Americans moved from Asia to North America and eventually South America. The students were required to record this in their notebooks. To promote academic success, NES [non-English-speaking] students were allowed to write the notes in their native language. Also, I had the students draw pictures in order to help them with the vocabulary and concepts. In addition, I always find ways to help the students feel at ease in my classroom through humor and acting out the lessons. I let them act out vocabulary words from the lesson.

One Classroom's Perspective (*continued*)

Affirming:

I used the strategy to support me in authentically assessing my students' understanding of the lesson, as evidenced by my modification of the U-C-ME model. I had the students cut out another version and place the oval in the middle and the other spokes and boxes around the oval. I then instructed the students to draw what they remembered from the lesson. They took their time and worked well together as a whole class. The students remembered a lot of what was in the lesson, as evidenced by their artwork.

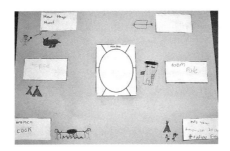

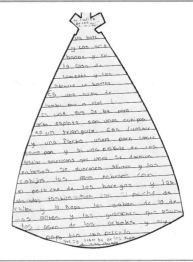

Student Voices

I liked being able to come up with my own questions about what I wanted to know and then find the answers in the story! It was really neat!

—*ELL Student
Intermediate Fluency*

Filling in the circles is really neat because I can ask my friends for help when I don't know the answer. We also look in the book.

—*ELL Student
Speech Emergent*

I really liked being able to make a poster after we filled out the U-C-ME chart. It was neat to use all the information from what we learned and put it on a big poster and see it in a new way!

—*ELL Student
Intermediate Fluency*

Uncover
Concentrate
Monitor
Evaluate

U-C-ME

Name: ______________________________

Date: ______________________________

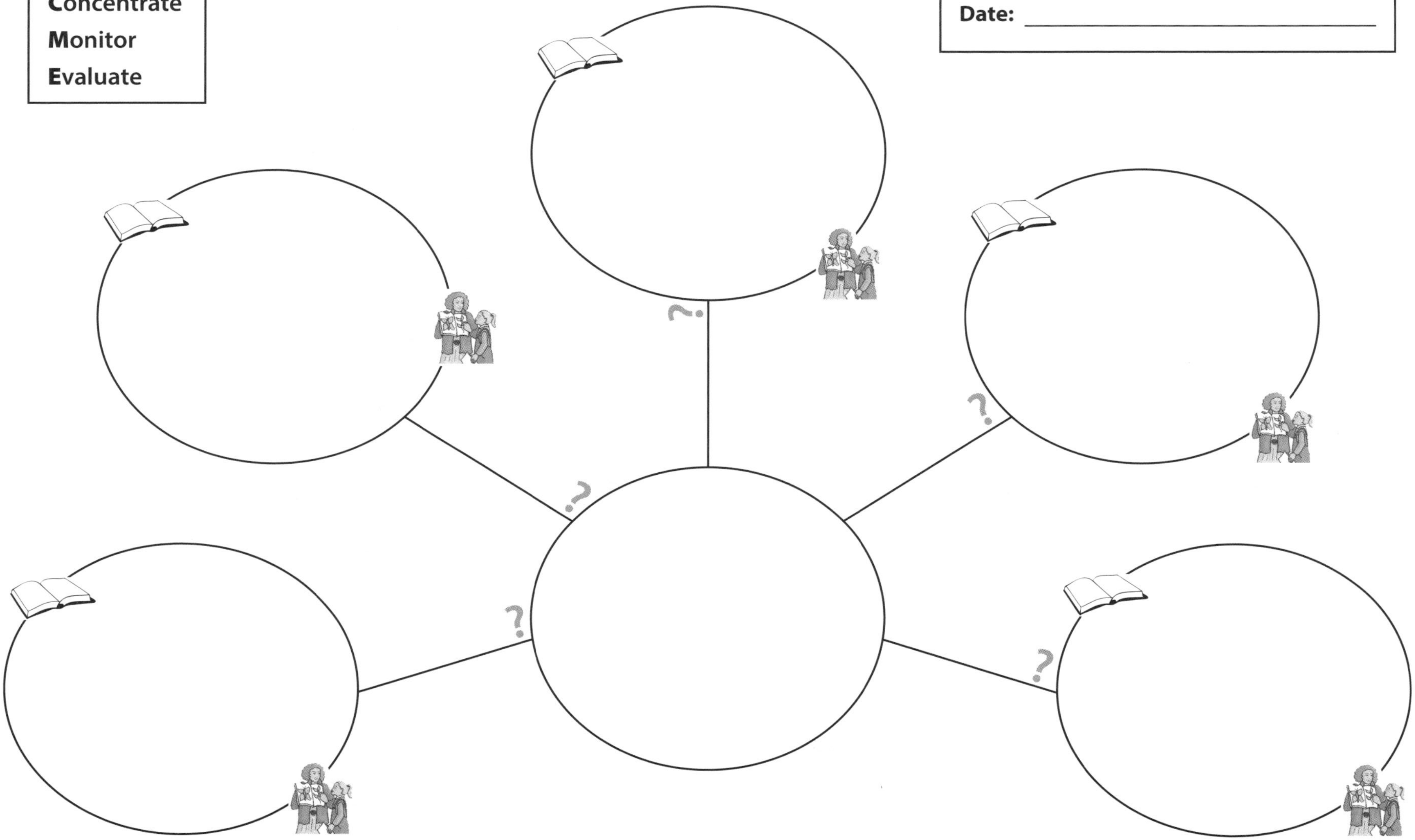

Available for free download and printing from www.tcpress.com

STRATEGY

Extension Wheel

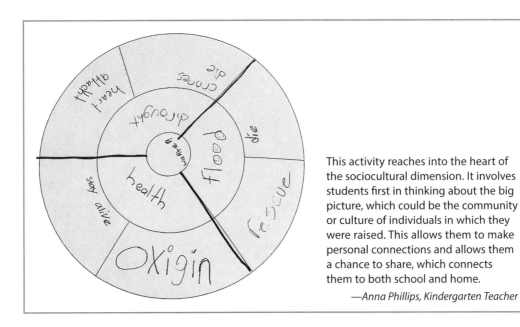

This activity reaches into the heart of the sociocultural dimension. It involves students first in thinking about the big picture, which could be the community or culture of individuals in which they were raised. This allows them to make personal connections and allows them a chance to share, which connects them to both school and home.

—*Anna Phillips, Kindergarten Teacher*

Where Theory Meets Practice

As teachers, some of most powerful things we hear in the classroom each day are the responses students give to the questions we ask and those they ask of each other. The cultural connections they make to their own lives and those of their peers never cease to amaze us! Each student approaches the lesson from a specific frame of mind. Herrera (2010) states that it is only when we as teachers "actively listen to the hidden messages of student talk" that we can guide learners to interact with the content in ways that stretch them to their zone of proximal development (p. 118). To do this, we need to find strategies that can help us access the individual biographies of our students, identify what it is they understand about the lesson, and expand upon their individual learnings in meaningful ways. The Extension Wheel is one such strategy.

The Extension Wheel is a strategy that guides CLD students to expand upon information gained in a lesson. The power of this strategy is that it stems from the students' own voices. The visual organizer provides CLD students with a framework for both the categorization of information (Zwiers, 2004/2005) and the progression of discussion as they move from the central topic to the related details to appli-

cations of the content in the real world (Center for Instructional Development and Research, 1999). In addition, it provides the students with multiple opportunities to engage in peer sharing as they discuss each addition to the wheel. The teacher is able to reinforce these ideas by revoicing what students have shared and validating students' personal connections. With each step, the Extension Wheel strategy provides students with the opportunity to reflect on their own understandings and extend their knowledge of the topic beyond the classroom.

The Extension Wheel strategy also lends itself to the exploration of numerous text structures, including cause/effect, compare/contrast, problem/solution, structural analysis, and point of view. Because the successful outcome of this strategy is highly dependent upon student-driven ideas and connections, it also enhances student ownership of the concepts and vocabulary (Blachowicz & Fisher, 2000). By helping learners organize their thoughts and ideas on the extension wheel worksheet, this strategy further supports their comprehension of the topic.

Materials Needed: Extension Wheel template (one per student) • curricular materials • paper • pencils/pens

ACTIVATION: A Canvas of Opportunity

Directions:

- Place students in small groups of three or four students.
- Give each student a blank Extension Wheel template.
- **I** Have students write the name of the topic/concept that is the focus of the lesson in the center circle of the wheel.
- Ask students to think about the topic/concept and draw an image that they associate with it in the center circle.
- **S** Next have students discuss their ideas and image with the members of their small group. Encourage students to think about cultural connections to the topic/concept.
- After students have finished sharing their ideas, ask them to look at the topic/concept in the middle of the

wheel and work in their small groups to think of and discuss two or three extensions/effects of the idea.

- As students are thinking of the extensions, explain to them that any idea can have negative as well as positive effects. For example, if the term in the middle is "rainfall," students might think of extensions such as *floods, crops,* and *monsoon.*
- Extensions will vary, depending upon the students' funds of knowledge, prior knowledge, and academic knowledge (especially knowledge related to their countries of origin).

- Encourage students to provide rationales for their ideas so that other group members will understand their perspective.
- As students share rationales behind their extension ideas, circulate around the room and silently listen as students discuss their thought processes.

Activating the "*i*"

How does this process activate CLD students' existing knowledge?

- **Sociocultural:** The collaborative learning component of this phase helps CLD students understand how ideas can be elaborated upon in multiple ways, depending on a person's point of view. By recognizing the validity of each perspective, students also gain a greater appreciation for other members of their classroom learning community.
- **Linguistic:** As students discuss extensions for the

vocabulary words, they further develop their English language skills.
- **Academic:** Discussion of possible extensions of the topic/concept allows students to consider multiple aspects of the topic/concept.
- **Cognitive:** This phase of the strategy helps students categorize their initial schematic connections to the topic/concept.

CONNECTION: The Broad & Narrow Strokes of Learning

Directions:

- **S** After students have finished discussing their initial extensions, ask them in their small groups to transfer the results of their oral discussions onto the first ring of the wheel.
  - As students complete this step, make sure to circulate to each group, look at their extensions, and direct their final ideas toward extensions that will connect best to the content of the lesson.
  - Revoicing can play a crucial role at this time, so you also may want to bring the class together to revoice some of the things that students put on their wheels. For example, a teacher might say, "I noticed that Yugang's group put _____ on the first ring. I really like that because it shows how they were personally connecting to the topic."
- Next have students connect to the topic through text or media. As you

share the content with the students, stop at several points and have them look for further extensions of the ideas on the first ring of the wheel. This time, the groups will add ideas to the second ring, two ideas/extensions per one extension from the first ring.

- **S** **T** After students finish putting the expanded ideas on the second ring, bring the class together and have groups share their ideas with the whole class or with another small group.
  - As one group is sharing, have the other students individually use their extension wheels to add details they are hearing.
- **S** Because the whole purpose of the activity is for students to expand upon their thought process, you may want the students to extend to an

added third ring as well. To do this, have students expand upon only certain ideas from the second ring.

- To support this additional extension process, visit each group and circle on the students' extension wheels the ideas you now want them to expand upon.
- Make sure to have students expand upon the things that will help them move toward your overall goal/outcome for the lesson.

Connecting to the "*i*+1"
How does this process move CLD students from the known to the unknown?

- **Sociocultural:** Students are able to learn from each other as they continue working on the expansions, thereby creating a community of learners.
- **Linguistic:** This phase provides students with opportunities to use listening, speaking, reading, and writing to convey their points of view, consider others' perspectives, and document learning.
- **Academic:** The continual expansion of ideas becomes a discovery process for each student, as he or she con-

nects to the academic concept at individual, local, and global levels.

- **Cognitive:** Students must reflect upon all the ideas shared by their peers as they make decisions about which ideas to record on the wheel. This process requires students to use higher-order thinking as they filter through the information and determine the most important and relevant details.

AFFIRMATION: A Gallery of Understanding

Directions:

- **I** **P** After groups finish recording ideas on the wheel, ask the students to write a narrative or expository summary of the points identified on the wheel. Students can complete this task individually or in pairs.
- You can incorporate student choice into this assessment by allowing students to choose which of the ideas from the wheel they would like to discuss in their writing.
- You can accommodate student preferences and varying levels of language proficiency by:

- Providing a multiple-choice or open-ended authentic assessment (be sure to allow CLD students to use their individual extension wheels as needed).
- Allowing students to alternatively create a pictorial summary that incorporates key terms and ideas.

- Having students write two or three sentences summarizing the key points learned from the lesson while using vocabulary/concepts from the extension wheel.

Author Talk: Affirmation

One of the many challenges teachers face is that of promoting students' comprehension. For CLD students, one of the keys to comprehension is determining what is most important and documenting this while reading. As teachers, we know that students need multiple pathways to comprehend text, and we are in the best position to help them find those pathways. Research has shown that effective reading comprehension requires that students have substantial vocabulary and background knowledge to understand and make inferences about the text being read (Konold, Juel, McKinnon, & Deffes, 2003; Lesaux & Siegel, 2003). Often

this requires significant vocabulary development, keeping in mind students' biographies and needs.

What is exciting about the Extension Wheel strategy is that it allows students to use academic vocabulary throughout the lesson as they work on the extension of their own ideas. Using the wheel as a template, students are able to document their background knowledge and then add their new understandings. This extension of students' ideas works like the ripple effect that is created when a pebble is dropped in a body of water. CLD students' language and comprehension expand as we start building upon the foundational knowledge of the topic that they bring to the lesson.

Affirming Student Ownership: "I" Get It!
How does this process celebrate CLD student learning?

- **Sociocultural:** The completed extension wheel provides students with a tangible product to share with peers and reinforces the idea that all students participate in the construction of knowledge.
- **Linguistic:** Since students' expansions are tied to a single concept, their associations help them elaborate on the topic and at the same time retain the new ideas.

- **Academic:** The Extension Wheel strategy can serve as a great tool to enhance students' thinking skills and as a medium for helping students make reading and writing connections as they use their wheels to record their summaries.
- **Cognitive:** As students complete their extension wheels, they are stretched cognitively as they expand upon the concept.

SPOTLIGHT: Early Literacy Connection

The Extension Wheel strategy is a great vehicle for allowing early literacy students to practice English grammar. Although research has shown there is a strong connection between oral and written language, explicit instruction is necessary because the two are not synonymous (Boyd-Batstone, 2006). Providing CLD students with activities such as the Extension Wheel strategy helps them distinguish between oral and written language (Sulzby & Teale, 2003).

How Many Ways Can You Say the Word?

For this variant of strategy, draw an extension wheel on a large piece of chart paper. Write "Action Words" in the center circle. In the first ring, write the words *walk, run,* and *jump*. Have the students listen attentively as you say each verb and model the action for the students. Then have them physically imitate your actions. For the next ring, have the students work with a partner to come up with two examples that could be built off each of these words. Examples might include *walking, walked*; *running, ran*; and *jumping, jumped*. Model this level of extension with the one of the action words (e.g., *walk*). Talk about the meaning of the two different words (*walking* means you are doing it now; *walked* means you did it in the past). Allow students to generate extension words for the remaining action words. Have pairs share their ideas with the rest of the class. Then have the students draw pictures to illustrate some of their action words. Next, help them write sentences describing each picture.

You can repeat this activity using more action verbs or any other words you would like to use to help students practice grammar in a fun, interactive way!

Biography-Driven Response to Intervention

Extension Wheel is a strategy that has great potential for use during core instruction. As teachers work with students on the strategy, teachers have unique opportunities to tailor the strategy for group work as well as to help students at their individual levels. Since the organization and expansion of thoughts and ideas are the primary focuses of the strategy, students can extend their ideas and thought processes into Tier 2 instruction with the same tool. This is a great strategy for helping students meet their language and content-specific goals during core and tiered instruction as they work with vocabulary and concepts.

One Classroom's Perspective

Activating:

Today was the first day we decided to work on the concept of area and perimeter. Our students need constant practice with these two skills, and I decided to focus on the topic by having students practice this using their Extension Wheel templates. The first thing I did was to divide students in small groups. Since this was a very content-based activity, I divided the students into the groups based on their academic and linguistic understandings.

I started the activity by giving all the students blank sheets of paper and having them first think about what they knew about the topic. I had them individually jot down some of the things they knew about the topic. At this time, I gave them the option to either write or draw the ideas. As students did their individual work, I went around and noted some of the ideas they were putting on paper so I could revisit these at a later time with them.

One Classroom's Perspective (*continued*)

Connecting:

Once the students were done putting their individual connections on the paper, I had them discuss their ideas with each other in their small groups. Next, I had them get started on their extension wheels. We started off by thinking of the three things that would impact us the most in math and the real world related to area and perimeter. The three things most students chose for this ring were *labels, real life,* and *definitions*. Since the students had already discussed the ideas in their small groups, I had them first work on the wheels independently. I gave them the option of using the papers on which they had brainstormed the ideas earlier. At this time, also, students had the option of either drawing or writing the ideas on the paper. As students finished the first ring of the wheel, I had them again discuss the things they covered in their small groups. After the students were done with the first ring, we worked on some word problems specific to the topic to help students

further expand upon the wheel. Once we revisited the problems, students further added their ideas to the next ring.

Affirming:

Once the students were done with the first two rings, I had them further expand upon the wheel by having them add more ideas to the wheel. As students worked on it, most of them talked about the fact that they would have to keep in mind the concept of area and perimeter when they are doing some construction at home or building a fence. A lot of my students also shared with each other how this activity helped them in remembering the formulas, and I was very pleased with that. After the students were done expanding their wheels, I had them share one more time the ideas they had on the wheel with each other at the table. The following day, we used our extension wheels to do some math problems specific to the topic. I feel like this was such a great introduction and review for my students to get into the topic of area and perimeter.

Student Voices

I liked being able to write about the weather and what happens in different kinds of weather. Making my wheel was fun!

—*ELL Student*
Speech Emergent

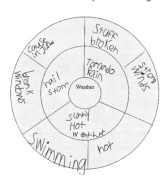

I didn't know that everything had a consequence. This helped me see them a lot easier because I could talk to my friend about it.

—*ELL Student*
Speech Emergent

I learned something new. Now I can use this again when I want to know about consequences and the effects of that.

—*ELL Student*
Intermediate Fluency

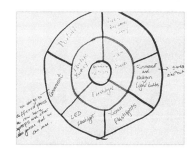

TEMPLATE: Extension Wheel

Name: _____

Date: _____

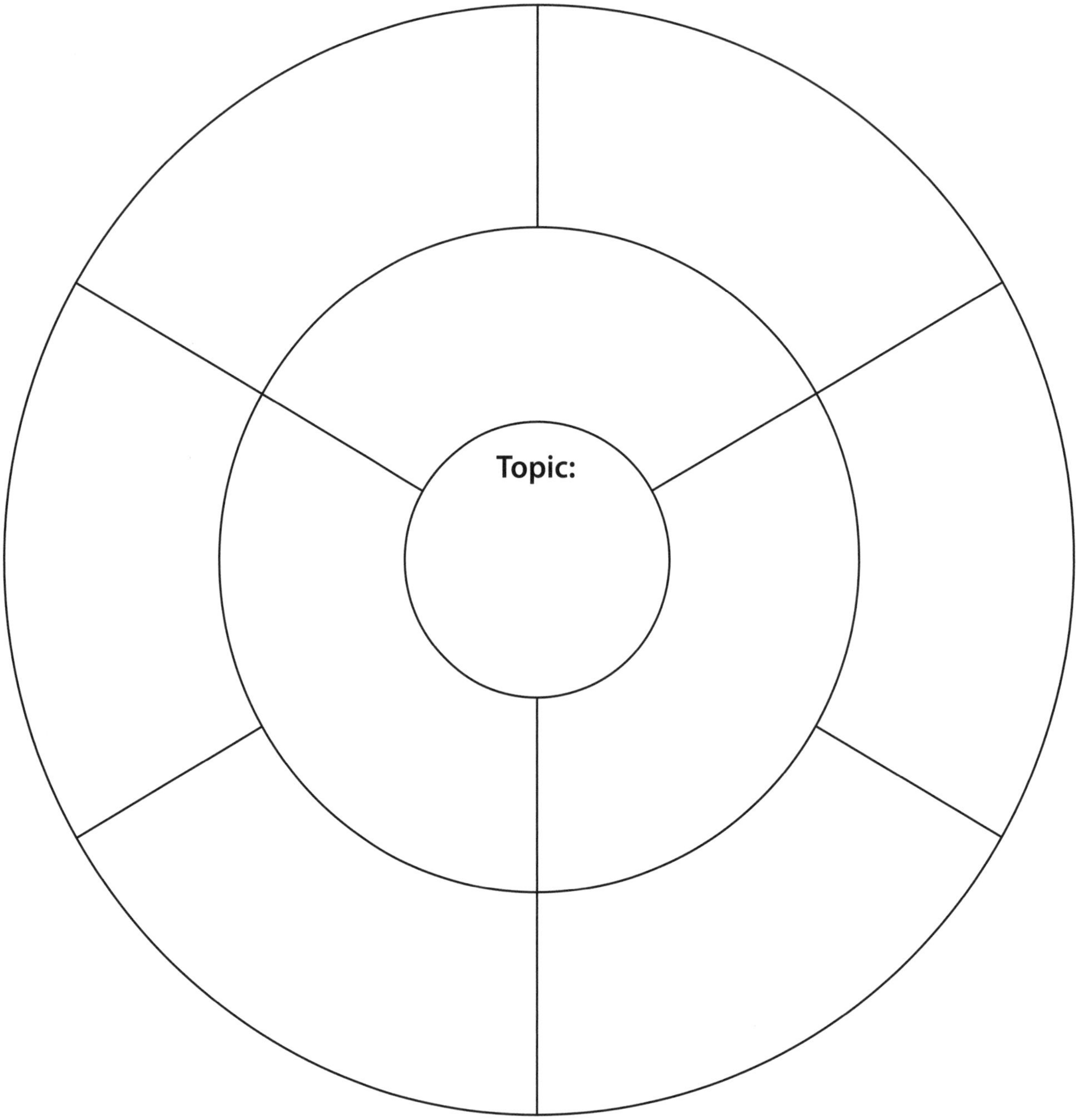

Topic:

STRATEGY

Hearts Activity

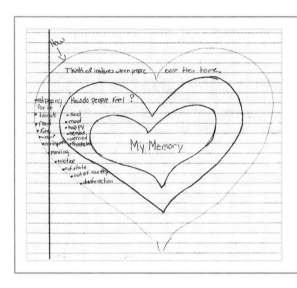

The Hearts Activity allows the teacher to reach the students academically. It helps us understand what they know, what they have gone through, and the academic connections they are making to the text so we can meet their needs. It also provides us with insight into their writing skills.

—*Jennifer Bowden, 6th-Grade Teacher*

Where Theory Meets Practice

The ability to articulate one's views about a topic or issue often requires the learner to made a connection to the topic, understand new information, and come to some conclusion related to what he or she believes about the topic. It is also necessary to have the language and vocabulary to make this happen. The Hearts Activity provides learners with a concrete tool to share what they already know, a way to think about what impact or emotional connection the topic may have on society, and, ultimately, a vehicle with which to make a personal connection to the topic/text/issue before the lesson begins. As an opening for a lesson, the strategy immediately creates the conditions for listening, speaking, reading, and writing to occur in a setting that supports instructional conversations (Tharp, Estrada, Dalton, & Yamauchi, 2000). According to Marzano (2004), listening to and observing what students bring as background knowledge greatly enhances teaching and learning in practice.

Research by Herrera (2010) elaborates on this concept, stating that "to understand what our students know and how they communicate that knowledge, we must first understand the cultural constructs that shaped them *before* they arrived in our classrooms" (p. 81). Yet getting at these cultural constructs can sometimes be difficult, particularly when students are hesitant to share information from their background knowledge.

The Hearts Activity helps us to understand these constructs by observing our students throughout the lesson as they make sense of, and make connections to, what we are teaching. In addition, it helps our CLD students conceptualize the contexts and situations that will allow them to voice their individual biographical roots in a structured way (Herrera, 2010). To help our students do this, we need to first tap into the funds of knowledge that they bring to the lesson.

After making biography-driven connections to the topic, CLD students are guided to make connections to the new information in the text. By moving from the "known" (students' biography-driven connections) to the "unknown" (new content knowledge), students are guided to make meaningful connections to the text as they draw first upon their existing knowledge.

Materials Needed: Blank sheet of paper or Hearts Activity template appropriate to grade level of students (nested hearts for Grades K–2 or split heart for Grades 3–6; one per student) • markers/colored pencils • pencils/pens

> *Note:* Given the specific nature of this strategy, two sets of directions are being provided. The first set, given in the standard format, is recommended for Grades K–2. The second set, which appears in a more condensed format on page 145, is recommended for Grades 3–6. Each set has its own template, and the directions have been written to reflect the specific academic, linguistic, and cognitive needs of the targeted grade levels. But the overall goal of helping students make meaningful connections to the text by linking the "known" to the "unknown" is the same for all grade levels, K–6.

ACTIVATION: A Canvas of Opportunity

Directions (Grades K–2):

- **T** Give each student a Grades K–2 Hearts Activity template.
- Explain to students that they are going to be doing an activity in which they will expand upon a topic through questioning.
- **I** Draw a model of the Hearts Activity template on the board or on a large piece of chart paper and write the name of the lesson topic at the top. Place this in the front of the room, where all the students can see. Have students individually write the topic on their template in the center heart (the "topic" heart).
- **T** To get students started, tell them they are going to *activate* their thinking. To do this, they need to first write the word "Activate" at the top of the largest heart. Pose one or two of the following questions to help them connect the topic to something happening in their community or the world:

- What personal connections do you have to _____ [the topic]?
- What are some things happening where you live related to _____ [the topic]?
- Have you seen anything on TV or heard your parents talk about _____ [the topic]?
- How do you feel or how do you think other people feel about this?
- **P** Have students discuss the question with a partner and individually write their responses in the outermost rim of the heart (depending on the age and language proficiency level of your students, this can be in the form of pictures, words, or abbreviated sentences) to document/register the ideas/thoughts they activated. Be sure to allow students to add any ideas learned from peers during this time.
- As partners are sharing, circulate from group to group and listen to what is being shared. As students are sharing,

write their responses on sticky notes. Put these sticky notes on the Hearts Activity template at the front of the room.
- **T** Return to the whole group and have students share with the class their individual responses. To support their sharing, revoice specific responses from the partner conversations by restating students' answers.

Activating the "*i*"

How does this process activate CLD students' existing knowledge?

- **Sociocultural:** The collaborative learning component helps CLD students understand how ideas can be elaborated in multiple ways, depending on a person's point of view (culture). By recognizing the validity of each perspective, as well as their own prior knowledge about the topic, students will realize they have words or images that set the stage for making associations and connecting to new learning.
- **Linguistic:** As the teacher actively listens to what students share with their peers, the teacher has an opportunity to gain insight into *how* students know what they

know. This gives the teacher links that he or she can use to connect to students' native language and known vocabulary during the working phase of the lesson.

- **Academic:** The initial phase of the Hearts Activity allows students to identify key academic vocabulary and sets the stage for peers at different levels to share the new vocabulary and the content knowledge they already bring to the lesson.
- **Cognitive:** This cognitive strategy helps students organize their thoughts related to the central topic and document them on paper as the lesson unfolds.

 CONNECTION: The Broad & Narrow Strokes of Learning

Directions (Grades K–2):

- **T** Next, have students use the middle heart (the medium-sized heart) to record their learnings. To guide students in doing this, have them write "Connect" at the top of the middle heart so they can record their specific connections to the text.
- Explain that you are going to give them a new set of questions that will help them set a purpose for their reading. These questions can be displayed for students on the board or with a projector.
- We recommend that you give your students a combination of literal and inferential questions. Questions for this stage could include
  - What is happening in the story/chapter related to the topic?
  - What are the characters feeling?
  - What do you think is the main idea of the story/text?

- How can we apply what we learned from the story in the real world?
- **S** Have students work together in small groups to preview the text and predict answers to one or more of the questions posed.
- **T S** Read a portion of the text and have students stop and discuss in their small groups the specifics of the topic as related to the questions posed.
- **S I** After students have finished their discussion, have each group agree on one answer for each question that they will individually record in the Connect section of their template and share with the whole class.
- **T** Call on each group to share their answer for each question with the whole class. As students share answers, record them on a sticky note and add them to the whole-class

Hearts Activity template at the front of the room.

- Have students continue this process of reading, discussing, and documenting their learnings until the text has been completed.
- Make sure to stop periodically to share responses among the whole class.

Connecting to the "*i*+1"
How does this process move CLD students from the known to the unknown?

- **Sociocultural:** Through instructional conversations, students and the teacher are provided the opportunity to listen to different perspectives. This is an essential component to creating an environment of mutual respect and understanding.
- **Linguistic:** Language is taken to *i*+1 when the conditions are set and opportunities given for use of both social and academic language. During the connection phase, the learner listens to and has opportunities to articulate what is important. Academic vocabulary must be rehearsed in authentic ways to establish its use in the future.

- **Academic:** As the teacher provides new information and facilitates talk among the students, he or she is also formatively assessing learning. Elaboration or clarification is essential to making strong connections to new learning. This phase also provides an opportunity for the teacher to connect the "known" (opening knowledge) to the "unknown" (new learning).
- **Cognitive:** The completed Hearts Activity template serves as a "tool in the hand." For the student, it provides a roadmap of what is important. For the teacher, it documents what and how the content knowledge and vocabulary have been processed.

 AFFIRMATION: A Gallery of Understanding

Directions (Grades K–2):

- Once students have completed the outer (Activate) and middle (Connect) rings of their heart, have them turn the page over.
- **1** On the reverse side of their heart, have students individually summarize their key learnings by focusing on at least one of the following types of connections:
  - Text to self
  - Text to text
  - Text to world

Note: Students at the preproduction or speech emergent stages of second language acquisition should be given the option of writing this passage in their native language or with the sup-

port of a more proficient peer or para-professional.
- Encourage students to provide an illustration to accompany their writing.
- **P** After students have completed their writing, have them read their work to a partner.
- Circulate around the classroom and listen to students' sharing of their summaries so you can revoice critical connections with the entire class.
- Depending on the text/topic, you can also have students:
  - Draw a visual representation of the text and write a short description.
  - Use the information on their heart

template to do a compare-and-contrast diagram/chart.
- Write questions about the story based on the information from their heart and use it to "quiz" their peers.

Affirming Student Ownership: "*I*" Get It!
How does this process celebrate CLD student learning?

- **Sociocultural:** Students are able to use their ideas from the Hearts Activity to help them summarize their learnings in their own words.
- **Linguistic:** The completed heart is evidence of the vocabulary that has been learned throughout the lesson. It provides a tool for scaffolding writing or oral presentation of learning.
- **Academic:** Completing the Hearts Activity template provides both the teacher and the learner with notes

on what has been discussed and read throughout the lesson. Creating this tool provides the learner many opportunities to listen for important information, write, speak, and read throughout the lesson.
- **Cognitive:** Students' completed hearts provide them with a "tool in the hand" that they can refer back to as they prepare to demonstrate their learnings. For the teacher, it documents how the student has learned the information.

DIRECTIONS: Hearts Activity for Grades 3–6

Activating:

- Explain to students that they are going to be doing an activity that will help them explore cultural and vocabulary connections to the text they will be reading.
- Give each student a Grades 3–6 Hearts Activity template.
- **T** Introduce the topic of the lesson and ask students to think about ways they connect to it by using personal experiences, information from books they have read, or things they have heard on the news or from other people (e.g., their family or friends).
- **S** Place students in groups of three or four and have them discuss the different connections they make to the topic.
- To extend the group discussion, pose the following types of questions to the whole group and have students take turns sharing one idea connected to the topic in their small groups:
  - Broad question: When you think of _____ [the topic] what comes to mind as it relates to the past, the world, or _____ [something else]?
  - What impact will this have, or how might/do people feel about it?
  - What personal connections do you have with _____ [the topic]?
- **I** Next, have students individually write ideas from their group discussion in the "Ignite" part of their individual hearts. Encourage students to draw pictures or write in words what they associate with the topic, being sure to allow students to write in their native language (L1) if they choose to do so.

Connecting:

- **T** Before you have students read the text, give them a new set of questions that will help them set a purpose for their reading. We recommend that you give your students a combination of direct and inferential questions. Keep the questions closely aligned with the first set of questions you asked during the opening of the lesson. Sample questions for this Connection phase, when students work with and practice vocabulary and learn new information, include
  - Broad question: When you think of _____ [the topic] what comes to mind as it relates to the past, the world, or _____ [something else]?
  - What impact will this have, or how might/do people feel about it?
  - What personal connections do you have with _____ [the topic]?
  - As you are reading/listening to the teacher or talking with your peers about what is happening in the story/text, what can you cite that would provide evidence of _____ [something]?
  - What makes you think that? Be specific, and choose words from the text to help support your answer.
  - What are the characters feeling?
  - What are some of the key issues the author is focusing on?
  - What are some of the main ideas or "lessons" we can take away from the story?
  - How can we apply in the real world some of the learnings we gained from the text?
- **S** After students have read a portion of the text or after you have led part of the discussion, have students stop and discuss specifics about the topic in small groups related to the questions posed.
- As students in their groups find answers, have them write their ideas in the "Connect" part of their individual hearts.
- **I** We recommend that, as "chunking" of the complex text occurs, teachers ask students to individually refer to their opening statements to find similarities and differences between their predictions/thoughts and those of the author.

Affirming:

- Once students have individually recorded their ideas in the Ignite and Connect parts of their heart, have them turn the page over.
- On the reverse side of the heart, have students individually summarize their learnings. Depending on the topic, students might:
  - **S** Work in small groups to role-play an exchange between characters in the story, explaining the causes for, as well as the effects of, the exchange.
  - **I** Individually write a persuasive paragraph explaining why a certain idea related to the topic is good or bad for the world.
  - **I** Use the ideas on their hearts to answer end-of-chapter questions individually.
  - **P** Work with a partner to compare and contrast their initial ideas with what was learned from the author.
- It is important for the learners to use the completed template as a tool for defending, articulating, and using key vocabulary as they write. So be creative in your closing activity, as long as it reflects the objectives of the lesson.

SPOTLIGHT: Early Literacy Connection

The Hearts Activity is a wonderful way to engage CLD students in meaningful connections with the text. Furthermore, it provides CLD students with a vehicle for using language in ways that allow them to interact with each other in meaningful ways. According to Boyd-Batstone (2006), this type of social interaction is a key pedagogical component of language development when working with young children.

In My Heart!

When doing this activity with younger CLD students, use a large piece of chart paper and draw the Hearts Activity template (Grades K–2 version). This allows the teacher to model the use of the strategy with all students. To begin, place the name of the topic/main idea in the center of the heart. When possible, add a visual cue to the center of the heart as well. Then ask the students to answer a personal question that will help them link to the overall message of the story you are going to be reading. As students respond, write down their answers in the middle (medium-sized) heart.

After completing this first phase, begin to read the story. Stop at key points and make connections back to what the students shared about their own feelings. After reading the story, ask another question that builds on the personal connections the students have made and ties to the text. This link from personal to text reinforces student learning and explicitly models how to make such connections.

Biography-Driven Response to Intervention

As teachers use the Hearts Activity strategy, the numerous opportunities for students to make connections to their background knowledge allow for a deeper understanding of the concepts, which is one of the primary goals of core instruction. Further, the strategy allows students to focus on connections with self and world as they proceed through the lesson. This particular aspect of the strategy works well for both core and tiered instruction. The questions associated with the different parts of the lesson provide a meaningful context for students to better understand abstract concepts that they encounter during core instruction; these connections can then be expanded upon during tiered instruction.

One Classroom's Perspective

Activating:

When planning this lesson I wanted to make sure my students understood different types of storms. The Hearts Activity was a great activity for getting to the heart of the Prism Model. Students had the opportunity to think about times they were frightened because of storms, to share experiences with each other, and to make connec-

tions with the main character in the story. Students interacted with and learned from each other. No matter what stage of language acquisition they were in, they were able to share and express their feelings and experiences and document them on their individual hearts.

One Classroom's Perspective (*continued*)

Connecting:

The second part of the Hearts Activity took students from the known to the unknown using all three memory functions (sensory, working, permanent) and helped my students make associations to new vocabulary. The use of individual, partner, team, and whole-group instruction further enhanced my students' learning. As we proceeded with the reading of the book, students used their background knowledge as a resource to learn new vocabulary.

By having them document their learning on their hearts, I was really able to take the lesson to an *i*+1 level using the information my students had already put on their hearts. One of the best things we discovered as a class was that there were many cognates (tornado, hurricane, torrential, typhoon, precipitation, catastrophe, temperature, map) that could be incorporated into the lesson.

Affirming:

At the end of the story, I had students compare/contrast their memories with the main character's experience. I encouraged my students to use information from their heart to support them with their writing. In particular, I emphasized using cognates to enhance their understanding. Not only did we model/share personal experiences, we also used the first page of our story

booklet to write/draw what they thought the title of the book, *Riding Out the Storm,* meant. They also used a map to share storm experiences by locating geographical areas for certain types of storms based on where students were from. After the students' stories were complete, we shared them as a whole class.

Student Voices

I liked being able to write about myself.

—*ELL Student
Speech Emergent*

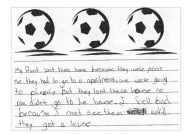

I really liked it. It helped me think about how my family felt and I was able to use the words I wrote in my heart to write.

—*ELL Student
Speech Emergent*

It made me happy to talk about my family and how much I missed them, especially my aunt.

—*ELL Student
Intermediate Fluency*

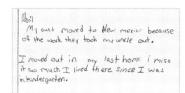

TEMPLATE: Hearts Activity (Grades K–2)

Name: _____

Date: _____

TEMPLATE: Hearts Activity (Grades 3–6)

Name: _____

Topic: _____   Date: _____

Ignite   Connect

STRATEGY

Active Bookmarks

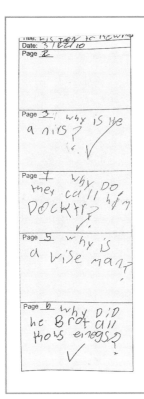 

This strategy allows students to check their progress and make sure they comprehend the material. It also allows them to take ownership of their learning. As the students write questions, note taking becomes part of this process, which leads toward prediction and summarization skills.

—*Sabina Hacker, ESL Coordinator*

Where Theory Meets Practice

Students often struggle to focus on key concepts when reading. One of the primary reasons for this difficulty is that they often get "lost" in all the text. When the goal of comprehension is not being achieved, explicit instruction on metacognitive reading strategies can help CLD students take corrective action and more effectively engage with the text (Herrera et al., 2010). By explicitly modeling how to monitor their thinking and assess their understanding, teachers promote CLD students' metacognition and text comprehension.

Active Bookmarks is a strategy that builds on the idea that readers will more fully comprehend what they are reading if they first construct a purpose for reading (Tovani, 2000). After having students make predictions about the overall text, Active Bookmarks guides students to pose questions about the information as they read. Using the text as the foundation for their questions helps students extract new content knowledge, and the bookmark provides them with a concrete tool for processing and organizing the information (Hill & Flynn, 2006). Additional benefits of Active Bookmarks for CLD students include

- Allowing students to take charge of their own learning as they decide on questions to write on their bookmark
- Focusing students' attention on key concepts/ideas
- Encouraging students to use their personal experiences to link to new content knowledge
- Providing students with a tool they can use to monitor their comprehension and scaffold their peer discussions

Finally, Active Bookmarks keeps CLD students engaged in all phases of the reading process: before, during, and after. Research has found that this type of active engagement is one of the essential characteristics of a good reader (Gregory & Burkman, 2012; Smartt & Glaser, 2010).

150

According to Harris, Graham, Mason, and Friedlander (2008), before, during, and after reading strategies can be translated as **TWA**, or:

- **THINK** before reading
- Think **WHILE** reading
- Think **AFTER** reading

Active Bookmarks ensures that all students are provided the support they need to participate in these reading processes.

Materials Needed: Active Bookmarks template (one per student) • curricular materials • pencils/pens

---

 ## ACTIVATION: A Canvas of Opportunity

Directions:

- **T** Introduce the Active Bookmark strategy by telling students that they are going to be monitoring their own learning as they read the text. They will do this by posing and answering questions as they interact with the text.
- **S** Place students in groups based on their language and academic proficiencies.
- **T** Share the title and the cover page of the story (or the chapter/section title of the text) with students. (*Note:* Alternatively, students can work in their small groups and use different books, one book per group.)
- **S** Have students in their small groups talk about their predictions related to the story/topic. As students predict what the story is about, ask them to reflect on their personal/background experiences to see if they can find a connection to the text.

- Circulate around the room to listen to students' predictions.
- Give each student an Active Bookmarks template.
- **T** To help students understand how to use the active bookmark, read a short piece of the text and model how we can pose questions during reading to make predictions and to further our understanding of the text. Also, explain to students that there are different ways we can find answers to the questions we pose. *Sometimes the answer is right there in the text, sometimes we have to read a little bit more to find the answer to our question, or sometimes we have to use what we know and our imagination to come up with an answer.*
- To help students generate questions, model the process for them:
  - Talk about your thinking process so students can "see" what you are doing.

- You might say something like the following: "I like how the text _____. But it makes me wonder _____. My question is: _____?
- Write your sample question on the active bookmark to show students how to document their questions. Be sure to explain that students should note the number of the page from the text that corresponds to their question.

Activating the "*i*"

How does this process activate CLD students' existing knowledge?

- **Sociocultural:** As students share their predictions about the text, they focus on their own background experiences that connect with the text.
- **Linguistic:** Through teacher modeling, students are provided with a language model to follow when doing the activity independently.

- **Academic:** Making predictions allows students to activate their prior knowledge about the topic so they are primed to make connections between the new information and what they already know.
- **Cognitive:** The Activation phase promotes cognition and engagement by scaffolding for students the process of interacting with text.

CONNECTION: The Broad & Narrow Strokes of Learning

Directions:

- **I** Have students individually work on their active bookmarks as they read a short section of the text/story.
- Encourage students to stop frequently (e.g., after every paragraph) to see if they have a question they could pose.
- **P** When students have finished with the short section of the text, have them work with a partner within their small group to share their questions.
  - Have them explicitly state for their peer how they came up with the question. This articulation of their thinking is a wonderful way for students to serve as models for each other.

- **I** After students have finished sharing their questions, ask them to individually find the answers to their questions by:
  - Re-reading the part of the text they have already read to see if any of their questions are answered there.
  - Continuing to read the text to find the answers.
  - Using what they already know and their imagination to make inferences about the answers.
- **P** Have the students write their answers on the back of their bookmark and then share their answers with their partner.

Title:
Date: 3-22-10
Page 2
why did the man was lost?

Page 4
why did the wise man just said it?

Page 6
how long was it?

Page 7
what if the man did not do the promies?

Page 9   how the got the tools?

Connecting to the "*i*+1"
How does this process move CLD students from the known to the unknown?

- **Sociocultural:** Students are encouraged to draw upon their background knowledge to infer answers to their text-related questions.
- **Linguistic:** Documenting their questions (and related answers) in writing provides students with an authentic reason to practice writing in English.

- **Academic:** The Connection phase supports students' comprehension of the text and the larger topic.
- **Cognitive:** The Active Bookmarks strategy helps students monitor their own learning. In addition, it supports greater investment in the learning process, as they select what they want to focus on when reading.

AFFIRMATION: A Gallery of Understanding

Directions:

- **S** Next, have each student within the small group switch partners. Have students take turns asking their questions to their new partner. Once the partner answers the question, the student who asked it gets to confirm/disconfirm the answer and share his or her response.
  - Encourage partners to think especially hard about questions that require the reader to make an inference. Pairs can then compare their answers and, if different, they can discuss the thought process they used to arrive at their answer. If

differences still remain, encourage students to share their perspectives with you. Capitalizing on these moments can yield insights that can be used to further the learning of the entire class.
- **T** Bring the class back together as a whole group and have volunteers share their questions and the process they went through to find the answers (i.e., did they find the answer in text, did they have to infer the answer, or would they have to seek out additional resources to find the answer?).

- **I** Have students use their completed bookmarks as a scaffold to write a summary of the text/story.

Author Talk: Affirmation

Teachers in the field have used the Active Bookmarks strategy to extend students' learning and language development while they engage in independent reading. However, we have also seen teachers pair students based on their biography-driven needs so that they can collaboratively pose and answer the questions on their bookmarks. For students in the initial stages of English language development, this approach is particularly effective because they can work with a more proficient peer to support their reading of the text.

To answer the self-generated questions, students often need to use higher-order thinking skills. Many times the answer is not explicitly stated in the text. As observers, we have had the pleasure of watching students actively engage in this process, seeing firsthand how this strategy builds their cognitive skills. Perhaps the power of this strategy is best illustrated by the experience of an ESL teacher, who

shared this story after implementing the strategy with her 6th-grade students:

> As I was walking around, I noticed students going slower instead of zooming through the text. I also noticed the students feeling at ease to share with their group and listening to their peers. I thought we had a variety of higher-level questions, and many of the questions asked were not in the text. The students realized they would need to look for outside resources to find the answer.

In this example, Active Bookmarks readily engaged students in the learning process and they took ownership of their learning. For such reasons, we feel this is one of the best strategies for helping CLD students become more independent learners. While the strategy still provides them with the scaffolding they need, it also requires them to be active thinkers.

Affirming Student Ownership: *"I" Get It!*
How does this process celebrate CLD student learning?

- **Sociocultural:** Students are able to hear peers' content-based connections/questions as well as to have their own voices heard.
- **Linguistic:** The active bookmark allows students to use academic language to articulate the answers to their questions.

- **Academic:** Students have an opportunity to hear and evaluate alternative perspectives on the answers to their questions, which helps to solidify their overall understanding of the text.
- **Cognitive:** Students' completed active bookmarks provide them with a tool they can refer back to as they synthesize their own learnings.

 SPOTLIGHT: Early Literacy Connection

The Active Bookmarks strategy is a great way to model the thought process a reader engages in when reading. For younger students, this modeling is particularly important, as they may not know how to ask questions when reading. Boyd-Batstone (2006) notes that shared experiences like this help students understand the way readers perceive and interpret the meaning of a story.

Our Questions

When performing this activity with younger CLD students, post a large piece of chart paper at the front of the class to document students' questions. Begin by reading a story aloud to students. Stop at key points and ask a question about what you are reading. Record these questions on the chart paper, along with the related page numbers from the text. This allows the class to easily refer back to the text.

After modeling this process several times for your students, ask them to pose questions they have. As students are sharing their questions, document them on the chart paper. Continue reading the story. As you encounter answers to the questions you and your students have posed, go back to the chart paper and document the answers.

Biography-Driven Response to Intervention

With the strategy of Active Bookmarks, we can focus on multiple skills needed for comprehension, a paramount goal of core instruction. Students start with prediction and proceed with the many steps of active monitoring as they use the active bookmark as a tool. Learners chunk textual information as they move through the text. The strategy can be a great way of differentiating instruction for learners as they generate questions at their own cognitive, academic, and linguistic levels.

One Classroom's Perspective

Activating:

As a whole group, we discussed different types of questions, such as fat questions and skinny questions. (*Fat questions* are those with lots of detail and meaning, whereas *skinny questions* are those that lack specific information and richness.) We then discussed why children work and child labor, incorporating the vocabulary words that would be in the text. After I was sure the students understood the meaning of the vocabulary words as well as writing questions, I then introduced the Active Bookmarks strategy. The students were instructed to read silently, stop at each paragraph, and write a question that was circling in their head. I emphasized the questions must be about the text. I also reminded them to write the page number next to their question.

Connecting:

As the students were reading quietly, I walked around the room to make sure everyone was on task. As soon as they were done with a question, students were allowed to share their question with their partner, and the partner was expected to answer the question. After the partner shared his or her thoughts, together they would discuss the question. As the students were working with their partners, I heard some interesting conversations.

Affirming:

I pulled the groups back together and asked specific students to share their questions and their thoughts. The students had no idea I was going to call on them, which made the discussion interesting. It kept everyone on their toes, and I was able to point out the higher-level questions.

Student Voices

It helped me to write questions—I could remember better.

—ELL Student
Speech Emergent

This was a great tool. I now have something I can use all the time when reading. The bookmark really helps me keep track of what I read!

—ELL Student
Advanced Fluency

I liked being able to ask my friends my questions. Sometimes I had such a hard question they couldn't even answer it! But then we looked up the information together.

—ELL Student
Intermediate Fluency

TEMPLATE: Active Bookmarks

Note: This template provides two distinct bookmarks to save paper when copying the bookmarks for distribution. In practice, the bookmarks are cut apart, and only one bookmark at a time is used per student.

Name:	**Name:**
Title:	**Title:**
Date:	**Date:**
Page _____	**Page** _____
Page _____	**Page** _____
Page _____	**Page** _____
Page _____	**Page** _____
Page _____	**Page** _____

STRATEGY

Mini Novela

Mini Novela really gave my students an alternate way of considering the ways to summarize learning. We started the activity by getting involved in a task that took shape with students' high interests. Students were able to use their understanding of the vocabulary words to create their personal summaries in the form of a mini novela. This strategy truly spoke to my students, and the best part was they were able to work in small groups and capitalize on each other's language skills.

—*Jessica Larsen, 6th-Grade Teacher*

Where Theory Meets Practice

Effective teachers seek to understand and build upon students' strengths and interests. Students from CLD families possess a wealth of cultural knowledge and experiences that can be used to enhance their literacy development (Moll & Gonzalez, 1994). The Mini Novela strategy taps into the cultural phenomenon of telenovelas (short-lived soap operas) that are shown in countries all over the world. These telenovelas are well known for their dramatic short stories of the characters' lives. Most run for only one season. Tapping into the storytelling aspect of telenovelas, Mini Novela combines cultural knowledge, drawing, and writing to help students understand key vocabulary and concepts within the texts they read.

When CLD students are able to use their cultural experiences, it gives them a sense of belonging and can increase their ability to learn the English language (Wong Fillmore, 2000). Thus, Mini Novela has been purposefully designed to allow students to share their cultural connections to key vocabulary terms at the beginning of the lesson. According to Herrera (2010), when educators begin the lesson by capitalizing on students' cultural connections, they greatly increase the likelihood of the students' active engagement throughout the lesson.

During the lesson, the Mini Novela strategy engages students in drawing to support their writing development. Routman (2005) found that allowing students to draw first stimulated their story writing. Therefore, in this strategy, drawing serves as a scaffold that encourages CLD students to become more independent writers. After students have drawn a visual representation of a portion of the text in their Mini Novela, they then write a sentence to explain their illustration. Students use their drawings to generate ideas about what to write and to further elaborate on their thinking. For those with limited English-speaking ability, the pictures they have drawn help them to recall and use a wider range of academic vocabulary words than they might otherwise incorporate. Because this strategy provides students with multiple opportunities to revisit the text and summarize it in their own words, it is ideal for supporting their metacognition (Chamot & O'Malley, 1994).

Materials Needed: Blank sheets of paper • curricular materials • scissors • stapler • pencils/pens

ACTIVATION: A Canvas of Opportunity

Directions:

- **T** **I** Following the directions at the end of this strategy description (page 163), either make mini books for the class ahead of time or provide students with the materials and guide them through the process of constructing their own mini books.
- Post six to eight vocabulary words specific to the topic on the board and give each student a blank piece of paper.
- Have students individually create their first impressions of the words by either illustrating what the word means or writing the meaning of the word.
- **P** After the students have finished documenting their initial connections to the words, have them turn to a partner and share their ideas with the partner. Tell students that at this time they can add their partner's words to their own words on the paper.
- As students discuss the words with each other, circulate around the room to listen to their ideas.

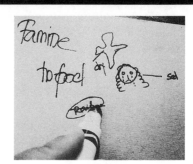

Activating the "*i*"

How does this process activate CLD students' existing knowledge?

- **Sociocultural:** The collaborative nature of the activity allows students to hear alternative perspectives and helps them create relationships with peers that can support their learning outcomes.
- **Linguistic:** The low-risk learning environment fostered by this strategy allows students to document their first impressions of the vocabulary words in a way meaningful to them. This, in turn, supports students' sharing of their perspectives with peers.

- **Academic:** This phase allows students to make and record their existing academic knowledge of the vocabulary words before being influenced by the perspectives of a peer.
- **Cognitive:** The kinesthetic task of creating the mini book increases student interest and engagement in the activities of this phase and throughout the lesson.

CONNECTION: The Broad & Narrow Strokes of Learning

Directions:

- **T** Share with the class that during the lesson they will be working to summarize their learning in the form of a mini novela. Explain to students that the Mini Novela strategy will involve their drawing visuals and using the language that is most meaningful to them.
- If you have access to technology, you can share a few short clips of a telenovela with students.
- Once you have explained the gist of the task, share with students the topic of the lesson or the book that will be read. If using a book, start by showing the cover of the book, and ask students to predict what the book will be about.
- **I** Allow students 1 minute to individually predict what the book or lesson might be about.
- **P** Have students share their thoughts with a partner.

- **S** Place students in small groups of three or four students and give each student a mini book (unless students created their own at the beginning of the strategy).
- **T** **S** Read the selected text (or cover the content of the lesson), stopping periodically (or at the end of every page or two) to have students discuss the content with their small group.
- **I** After students have finished discussing their ideas about a given text selection/concept, have them use one page of the blank mini book to draw a description of their individual summary, using a mini novela format. In order to do this:
  - Have them reflect back on the clips they watched and think of the ways the language was being used.

- Explain that the purpose of the mini novela is to make their summaries interesting and appear like a story.
- Next encourage students to write a narrative to accompany their illustrations. Encourage them to incorporate the target vocabulary words.
- Continue this process until you have finished the entire book or lesson.

Connecting to the "*i*+1"
How does this process move CLD students from the known to the unknown?

- **Sociocultural:** This phase encourages students to connect to their background knowledge as they make predictions about the text/topic.
- **Linguistic:** Discussing their personal learning and understandings with peers supports CLD students' ability to extend upon their vocabulary and written language skills in their summaries.

- **Academic:** As students work on the summaries, they have the opportunity to monitor their comprehension of the lesson's concepts and vocabulary.
- **Cognitive:** When students create their own summaries at the end of every passage/concept discussion, they are supported in comprehending manageable chunks of the text/segments of the lesson.

AFFIRMATION: A Gallery of Understanding

Directions:

-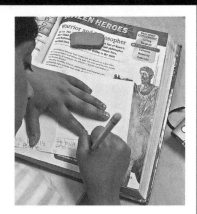
- **I** Have students put the finishing touches on their mini novelas.
- **S** Then have students take turns sharing their mini novelas with each other in their small groups.
- As students are sharing their ideas, have them add to their summaries if they come across anything interesting that can also add to their summaries.
- **I** Once the students have finished sharing their summaries, have them return to the initial impressions of the vocabulary words that they recorded during the Activation phase. Ask students to confirm/disconfirm their original thoughts by underlining ideas related to the lesson. Have them add new learning as needed to clarify the meaning of the words.
- *Extension activity:* If the strategy was used with a picture book, show students the book's illustrations and have them compare those illustrations with their own.

Author Talk: Affirmation

Mini Novela is a great strategy to share with CLD families. Many countries around the world have types of television programs much like the telenovelas that are so popular in Spanish-speaking countries. The Mini Novela strategy encourages students and their families to use their imagination, create visual images, and actively participate in the act of storytelling. Storytelling is a tool for socialization through which ideas, perspectives, and cultural customs are passed down to future generations. Stories shared within a family setting are a treasure trove of cultural information and insight into students' lives.

Teachers can encourage families to make their own mini novelas and then have the students bring these stories back to the classroom to share with their classmates. Parents should be encouraged to create the stories in their native language. They can also be invited to read the stories aloud to the class. The drawings start to tell the story regardless of the language of the text. Students can then translate and explain the story to the class in English.

Affirming Student Ownership: *"I" Get It!*
How does this process celebrate CLD student learning?

- **Sociocultural:** A continual sharing of ideas helps students appreciate the knowledge and ideas of their peers and become more confident in themselves as learners.
- **Linguistic:** As students share their mini novelas, they gain experience in orally articulating their written work.

- **Academic:** The completed mini novela serves as a showcase of each student's understanding of the language and concepts of the lesson.
- **Cognitive:** As students review their initial impressions related to the vocabulary words, they are able to evaluate the accuracy/relevance of their prior knowledge.

SPOTLIGHT: Early Literacy Connection

Some CLD students may be able to draw detailed pictures; however, they may not have the ability to communicate the details verbally or in writing because they lack sufficient skills in the English language. The Mini Novela strategy allows students to rely on visuals to help them relay their understanding of the concept. Young learners may not be developmentally ready to produce writing to accompany their visuals. Some of the ways teachers have made connections between this strategy and early literacy include the following techniques.

About Me

At the beginning of the school year, teachers always ask their students to share a little something about themselves. Mini Novela can help students share about themselves in a very nonthreatening yet meaningful way. Give each student in the class a blank mini book or four or five pieces of paper stapled together. As you hand out the mini books, ask students to create a story about themselves. They can simply draw pictures or they can draw and write on the paper. After the students have finished creating their mini novelas, they can be allowed to take them home to share with their parents.

Show Me the Pictures

As you read a book to students, have them use blank mini books to create their own mini novela summaries using only pictures. After students have finished, have them share their mini novela with a partner.

Biography-Driven Response to Intervention

Mini Novela is a strategy that can help students connect with language and content while at the same time providing opportunities for them to share with others their sociocultural backgrounds. It supports students' summarization skills and provides them with a tool that is meaningfully rooted in the context of the text being used. For additional support during tiered instruction, students can work in pairs to create their mini novelas. As an extension of Tier 1 support, the strategy can be modified for small-group instruction by simply having students work in strategically configured small groups to create their summaries.

One Classroom's Perspective

Activating:

Today was the first day we were working with the topic of the life of Marcus Aurelius in our social studies unit. In my small group of students that I was working with as a Tier 2 group, I have students who are from many different countries. My students are at multiple language levels. I knew that I wanted an activity that would provide students with an opportunity to express themselves in a meaningful way and that would include students' own words.

So I started the lesson by pulling six words from the chapter and sharing them with students on sticky notes. I put the sticky notes with one word each on a big poster paper. As I posted the words, I had my students create their impressions by talking to each other about the word. This activity really helped my students activate their understanding, since I have students at multiple levels of language proficiency in my class.

One Classroom's Perspective (*continued*)

Connecting:

Once we were done sharing the words, I explained to my students that they were going to be creating mini novelas using their booklets. First I shared with them a short clip of how a novela looks. Since I have a lot of students from Latin American countries, my students were able to connect to them right away. Next I shared with them that they were going to create their own summaries in a mini novela format. This was a great opportunity for my students since a lot of them like to draw their ideas.

We started the activity by first reading a little from the book. At specific points we stopped and discussed what we read. After the discussions and the sharing, students proceeded with creating their own mini novelas. Individually they took their mini books and created the pictures that came to their mind as they thought of the life of Marcus Aurelius. At the same time, they gave phrases to their visuals to make them sound like dialogues from a novela.

Some of them did a description of Marcus's life as if he was living in present times and sharing his own story in a novela format.

Affirming:

Once the students were done creating their novelas, I had them go to their social studies book one last time and add any other ideas specific to Marcus Aurelius's life, to help them connect with the text and look for more details. Once students were done with that, I had everyone come to the front of the room and share their novelas with the class. This was a great activity since it really helped my students see how they

can represent the life of a historic figure using their own summaries. My students took great pride in creating these mini books. As students finished sharing their novelas, we looked at our social studies book and compared our illustrations with those in the book. At this time I also allowed students to add more descriptions to their novelas if they found something interesting in

their peers' summaries. I plan on using this strategy to teach students the skill of summarizing.

Student Voices

I loved drawing the pictures on my mini book. Sometimes social studies has really hard concepts but by drawing the pictures I was able to learn. Since my family watches novelas it was great.

—*ELL Student*
Speech Emergent

I enjoyed working with a partner since we were able to share ideas with each other. Also looking at the vocabulary really helped me at the beginning since I was able to write my sentences on the topic too.

—*ELL Student*
Speech Emergent

I liked working on the strategy since each of us had our own books and we could draw however we thought the story worked. Since it is about someone's life, I drew pictures that showed Marcus's life in my mini book. I am going to keep my mini book with me and use it to study for the test.

—*ELL Student*
Intermediate Fluency

INSTRUCTIONS: Creating Your Mini Novela

Materials: A single Mini Novela will require one sheet of paper and a pair of scissors.

Step 1:	Take a piece of paper, making sure it is in landscape orientation (long edges at top and bottom), and fold it in half from left to right, making a sharp crease.
Step 2:	Turn the page so it is once again in landscape orientation. Then fold it in half from left to right and make a sharp crease.
Step 3:	One last time, turn the page so it is in landscape orientation. Once again, fold it in half from left to right and make a sharp crease.
Step 4:	Unfold the paper until you have four rectangles (the paper will be folded in half at this point). Take a pair of scissors and, *on the fold side*, cut along the center fold, making sure you **cut only to the middle fold** of the paper. When you open the paper, you should have one horizontal slit in the middle of the paper.
Step 5:	To make your mini novela, slip one hand through the slit in the middle of the paper. Using your other hand, grab one side of the paper and pull it out slightly to make the shape of half of a diamond.
	Slowly take your first hand out of the paper. With your this hand, grab the other side of the paper and pull it out to complete the diamond.
Step 6:	Holding the top and bottom points of the diamond, pull them away from each other as far as possible to make the pages of your mini novela.
Step 7:	You should have eight pages in total. Simply flatten them together, making sure that each page has a solid crease.

STRATEGY

Word Drop

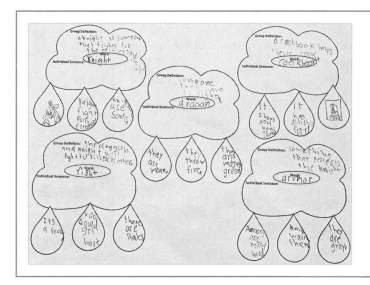

Students now understand and comprehend the vocabulary and can now write and understand characters in stories better because of the connections they have made. The students like to take ownership in activities, and I believe that the students learned more from this activity because they worked together to complete it.

—*Tammie Heathman, 2nd-Grade Teacher*

Where Theory Meets Practice

Research has shown that one of the keys to building vocabulary is to engage students in the study of words through word collections, active involvement, and explicit vocabulary instruction (Herrell & Jordan, 2012). Word Drop is a strategy that not only addresses all of these considerations but also helps promote students' comprehension as they take their initial connections to the word and link them to text. According to research by Allen (2000), this focused attention on the development of vocabulary and comprehension is essential to successful and fluid comprehension in reading.

Word Drop is also an excellent social/affective strategy in that it provides students with the opportunity to discuss key information with peers throughout the lesson. Such collaboration provides CLD students with a scaffold for individual reading and writing tasks. According to Herrera (2010), situations and strategies such as these prompt students to become more self-sufficient learners who are less dependent on the teacher. Students are guided to make and elaborate on key connections to the critical concepts presented in the lesson based on their own understanding and background knowledge. Teachers further enhance the power of strategies like Word Drop when they configure groups based on students' biographies to ensure student pairings and groupings that will result in challenging yet low-risk and supportive environments (Herrera, 2010).

Word Drop ensures that CLD students are held to the same high expectations for learning the academic content and vocabulary of the lesson as all other students. However, the strategy also provides the necessary support structures to enable all students, regardless of English language proficiency level, to experience success and come away with new knowledge. The graphic organizer in this strategy is used to capture students' background knowledge, provide a tool for note taking, and support students' application and summarization of their learning. A spin-off the Word Drop activity commonly used in classrooms, this strategy is sure to resonate with teachers who are ready to take their instruction to the next level.

Materials Needed: Word Drop template • curricular materials • pencils/pens

ACTIVATION: A Canvas of Opportunity

Directions:

- Select five key vocabulary words that are crucial to students' comprehension of the lesson concepts.
- Place students in small groups of four or five students. (*Note:* Strategically use your knowledge of students' L1 and English language proficiency levels to create supportive groups.)
- **I** Pass out a Word Drop template to each student. Have students individually write the preselected vocabulary words in the center of each of the five clouds (one word per cloud).

- Have students make three connections to each word and write those connections in the three raindrops below the clouds.
  - Encourage students to use L1 and/or picture prompts as needed.
  - Allow only 3–4 minutes for students to drop their words/pictures on the page.
- **P** Have students share their connections with a partner.
- As students complete this activity, circulate around the room and note

the academic vocabulary that students have already recorded on their templates. Listen for connections that you can later revoice for the entire class.

Activating the "*i*"

How does this process activate CLD students' existing knowledge?

- **Sociocultural:** Word Drop allows each student to quickly show the teacher how his or her life experiences might manifest themselves within the lesson, especially in relation to the key vocabulary words that will be taught.
- **Linguistic:** Allowing use of the native language and/or visuals gives all CLD students a way to document what they already know about the academic vocabulary.

- **Academic:** The Activation phase provides students with the opportunity to examine what they already know and begin exploring other perspectives on the vocabulary words.
- **Cognitive:** Students are provided with a low-risk opportunity for actively entering the lesson without fear of failure.

CONNECTION: The Broad & Narrow Strokes of Learning

Directions:

- Begin the lesson by reading the text aloud with the whole class.
- **S** As the key vocabulary words are encountered in text, have students work in their small groups to create a group definition for the word, which they will then write in the top half of each cloud.
  - Remind students to use information from the text as well as the information that they and/or other students had already "dropped" on their raindrops to help them come up with the definition.

- Reminding students to revisit their initial connections will help them create a more meaningful and comprehensive definition. They will be able not only to confirm/disconfirm their initial understanding but also to embed personal associations with the vocabulary word.
- Circulate around the room and support groups as needed as they create their definitions.
- Have each group share their definition with the whole class before continuing on with the reading.

- Proceed with the reading until all definitions have been completed and shared with the class.

Connecting to the "*i*+1"
How does this process move CLD students from the known to the unknown?

- **Sociocultural:** The collaborative negotiation of appropriate definitions among students helps them build skills for effective communication with peers.
- **Linguistic:** CLD students are able to use both basic interpersonal communication skills and cognitive academic language proficiency (BICS and CALP) to help them deconstruct the vocabulary and interpret it in meaningful ways.

- **Academic:** The focus on definitions that take into account the context of the lesson and students' prior knowledge allows learners to better understand the words and related concepts.
- **Cognitive:** Students practice the cognitive strategy of taking notes while reading as they record their group's definitions.

 AFFIRMATION: A Gallery of Understanding

Directions:

- **I** To assess students' individual understanding of the target vocabulary, have them write a sentence in the bottom half of each cloud in which they use the corresponding vocabulary word.
- Next have students individually write a summary of what they learned over the course of the lesson on the back of their Word Drop template.
  - Ask students to use at least three vocabulary words that were most meaningful to them.

- For students who need extra linguistic support, consider accommodations such as the following:
  - Allow students to work with a partner.
  - Provide students with a cloze paragraph.
  - Allow students to use both their native language and English, incorporating pictures where necessary to communicate their understanding.

- **P** Have students share their summaries with a partner to show all that they have learned.

Author Talk: Affirmation

Have you ever heard the saying "the classroom was alive and buzzing with activity"? This is exactly the type of learning environment that the Word Drop strategy fosters. It actively engages CLD students in the learning process and promotes student interaction throughout the lesson. When observing this strategy in practice, it is always fascinating to see the transformation that takes place: students are up and out of their seats, actively engaging in discussion, and sharing ideas that promote their learning and comprehension. As Kerry Wasylk, a 4th-grade teacher, noted:

This strategy gave my students a chance to organize their own thoughts before being taught new content.

They were each allowed to enter the lesson on their own level. They had the choice of writing or drawing their thoughts on the page. Next, my students were able to meet their social needs by having role models in the classroom during partner and small-group discussion. Students of all abilities would be able to participate in this lesson on their level while learning important grade-level content.

The more we can do as educators to promote our students' cross-cultural interactions and connections to key vocabulary through strategies such as this, the more likely we are to promote meaningful and long-term content learning for our CLD students.

Affirming Student Ownership: *"I"* Get It!
How does this process celebrate CLD student learning?

- **Sociocultural:** Having students self-select the key vocabulary that is most meaningful to them when writing their summaries gives them a voice in the learning process.
- **Linguistic:** CLD students are able to apply the new academic vocabulary from the lesson as they write about their learning while using their completed Word Drop template as a reference.

- **Academic:** Word Drop stretches students to the $i+1$ and allows for individual accountability by challenging them to individually create sentences using the key vocabulary.
- **Cognitive:** The Affirmation phase supports students' understanding of the value of taking notes as they use the completed Word Drop template as a scaffold for the cognitively complex task of summarizing their learning.

SPOTLIGHT: Early Literacy Connection

The Word Drop strategy is an excellent strategy for promoting young learners' exposure to, and active discussion of, key content vocabulary. Research has shown that students best understand the meaning of words when their senses, background knowledge, and emotional responses are engaged (Boyd-Batstone, 2006; Marzano, 2003). Multisensory instruction, for example, helps learners use their senses (visual, auditory, tactile, and kinesthetic) to store and retrieve information (Birsh, 2001). Such instruction sends information to the brain simultaneously along multiple pathways (Currie & Wadlington, 2000).

Creative Connections

To modify the Word Drop strategy, you will need a poster-sized version of the Word Drop template so that all the students can see it. Introduce each word by saying it aloud; have the students repeat the word. Next, write the vocabulary word in the center of one of the clouds. As you spell the word, have the students practice spelling the word through skywriting (writing the word in the air). After all the words have been recorded on the Word Drop

poster, orally discuss the words and any connections that the students can make with the vocabulary. You can incorporate pictures from the text or other visuals related to the vocabulary. Such pictures, photos, or illustrations provide concrete, visual support for students' understanding. This strategy also provides a great opportunity to bring in multimedia resources such as videoclips, auditory samples, and so forth to help enhance students' multisensory connections to the newly introduced vocabulary.

Next, share a student-friendly definition of each word in the "group definition" section. This will start to build or clarify students' background knowledge about the vocabulary. As you encounter the words in the context of meaningful literature, pause to discuss how the words are used in that context. This further extends students' learning and understanding of the words. After the entire story has been read aloud, revisit the Word Drop poster and discuss how each of the words could be used in a sentence. Have several students share possible sentences and then write one of those sentences on the poster.

Biography-Driven Response to Intervention

Word Drop is a strategy that exposes students to vocabulary at many levels. The pictorial and linguistic representations help students work with the vocabulary words by first using their own personal connections. As students then are challenged to manipulate the words throughout the strategy, they enhance their understanding of the topic. Student-created summaries at the end of the lesson can be used both as a gauge for reintroducing the same words during Tier 2 interventions and as a summative assessment to plan further instruction.

One Classroom's Perspective

Activating:

Before the lesson I wanted to encourage the students to write in their native language or draw what they thought of when they heard the target vocabulary words from our story, *The Knight and the Dragon,* by Tomie DePaola. The Word Drop strategy is perfect for 1st-graders to use because the more advanced students can write the words in English and my students who are still acquiring English can either draw a representation of the word or write words in their native language. But what I have found that the students like most is being able to share their connections with a partner or small group as soon as they are done "dropping" all of their own knowledge about each word onto the page. As a teacher, this is also an eye-opening experience for me, because I get to see the background knowledge that the students already bring to the lesson. This insight helps me to know where to begin my instruction before I even open the book!

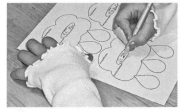

Connecting:

I told the students before I started reading the story that their job was going to be to listen for the key vocabulary words on their Word Drop templates. When I got to one, they had to raise their hands so I knew that we would have to stop at the end of that page and discuss the word. As I began reading, I was really surprised at how attentive the students were. They really listened for the key vocabulary and were quick to signal me when they heard one of the words. After the students had signaled me, I would stop at the end of the page and we would identify which word(s) they had heard and discuss them as a whole group. Then I told them their job was to come up with a definition for the word in their small groups based on our discussion. As each group discussed and wrote down their definitions, I checked to make sure they were on the right track by talking to each group separately. After all the groups were done, I had them share their definitions with the class before we continued reading the story. By the time we finished the story, all the students had their group definitions of the vocabulary words filled out on their Word Drop templates.

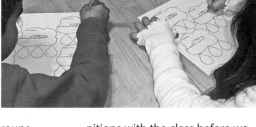

Affirming:

To be sure the students really understood the meaning of the words, I had them individually use each word in a sentence. I told the students to be sure to use the words and pictures as well as the group definitions they created from our story to help them come up with meaningful sentences. Finally, to assess students' overall comprehension of the story, I asked each one to write a summary of what the story was about on the back of their Word Drop template. The only rule was that they had to use as least three of the vocabulary words from the front of the Word Drop in their summary. After reading the individual student sentences and summaries, I could see the students had a much deeper understanding of the terms and the story. This was especially evident with the more limited English speakers, who were able to create much richer and more detailed sentences than they had in previous lessons!

Student Voices

I really liked doing this because I got to write and draw what I knew about the words first. Then I got to talk to my friends and we wrote down what the word meant.

—*ELL Student*
Intermediate Fluency

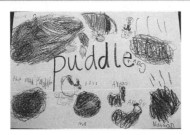

This helped me see if I really knew what the word was or if I just thought I knew what it was.

—*ELL Student*
Speech Emergent

I really liked doing this activity, and I wish we could do it all the time! I really liked talking to my friends about the words!

—*ELL Student*
Intermediate Fluency

Word Drop

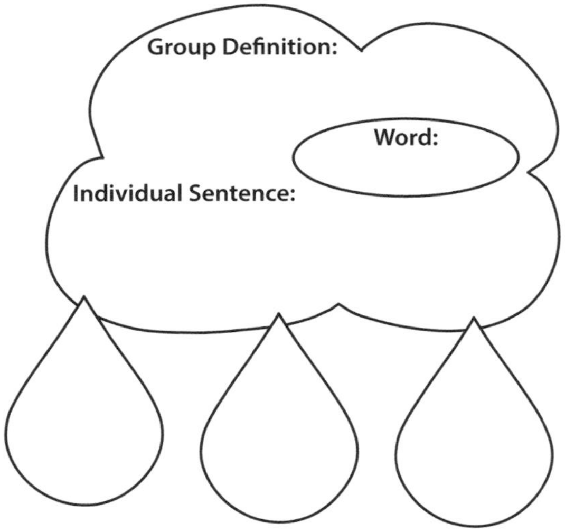

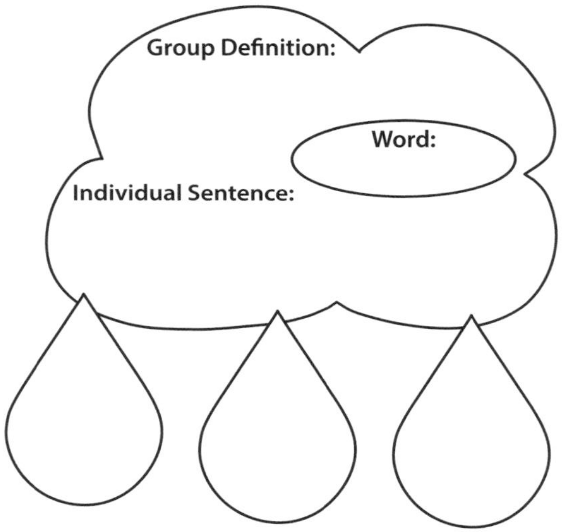

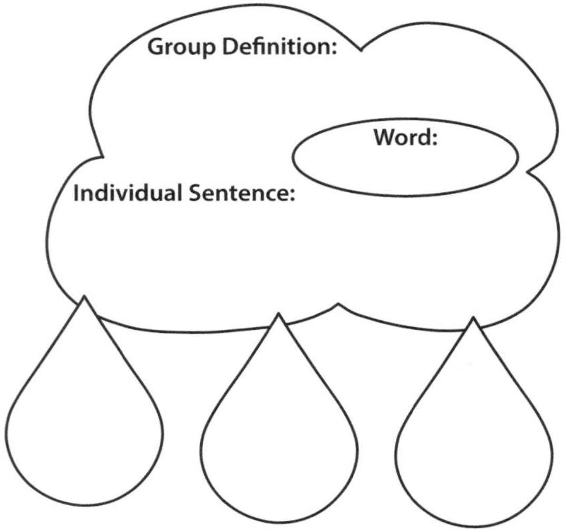

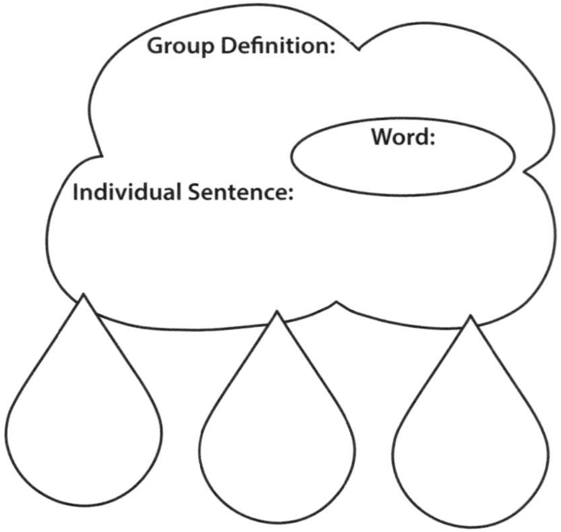

Group Definition:

Word:

Individual Sentence:

Group Definition:

Word:

Individual Sentence:

Group Definition:

Word:

Individual Sentence:

Group Definition:

Word:

Individual Sentence:

Group Definition:

Word:

Individual Sentence:

Name: _____

Date: _____

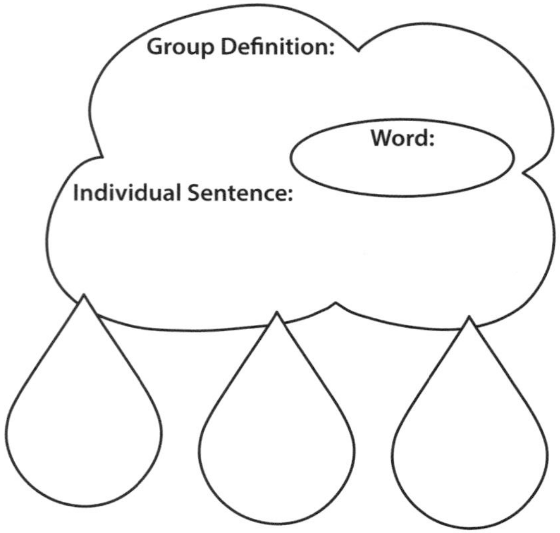

PART III

On the Path to Standards-Driven Outcomes and Student Success

Teachers should develop a learning environment that is relevant to and reflective of their students' social, cultural, and linguistic experiences. They act as guides, mediators, consultants, instructors, and advocates for the students, helping to effectively connect their culturally- and community-based knowledge to the classroom learning experiences. (M. Wilson-Portuondo, quoted in The Education Alliance, 2006, section 7)

Through our work at the Center for Intercultural and Multilingual Advocacy, we have seen the power of teachers who create learning environments and instructional conditions such as those described in the passage above. These teaching and learning dynamics are made possible when teachers develop relationships of care and trust with the students in their classrooms. Their learning environments are responsive to CLD students' sociocultural, linguistic, and academic needs. All students see themselves as valuable contributors to the classroom community. Each student knows that he or she will receive the support needed to achieve academic success. To support grade-level teachers as they take the next step toward creating this kind of teaching and learning environment, we have emphasized the implementation of biography-driven instructional (BDI) strategies. These strategies have evolved as a reflection of more than a decade of work in K–8 classrooms, and they provide pathways for translating theory and research into practice with CLD learners.

Our emphasis on the CLD student biography throughout a lesson is what we believe sets our work apart. Biography-driven instruction looks at all four dimensions of the CLD student biography—sociocultural, linguistic, cognitive, and academic—and strives to articulate what it takes to deliver instruction that promotes linguistic and academic achievement by CLD students. In a system of education where the cultures, languages, and experiences of students often are undervalued or in conflict with current pedagogical practices and one-size-fits-all curricula, such an approach to instruction is more critical than ever. As researchers and educators, we have found that by framing lessons in ways that maximize overlap with students' biographies, we unleash the potential of learners to use their assets as they collaborate with peers to achieve standards-driven outcomes.

The Framework

As illustrated throughout this book, we believe that no matter what strategy is being implemented, teachers must attend to the following three processes in every lesson:

- *Activation of Student Knowledge.* Teachers create a *canvas of opportunity* for students to share their background knowledge at the beginning of the lesson. By providing this opportunity, the teacher is afforded a chance to preassess and learn more about individual students.
- *Connection to New Learning.* During the lesson, the teacher creates conditions that enable students to make schematic connections with new content and language. As the teacher introduces both the topic and the target vocabulary of the lesson, links are made to students' initial thoughts or vocabulary. These connections then are expanded upon through the lens of each student's existing knowledge base. Frequently, academic dialogue among peers is used to promote the making and sharing of such connections. Purposeful observation of students as they use language to negotiate their understanding of the content and language makes it possible for the teacher to route and reroute students to ensure the highest levels of comprehension.

171

- *Affirmation of Student Learning.* Having documented what has taken place throughout the lesson; the teacher is able to affirm for students at the end of the lesson what they have learned along the way. The strategies implemented throughout the lesson provide a natural scaffold for postinstructional assessment and yield learning tools that students can use for future endeavors.

Figure 2 highlights some of the fundamental concepts that are part of what we have found to be most effective in meeting the needs of CLD student populations.

Standards-Driven Outcomes

At the end of the day, no matter what curriculum or program is being implemented, every teacher across the country is asked the same question: Did you meet the standards? Many teachers today feel so much pressure to have students achieve higher scores on standardized tests that they frequently place standards above effective pedagogy. In reality, the two work together to achieve the same goal: higher levels of student learning. As demonstrated in Figure 3, through the implementation of BDI strategies, teachers can support learners in meeting the student outcomes set forth in standards such as the Common Core State Standards (NGA & CCSSO, 2010).

The key to effective implementation is viewing standards as the starting point for instruction. From these, learning goals are derived that set the stage for student learning across the three phases of lesson delivery (activation, connection, and affirmation). As teachers, it is important to consider the strategy that will be implemented throughout the lesson, because the strategy builds in opportunities for

| **FIGURE 2** |
| *Concepts Critical to Biography-Driven Instruction* |

Concept	Description
Culturally and linguistically diverse (CLD)	The term used to describe an individual whose culture or language differs from that of the dominant culture and language in the school system
CLD student biography	The four interrelated dimensions of a student—sociocultural, linguistics, cognitive, and academic—that influence his or her linguistic and academic development
Background knowledge	Accumulated knowledge related to language and concepts derived from the student's funds of knowledge (home), prior knowledge (community), and academic knowledge (school)
Schematic connections	Links made between new material and the students' existing background knowledge and frames of reference
Strategic grouping configurations	Arrangements of students, such as pairs or small groups, that reflect considerations for individual student biographies and that increase social and academic interactions in order to build classroom community and promote linguistic and academic development
Revoicing	Observing students, listening to what they say, and repeating their understanding (through repetition, expansion, rephrasing, summarizing, or reporting) to validate, encourage elaboration, or reroute student understanding
Confirming	Validating students' thinking in the learning process
Disconfirming	Identifying students' misconceptions to clarify or redirect learning
Negotiation of learning	Students' active process of constructing meaning as they draw upon background knowledge and interact with peers to learn language and content

FIGURE 3

FIGURE 3
Pedagogical Constructs That Support Standards-Driven Outcomes

Activation Phase

- Activate CLD students' funds of knowledge, prior knowledge, and academic knowledge.
- Provide opportunities for students to share, or make public, what they know.
- Support students in making meaningful links to new learning.

Teacher Dynamics

The teacher:
- Acts as a silent observer.
- Provides opportunities to make public what students know.
- Documents connections that students provide between their background knowledge and key concepts and vocabulary of the lesson.

Student Dynamics

The student:
- Makes links between the new material and his or her existing background knowledge as shared.

Student Outcomes
- Make links to background knowledge.
- Make predictions.
- Determine the topic of a text or lesson.
- Feel an increased sense of belonging in the learning community.

Connection Phase

- Create conditions that encourage learners to practice and apply new vocabulary and concepts in meaningful and interactive ways.
- Engage students in a variety of grouping configurations to promote dialogue and academic development.
- Support students' thorough understanding of the content through confirming, disconfirming, and revoicing.

Teacher Dynamics

The teacher:
- Uses information acquired from students before the lesson to make connections between what they know and the new information being presented.
- Facilitates instruction and ensures input is comprehensible.
- Implements instructional formative assessments.

Student Dynamics

The student:
- Monitors his or her own understanding to construct knowledge.
- Practices and applies new vocabulary and concepts.

Student Outcomes
- Determine the meaning of academic vocabulary.
- Increase understanding of the academic content.
- Take ownership of the new information and learning strategies.
- Interact with peers to hear multiple perspectives and stretch learning to the next level.

Affirmation Phase

- Let students know their effort during the lesson was worth it and that they learned.
- Provide opportunities for all students to individually demonstrate their learning.

Teacher Dynamics

The teacher:
- Celebrates students' learning and uses summative assessment to inform subsequent instructional decisions.

Student Dynamics

The student:
- Celebrates progress and demonstrates what he or she has learned individually and as a member of the classroom community.

Student Outcomes
- Comprehend and evaluate personal understanding of complex texts.
- Summarize main ideas and key supporting details from the text or lesson.
- Apply learnings in practice.

Standards Curriculum: Learning Goals
(Content Objectives/Language Objectives)

students to use language and make meaningful links to the content. The ideas and language that students generate inform the teacher's subsequent decisions about how best to advance learning and promote students' continued engagement with the academic vocabulary and concepts. This interplay between student dynamics and teacher dynamics makes it possible for students to take ownership of their learning and ultimately demonstrate the learning outcomes that we desire for each member of the classroom community.

Making BDI Strategies Your Own

As we bring closure to this book, we would like to share two final examples of the work of elementary teachers who have taken the BDI strategies and made them their own by implementing them in their math and science curricula. These applications illustrate the possibilities for student learning that exist when teachers combine the versatility of BDI strategies with their own creativity.

One Classroom's Perspective: Thumb Challenge (Mathematics)

Activating:

While planning this lesson I took into consideration what my students have been taught about transformations in the previous year and in lessons they had already worked on in my class. To begin the lesson and build CLD students' confidence throughout the lesson while engaged in the Thumb Challenge, I had all the students start by drawing and acting out/demonstrating the transformations. Once I had made sure all the students' drawings were correct by walking around the room and informally assessing them, and all the students had acted out/demon-

strated the terms, I paired up the students to do the Thumb Challenge. The CLD students' sociocultural dimension was considered because the activity involved working with a partner, which helped to lower the CLD students' affective filter (preselecting the partners helped me get the most benefit from partnering). The CLD students' language development was also considered because CLD students were encouraged to build on what they already knew about the language of the transformations to help them make a connection between the unknown

language and their existing knowledge put into action. The CLD students' academic development was promoted by developing grade-level vocabulary.

Connecting:

During the lesson, I used the Thumb Challenge to allow CLD students to work with a partner to review the transformation vocabulary words. The oral response allowed students to state the answer and work together. As one partner shared the answer, the other student learned from his or her partner. If

the partner got stuck on a vocabulary term, the two students had the opportunity to share their answers, which stretched their comprehension to the next level. To make sure all students participated in the Thumb Challenge, I had all students repeat the Thumb Challenge two times with their partners.

Affirming:

After the Thumb Challenge, students had to individually demonstrate what they had learned. Each student was given a paper with the transformation vocabulary discussed during the Thumb Challenge. Students were asked to tell me what each transformation word meant to them. They were asked to use short sentences or words and draw a

picture to demonstrate a sample of the transformation. Students also completed the worksheet from their math book independently. In the past, my CLD students had struggled to complete this worksheet on their own, but I saw that as a result of the Thumb Challenge assessment my CLD students were able to construct responses very easily.

One Classroom's Perspective: Vocabulary Quilt (Science)

Activating:

I knew that using the Vocabulary Quilt would provide an opportunity for my students to express their individual background knowledge about the vocabulary words. This strategy gave my students a chance to organize their own thoughts before being taught new content. They were each allowed to enter the lesson on their own level. They had the choice of writing or drawing their thoughts on the page. My students were able to meet their social needs by having role models in the classroom during partner and small-group discussion. Students of all abilities were able to participate in this lesson on their level while learning important grade-level content. As I observed the students, I was surprised by how much they already knew about some of the words. For example, most students had some pretty solid prior knowledge about "force," even those I might not have expected.

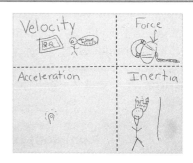

Connecting:

As I taught the lesson, I had the students fill in their Vocabulary Quilt as we came across the vocabulary words. The students were in a "total group" configuration as I read from their science book. Then they worked with partners to discuss what they were learning about the vocabulary words. They also had a chance to discuss their learnings in their small table groups. Once they reached consensus on a group definition, they wrote the definition for the word on the back of their individual Vocabulary Quilt. Throughout the lesson, the Vocabulary Quilt helped to open the doors of communication between my CLD students and their monolingual English-speaking peers.

Affirming:

After the lesson, my students acted out the vocabulary words. I did this for a few reasons. The first reason is that I wanted to assess my students in a way that didn't involve writing or verbal communication. They demonstrated their knowledge using actions. As the students acted out the vocabulary words, I was able to question the rest of the class to determine their understanding of the vocabulary words. I also had my students act out the words because I knew that it would help them commit the words to memory and I knew that was important considering the complex vocabulary words we were learning. After the students had acted out the vocabulary words, they wrote sentences using the vocabulary words on 3×5 cards. These cards also helped me determine if the students understood the vocabulary.

In her mathematics lesson with 4th-grade learners, Mrs. Brown used her math standards as a guide for establishing learning goals that met the needs of both her CLD students and her monolingual English speakers. By providing opportunities for students' activation of background knowledge, articulation of learning using the Thumb Challenge, and individual assessment, she was also able to solidify her students' comprehension of the academic vocabulary and content.

Mrs. Wasylk, who conducted the science lesson shown, has a very diverse 5th-grade classroom with Caucasian, African American, Hispanic, and Asian students who come from homes where multiple languages are spoken. Given the variety of backgrounds, cultures, and languages that her students bring, she is always looking for strategies that help her capitalize on their assets. She also recognizes the need for each student to become a proficient user of the content-specific vocabulary, and she knows that she must provide the necessary support to ensure that all learners reach this goal.

From her implementation of the Vocabulary Quilt, in addition to other BDP strategies, Mrs. Wasylk discovered that her CLD students' increased comprehension of academic vocabulary supported their increase in academic achievement. More importantly, she noted that this strategy helped her to "see on paper what my students were thinking so I could use this information to inform my teaching." As educators, uncovering what our students already know, and using these findings to inform our instruction, is one of the most powerful things we can do to promote their success!

Final Reflections

Biography-driven instruction is all about the learner. As educators, we need to be aware of the individual biographies of the students that sit before us. The strategies we employ in the classroom must build upon these biographies and serve as the *action* component of our larger plan to ensure that all students have access to academically challenging and individually meaningful educational experiences. The more we reflect upon and understand pedagogy from a biography-driven perspective, the more adept we become at connecting our instruction to the lived experiences of our students.

As CLD students witness their knowledge, skills, experiences, and perspectives being valued and maximized in the classroom, they become increasingly invested in taking their learning to the next level. In biography-driven classrooms, we orchestrate the conditions that allow students to see the depth of their own potential and that of their peers. By acting on our commitment to support each student in attaining our shared learning goals, we become advocates capable of changing lives, communities, and indeed the world.

APPENDIX

Strategy Rubrics and Checklists

CHAPTER 1 *Images as Catalysts for Predictions and Connections*

Pictures and Words: Student Academic Behavior Checklist   178

Mind Map: Student Assessment Rubric   179

Listen Sketch Label: Student Academic Behavior Checklist   180

CHAPTER 2 *Words and More Words*

DOTS Chart: Student Academic Behavior Checklist   181

Tic-Tac-Tell: Student Assessment Rubric   182

Vocabulary Quilt: Student Academic Behavior Checklist   183

Thumb Challenge: Student Academic Behavior Checklist   184

CHAPTER 3 *From Word Knowledge to Comprehension*

U-C-ME: Student Assessment Rubric   185

Extension Wheel: Student Assessment Rubric   186

Active Bookmarks: Student Academic Behavior Checklist   187

All of these rubrics and checklists are available for free download and printing
from www.tcpress.com

Pictures and Words

Student Academic Behavior Checklist

Name: _____   Topic: _____

Academic Behaviors	Score*			Comments
	1	2	3	
Assesses personal understanding of the word at the beginning of the lesson.				
Shares background knowledge and academic connections to the words with a peer.				
Makes connections between his or her background knowledge and the topic/vocabulary, and documents the connections in writing and/or with nonlinguistic cues (pictures).				
Participates in collaborative conversations with peers and listens in ways that demonstrate care and respect.				
Works with peers to define the meaning of key vocabulary from the text and helps group reach a consensus.				
Builds on and makes meaningful links between comments shared by others about the summary of key learnings at the end of the lesson.				

*Scoring (Optional):   1 = Beginning   2 = Developing   3 = Accomplished

Mind Map

Student Assessment Rubric

Name: _____ Topic: _____

Category	Beginning 1	Emerging 2	Developing 3	Accomplished 4
Linguistic and Nonlinguistic Representations	Only one type of representation, linguistic or nonlinguistic, is included on completed mind map. Few words or pictures reflect the topic.	Both types of representation are included on completed mind map. Some words and pictures reflect the topic.	Both types of representation are included on completed mind map. Most words and pictures reflect the topic.	Both types of representation are included on completed mind map. Words and pictures reflect high levels of topic comprehension.
Vocabulary Development	Completed mind map does not include any key vocabulary words.	Completed mind map includes few key vocabulary words and no connections to the content.	Completed mind map includes key vocabulary words with connections to the content that demonstrate some level of comprehension.	Completed mind map includes key vocabulary words with connections to the content that demonstrate a high level of comprehension.
Connections between Mind Map and Summary Paragraph	No connections are made between concepts on the mind map and the final summary paragraph.	Minimal connections are made between concepts on the mind map and the final summary paragraph.	Some concepts and details on the mind map are integrated into the final summary paragraph.	Numerous concepts and details on the mind map are integrated into the final summary paragraph.

Comments

Listen Sketch Label

Student Academic Behavior Checklist

Name: _____   Topic: _____

Academic Behaviors	Score*			Comments
	1	2	3	
Individually produces an example of figurative language in the native language or in English.				
Willingly shares with peers an example of figurative language from background knowledge.				
Works collaboratively with peers to interpret student-generated examples of figurative language.				
Works collaboratively with peers to distinguish connotations (associations) from denotations (definitions) of figurative language in context.				
Individually sketches pictures that illustrate the meaning of figurative language in context.				
Individually labels each sketch in a way that demonstrates understanding of the figurative language, word relationships, and nuances of word meanings.				

*Scoring (Optional):   1 = Beginning   2 = Developing   3 = Accomplished

DOTS Chart
(<u>D</u>etermine, <u>O</u>bserve, <u>T</u>alk, <u>S</u>ummarize)
Student Academic Behavior Checklist

Name: _____   **Topic:** _____

Academic Behaviors	Score*			Comments
	1	2	3	
Writes words (in L1 or L2) or draws pictures in the boxes that represent his or her background knowledge (family, community, school).				
Orally shares initial connections to the topic with a peer and responds to the peer by asking questions to clarify ideas or seek additional information.				
Participates in discussion with peer(s) and builds upon ideas, as demonstrated through oral conversation and/or "borrowing" words and writing them on the DOTS chart.				
Independently connects words inside the DOTS chart to the target vocabulary as his or her understanding of the words in context expands throughout the lesson.				
During the lesson, places additional words related to the topic inside the DOTS chart to show increased knowledge of the academic concepts and language.				
Writes summary sentences/paragraphs that explicitly show connections between his or her her own words and the target vocabulary.				
Presents a clear and coherent summary that demonstrates his or her understanding of the topic, is well organized, and is written at his or her linguistic level.				

*Scoring (Optional):   1 = Beginning   2 = Developing   3 = Accomplished

Tic-Tac-Tell

Student Assessment Rubric

Name: _____   **Topic:** _____

Category	Beginning 1	Emerging 2	Developing 3	Accomplished 4
Word Selection	Words selected to create sentences are random and unconnected.	Words selected to create sentences demonstrate some thought and connection.	Words selected to create sentences are well thought out and connected.	Words selected to create sentences reflect advanced understanding of relationships among key concepts and vocabulary.
Key Vocabulary	Sentences do not include the required number of key vocabulary words.	Sentences include the required key vocabulary words, but do not demonstrate comprehension of the key vocabulary.	Sentences include all of the required key vocabulary words and demonstrate comprehension of the key vocabulary.	Sentences include all of the required key vocabulary words, demonstrate comprehension of the key vocabulary, and incorporate general academic and domain-specific words and phrases.
Sentence Structure	No complete sentences; only isolated words and/or phrases.	Complete sentences, but significant errors in syntax (grammar) or semantics (meaning).	Complete sentences with only minor errors in syntax or semantics.	Complete sentences with appropriate use of syntax and semantics that creates cohesion within and among the sentences.

Comments

Vocabulary Quilt

Student Academic Behavior Checklist

Name: _____   Topic: _____

Academic Behaviors	Score*			Comments
	1	2	3	
Individually documents connections to background knowledge (home, community, school) using pictures and/or words in L1 or L2.				
Shares written or pictorial associations with peers and articulates his or her rationales for the word(s) or picture(s) used.				
Predicts what the lesson or text will be about based on the key vocabulary words on the vocabulary quilt.				
Writes the definitions of key vocabulary words in his or her own words as they are encountered in text and documents these definitions (i.e., using sticky notes) for verification.				
Works collaboratively with peers to come to consensus on the definitions of key vocabulary words by using context cues from the reading and discussions about the academic content.				
Writes a summary, individually or with a partner, that demonstrates his or her understanding of the key vocabulary in context.				

*Scoring (Optional):   1 = Beginning   2 = Developing   3 = Accomplished

Thumb Challenge

Student Academic Behavior Checklist

Name: _____   Topic: _____

Academic Behaviors	Score*			Comments
	1	2	3	
Records individual connections on sticky notes using words (L1 or L2) and/or pictures.				
Willingly shares background knowledge connections to the key vocabulary with a peer.				
Interacts with a peer by taking turns to define the key vocabulary.				
Clearly explains to a peer the meaning of each vocabulary word with relevant details from the text or lesson.				
Writes sentences/paragraphs that demonstrate his or her understanding of the key vocabulary words.				

*Scoring (Optional):   1 = Beginning   2 = Developing   3 = Accomplished

U-C-ME
(Uncover, Concentrate, Monitor, Evaluate)
Student Assessment Rubric

Name: _____   Topic: _____

Category	Beginning 1	Emerging 2	Developing 3	Accomplished 4
Individual Connections	Includes only one individual connection in the center of the U-C-ME chart.	Includes two or three individual connections in the center, but they are vague and show no evidence of the peer discussion.	Includes four or more individual connections in the center that are clear and reflect the peer discussion.	Individual connections (four or more) in the center are clear and show extensive connections to the peer discussion.
Posed Questions	Questions posed are limited to yes/no questions.	Questions posed require some thoughtful consideration regarding the topic.	Questions posed elicit elaboration and discussion related to the topic.	Questions posed require in-depth analysis, elaboration, and higher-order thinking.
Summary	Summary does not include key information from the U-C-ME chart.	Summary includes some of the key information from the U-C-ME chart and is somewhat well organized.	Summary includes most of the key information from the U-C-ME chart and is well organized.	Summary includes all of the key information from the U-C-ME chart, and its organization reflects relationships among the questions and key details.

Comments

Extension Wheel

Student Assessment Rubric

Name: _____   Topic: _____

Category	Beginning 1	Emerging 2	Developing 3	Accomplished 4
Expansion of Ideas	Information presented on the different rings is disjointed and not connected to the topic.	Information presented on the different rings is somewhat connected to the topic, and there are minimal connections between the concepts in different rings.	Information presented on the different rings is connected to the topic, and there are some connections between the concepts in different rings.	Information presented on the different rings is explicitly connected to the topic, and the concepts in each ring build upon those in the ring at the level below.
Ties to Key Vocabulary and Critical Concepts	Information on the rings does not include key vocabulary or reflect critical concepts.	Information on the rings minimally includes key vocabulary or reflects critical concepts.	Information on the rings includes some key vocabulary and somewhat reflects critical concepts.	Information on the rings includes most key vocabulary and reflects critical concepts.
Sentence Formation	Student-created sentences do not include information from the wheel.	Student-created sentences include some information from the wheel and allude to the topic, but do not clearly demonstrate the relationships between the two.	Student-created sentences include key words and phrases from the wheel and somewhat demonstrate the relationships between the critical concepts and the topic.	Student-created sentences include a high level of information from the wheel and demonstrate the relationships between the critical concepts and the topic.

Comments

Active Bookmarks

Student Academic Behavior Checklist

Name: _____   Topic: _____

Academic Behaviors	Score*			Comments
	1	2	3	
Makes predictions that are logical, sequenced, and reflect personal connections to the text.				
Willingly shares predictions with peers.				
Determines relevant questions and provides a rationale for questions posed when asked.				
Reads and finds answers to questions posed.				
Participates in peer discussions regarding predictions, questions, and connections to the text.				
Produces a written summary that incorporates information from his or her individual active bookmark and clearly demonstrates his or her point of view or understanding of the text.				

*Scoring (Optional):   1 = Beginning   2 = Developing   3 = Accomplished

References

Allen, V. (2002). *Techniques in teaching vocabulary.* Shanghai: Shanghai Foreign Language Education Press.

Anderson, N. J. (1999). *Exploring second language reading: Issues and strategies.* Boston: Heinle and Heinle.

Anderson, N. J. (2002). The role of metacognition in second language teaching and learning. *ERIC Digest* (EDO-FL-01-10). Retrieved April 6, 2013, from http://www.cal.org/resources/digest/digest_pdfs/0110_Anderson.pdf

Anderson, R. C., & Pearson, P. D. (1984). A schema-theoretic view of basic processes in reading. In P. D. Pearson, R. Barr, M. L. Kamil, & P. Mosenthal (Eds.), *Handbook of reading research* (pp. 255–291). White Plains, NY: Longman.

Anderson, V., & Roit, M. (1993). Planning and implementing collaborative strategy instruction for delayed readers in grades 6–10. *Elementary School Journal (Special Issue: Strategies Instruction), 94*(2), 121–137.

August, D. (2004, May 1). *The work of the national literacy panel.* Presentation at the Reading Research Institute of the International Reading Association, Reno, NV.

August, D., Carlo, M., Dressler, C., & Snow, C. (2005). The critical role of vocabulary development for English language learners. *Learning Disabilities Research and Practice, 20*(1), 50–57.

August, D., & Collins, M. (2005). *Vocabulary development in Spanish-speaking English-language learners in the U.S.* Paper presented at the annual meeting of the International Reading Association, San Antonio, TX.

August, D., & Hakuta, K. (Eds.). (1997). *Improving schooling for language minority students: A research agenda.* Washington, DC: National Academy Press.

Bean, T. W., & Steenwyk, F. L. 1984. The effect of three forms of summarization instruction on sixth graders' summary writing and comprehension. *Journal of Reading Behavior 16,* 297–306.

Beaty, J. J., & Pratt, L. (2007). *Early literacy in preschool and kindergarten: A multicultural perspective* (2nd ed.). Columbus, OH: Prentice Hall.

Beck, I. L., McKeown, M. G., & Kucan, L. (2002). *Bringing words to life: Robust vocabulary instruction.* New York: Guilford Press.

Birsh, J. (2001). *Multisensory teaching of basic language skills.* Baltimore: Brooks.

Blachowicz, C. L. Z., & Fisher, P. J. (2000). Vocabulary instruction. In M. L. Kamil, P. B. Mosenthal, P. D. Pearson, & R. Barr (Eds.), *Handbook of reading research* (Vol. 3, pp. 503–523). Mahwah, NJ: Lawrence Erlbaum.

Blachowicz, C. L. Z., & Fisher, P. J. (2006). *Teaching vocabulary in all classrooms.* Upper Saddle River, NJ: Pearson Education.

Bortnem, G. (2008). Teacher use of interactive read alouds using nonfiction in early childhood classrooms. *Journal of College Teaching & Learning, 5*(12), 29–44.

Boyd-Batstone, P. (2006). *Differentiated early literacy for English language learners: Practical strategies.* Boston: Allyn & Bacon.

Bredekamp, S., & Copple, C. (1997). *Developmentally appropriate practice in early childhood programs.* Washington, DC: National Association for the Education of Young Children.

Bromley, K. (2002). *Stretching students' vocabularies.* New York: Scholastic.

Buzan, T. (1989). *Use both sides of your brain* (3rd ed.). New York: Plenum.

Buzan, T. (2003). *The mind map book: How to use radiant thinking to maximize your brain's potential.* London: BBC Books.

Byers, P., & Byers, H. (1985). Nonverbal communication and the education of children. In C. B. Cazden, V. P. John, & D. Hymes (Eds.), *Functions of language in the classroom* (pp. 3–31). Prospect Heights, IL: Waveland.

Calderón, M. (2007). *Teaching reading to English language learners, grades 6–12: A framework for improving achievement in the content areas.* Thousand Oaks, CA: Corwin.

Calderón, M., August, D., Slavin, R., Durán, D., Madden, N., & Cheung, A. (2005). Bringing words to life in classrooms with English language learners. In E. H. Hiebert & M. L. Kamil (Eds.), *Teaching and learning vocabulary: Bringing research to practice* (pp. 115–136). Mahwah, NJ: Lawrence Erlbaum.

Center for Instructional Development and Research. (1999). Teaching through discussion. *CIDR Teaching & Learning Bulletin, 2*(3). Available at http://www.washington.edu/teaching/files/2012/12/Discussion.pdf

Center for Research on Education, Diversity & Excellence (CREDE). (2002). *The standards for effective pedagogy and learning.* Retrieved January 5, 2010, from http://gse.berkeley.edu/research/credearchive/standards/stand_indic.shtml

Chamot, A. U., & O'Malley, J. (1994). The cognitive academic learning approach: A model for linguistically diverse classrooms. *Elementary School Journal, 96,* 259–273.

Coady, M., Hamann, E. T., Harrington, M., Pacheco, M., Pho, S., & Yedlin, J. (2003). *Claiming opportunities: A handbook for improving education for English language learners through comprehensive school reform.* Providence, RI: Brown University and the Northeast and Islands Regional Laboratory.

Cooper, J. D. (1986). *Improving reading comprehension.* Boston: Houghton Mifflin.

Cooperstein, S. E., & Kocevar-Weidinger, E. (2004). Beyond active learning: A constructivist approach to learning. *Reference Services Review, 32*(2), 141–148.

Cooter, R. B., & Cooter, K. S. (2010, November 6). *Improving content literacy in urban, high poverty middle schools: An inter-professional staff development model.* Paper presented at the conference of the Association of Literacy Educators and Researchers, Omaha, NE.

Coyne, M. D., McCoach, D. B., Loftus, S., Zipoli, R., & Kapp, S. (2009). Direct vocabulary instruction in kindergarten: Teaching for breadth vs. depth. *Elementary School Journal, 110,* 1–18.

Crow, J. T., & Quigley, J. R. (1985). A semantic field approach to passive vocabulary acquisition for reading comprehension. *TESOL Quarterly, 19,* 497–513.

Cummins, J. (1981). The role of primary language development in promoting educational success for language minority students. In C. F. Leyba (Ed.), *Schooling and language minority students: A theoretical framework* (pp. 3–49). Los Angeles: California State University at Los Angeles, Evaluation, Dissemination and Assessment Center.

Cummins, J. (1989). Language and affect: Bilingual students at home and at school. *Language Arts, 66,* 29–43.

Cummins, J. (2000). This place nurtures my spirit: Creating contexts of empowerment in linguistically diverse schools. In R. Phillipson (Ed.), *Rights to language: Equity, power and education* (pp. 249–258). Mahwah, NJ: Lawrence Erlbaum.

Cummins, J. (2001). *Language, power, and pedagogy: Bilingual children in the crossfire.* Philadelphia: Multicultural Matters.

Cunningham, P. M., Moore, S. A., Cunningham, J. W., & Moore, D. W. (1995). *Reading and writing in elementary classrooms: Strategies and observations* (3rd ed.). White Plains, NY: Longman.

Currie, P., & Wadlington, E. (2000). *The source for learning disabilities.* East Moline, IL: Linguisystems.

Curtis, A., & Bailey, K. M. (2001). Picture your students talking: Using pictures in the language classroom. *ESL Magazine, 4*(4), 10–11.

Darling-Hammond, L., & Bransford, J. (Eds.). (2005). *Preparing teachers for a changing world: What teachers should learn and be able to do.* San Francisco: Jossey-Bass.

de Jong, E. J., & Harper, C. A. (2005). Preparing mainstream teachers for English language learners: Is being a good teacher good enough? *Teacher Education Quarterly, 32*(2), 101–124.

Donovan, M. S., & Bransford, J. D. (Eds.). (2005). *How students learn: History, mathematics, and science in the classroom.* Washington, DC: The National Academy Press.

Dubetz, N., & de Jong, E. J. (2011). Teacher advocacy in bilingual programs. *Bilingual Research Journal, 34*(3), 248–262.

Duke, N. K., & Pearson, P. D. (2001). How can I help children improve their comprehension? Ann Arbor, MI: Center for the Improvement of Early Reading Achievement (CIERA).

Echevarría, J., Vogt, M. E., & Short, D. (2010). *Making content comprehensible for elementary English learners: The SIOP model.* Boston: Pearson Education.

The Education Alliance. (2006). Culturally responsive teaching [summary of a panel discussion on Cultural Relevance in Teaching; S. Nieto, K. Serverian-Wilmeth, M. Wilson-Portuondo, & J. Taylor-Gibson, participants]. *Teaching Diverse Learners.* Retrieved April 6, 2013, from http://www.alliance.brown.edu/tdl/tl-strategies/crt-principles.shtml

ERIC Clearinghouse on Languages and Linguistics. (1994). *Funds of knowledge: Learning from language minority households.* Washington, DC: Author. (ED367146)

Fisher, D., & Frey, N. (2009). Feed up, back, forward. *Educational Leadership, 67*(3), 20–25.

Flavell, J. (1976). Metacognitive aspects of problem-solving. In L. Resnick (Ed.), *The nature of intelligence* (pp. 231–236). Mahwah, NJ: Lawrence Erlbaum.

Forman, E. A., Larreamendy-Joerns, J., Stein, M. K., & Brown, C. A. (1998). "You're going to want to find out which and prove it": Collective argumentation in a mathematics classroom. *Learning and Instruction, 8*(6), 527–548.

Freeman, D. E., & Freeman, Y. S. (2000). *Teaching reading in multilingual classrooms.* Portsmouth, NH: Heinemann.

García, E. E. 2005. *Teaching and learning in two languages: Bilingualism and schooling in the United States.* New York: Teachers College Press.

Gay, G. (2000). *Culturally responsive teaching: Theory, research, and practice.* New York: Teachers College Press.

Gentry, J. R. (1987). *Spel . . . is a four-letter word.* Portsmouth, NH: Heinemann.

Gersten, R., Dimino, J., Jayanthi, M., Kim, J., & Santoro, L. (2007). *Teacher study groups as a means to improve reading comprehension and vocabulary instruction for English learners: Results of randomized controlled trials.* Signal Hill, CA: Instructional Research Group.

Geva, E., & Yaghoub Zadeh, Z. (2006). Reading efficiency in native English-speaking and English-as-a-second-language children: The role of oral proficiency and underlying cognitive-linguistic processes. *Scientific Studies of Reading, 10*(1), 31–57.

Gipe, J. P. (2006). Multiple paths to literacy: Assessment and differentiated instruction for diverse learners, K–12 (6th ed.). Upper Saddle River, NJ: Pearson Education.

Goldenberg, C. (2008, Summer). Teaching English language learners: What the research does—and does not—say. *American Educator, 2*(2), 8–44.

Greenberg, J. B. (1989, April). *Funds of knowledge: Historical constitution, social distribution, and transmission.* Paper presented at the annual meeting of the Society for Applied Anthropology, Santa Fe, NM.

Greenwood, C. R. (2001). Science and students with learning and behavior problems. *Behavior Disorders, 27*(1), 35–50.

Gregory, G. H., & Burkman, A. (2012). *Differentiated literacy strategies for English language learners: Grades K–6.* Thousand Oaks, CA: Corwin.

Gregory, G. H., & Kuzmich, L. (2004). *Data driven differentiation in the standards-based classroom.* Thousand Oaks, CA: Corwin.

Gunning, T. G. (2006). *Closing the literacy gap.* Upper Saddle River, NJ: Pearson Education.

Harris, K. R., Graham, S., Mason, L. H., & Friedlander, B. (2008). *Powerful writing strategies for all students.* Baltimore: Brookes.

Harvey, S., & Goudvis, A. (2000). *Strategies that work: Teaching comprehension to enhance understanding.* York, ME: Stenhouse.

Herrell, A. L., & Jordan, M. L. (2012). *Fifty strategies for teaching English language learners* (4th ed.). Boston: Pearson Education.

Herrera, S. (2010). *Biography-driven culturally responsive teaching.* New York: Teachers College Press

Herrera, S., Kavimandan, S. K., & Holmes, M. A. (2011). *Crossing the vocabulary bridge: Differentiated strategies for diverse secondary classrooms.* New York: Teachers College Press.

Herrera, S. G., & Murry, K. G. (2005). *Mastering ESL and bilingual methods: Differentiated instruction for culturally and linguistically diverse (CLD) students.* Boston: Allyn & Bacon.

Herrera, S. G., & Murry, K. G. (2011). *Mastering ESL and bilingual methods: Differentiated instruction for culturally and linguistically diverse (CLD) students* (2nd ed.). Boston: Allyn & Bacon.

Herrera, S. G., Murry, K. G., & Morales Cabral, R. (2007). *Assessment accommodations for classroom teachers of culturally and linguistically diverse students.* Boston: Allyn & Bacon.

Herrera, S. G., Perez, D. R., & Escamilla, K. (2010). *Teaching reading to English language learners: Differentiated literacies.* Boston: Allyn & Bacon.

Herrera, S., Perez, D., Kavimandan, S., Holmes, M. A., & Miller, S. (2011, April). *Beyond reductionism and quick fixes: Quantitatively measuring effective pedagogy in the instruction of culturally and linguistically diverse students.* Paper presented at the annual conference of the American Educational Research Association, New Orleans, LA.

Hill, J., & Flynn, K. (2006). *Classroom instruction that works with English language learners.* Alexandria, VA: Association for Supervision and Curriculum Development.

Hoyt, L. (1999). *Revisit, reflect, retell.* Portsmouth, NH: Heinemann.

Irvine, J. J. (1990). *Black students and school failure: Policies, practices, and prescriptions.* New York: Praeger.

Jensen, E. (2000a). *Brain-based learning* (rev. ed.). San Diego: The Brain Store.

Jensen, E. (2000b). Brain-based learning: A reality check. *Educational Leadership, 57*(7), 76–80.

Jensen, E. (2006). *Enriching the brain.* San Francisco: Jossey-Bass.

Jensen, E. (2008). *Brain-based learning: The new paradigm of teaching* (2nd ed.). Thousand Oaks, CA: Corwin.

Kinsella, K. (2005). *Preparing for effective vocabulary instruction.* A publication of Aiming High: A Countrywide Commitment to Close the Achievement Gap for English Learners. Retrieved from http://www.scoe.org/docs/ah/AH_kinsella1.pdf

Kinsella, K., & Feldman, K. (2003). *Active learning: Structures to engage all students. High school teaching guidebook for universal access.* Upper Saddle River, NJ: Pearson Education.

Konold, T. R., Juel, C., McKinnon, M., & Deffes, R. (2003). A multivariate model of early reading acquisition. *Applied Psycholinguistics, 24,* 89–112.

Krashen, S. (1985). *The input hypothesis: Issues and implications.* London: Longman.

Krashen, S., & Terrell, T. (1983). *The natural approach: Language acquisition in the classroom.* Oxford: Pergamon.

Lado, A. (2004). *Reading stories with the earliest-stage children.* Handouts for the Preconvention Institute on March 30, 2004, at the 38th annual convention and exhibit, TESOL 2004, Long Beach, CA.

Ladson-Billings, G. (1994). *The dreamkeepers: Successful teachers for African-American children.* San Francisco: Jossey-Bass.

Langer, J. A. (2001). Beating the odds: Teaching middle and high school students to read and write well. *American Educational Research Journal, 38,* 837–880.

Lenters, K. (2005). No half measures: Reading instruction for young second-language learners. *The Reading Teacher, 58,* 328–336.

Lesaux, N., & Siegel, L. (2003). The development of reading in children who speak English as a second language. *Developmental Psychology, 39,* 1005–1019.

Maria, K. (1990). *Reading comprehension instruction: Issues and strategies.* Parkton, MD: York Press.

Marzano, R. J. (2003). *What works in schools: Translating research into action.* Alexandria, VA: Association for Supervision and Curriculum Development.

Marzano, R. J. (2004). *Building background knowledge for academic achievement: Research on what works in schools.* Alexandria, VA: Association for Supervision and Curriculum Development.

Marzano, R. J., & Pickering, D. J. (2005). *Building academic vocabulary: Teacher's manual.* Alexandria, VA: Association for Supervision and Curriculum Development.

Marzano, R. J., Pickering, D. J., & Pollock, J. E. (2001). *Classroom instruction that works: Research-based strategies for increasing student achievement.* Alexandria, VA: Association for Supervision and Curriculum Development.

McGee, L. M., & Richgels, D. J. (2003). *Designing early literacy programs.* New York: Guilford Press.

Moll, L. C., Amanti, C., Neff, D., & Gonzalez, N. (1992). Funds of knowledge for teaching: Using a qualitative approach to connect homes and classrooms. *Theory into Practice, 31*(2), 132–141.

Moll, L. C., & Gonzalez, N. (1994). Critical issues: Lessons from research with language-minority children. *Journal of Reading Behavior, 2*(6), 439–456.

Moore, D. W., Alvermann, D. E., & Hinchman, K. A. (2000). *Struggling adolescent readers: A collection of teaching strategies.* Newark, DE: International Reading Association.

Nagy, W. E. (2003). *Teaching vocabulary to improve reading comprehension.* Urbana, IL: National Council of Teachers of English.

National Governors Association Center for Best Practices & Council of Chief State School Officers (NGA & CCSSO). (2010). *Common core state standards for English language arts & literacy in history/social studies, science, and technical subjects.* Washington, DC: Author.

National Reading Panel (NRP). (2000). *Report of the National Reading Panel: Teaching children to read. Reports of the subgroups.* (NIH Publication No. 00-4754) Washington, DC: U.S. Government Printing Office.

National Research Council. (1998). *Preventing reading difficulties in young children.* Washington, DC: National Academy Press.

Neitzel, S. (1989). *The jacket I wear in the snow.* New York: Scholastic.

Neuman, S., & Roskos, K. (1993). *Language and literacy learning in the early years: An integrated approach.* Fort Worth, TX: Harcourt Brace Jovanovich.

Nieto, S. (2002). *Language, culture, and teaching: Critical perspectives for a new century.* Mahwah, NJ: Lawrence Erlbaum.

O'Connor, M. C., & Michaels, S. (1996). Shifting participant frameworks: Orchestrating thinking practices in group discussion. In D. Hicks (Ed.), *Discourse, learning and schooling* (pp. 63–103). Cambridge: Cambridge University Press.

Osterman, E. (2000, November–December). Literature for my classroom: What's out there. *The Voice: Newsletter of the National Writing Project.*

Oxford, R. L. (1990). Styles, strategies, and aptitude: Important connections for language learners. In T. S. Parry & C. W. Stansfield (Eds.), *Language aptitude reconsidered* (pp. 67–125). Englewood Cliffs, NJ: Prentice Hall.

Peregoy, S. F., & Boyle, O. F. (2001). *Reading, writing, and learning in ESL: A resource book for K–12 teachers* (3rd ed.). New York: Longman.

Piper, T. (2007). *Language and learning: The home and school years* (4th ed.). Upper Saddle River, NJ: Pearson Merrill/Prentice Hall.

Pressley, M., & Afflerbach, P. (1995). *Verbal protocols of reading: The nature of constructively responsive reading.* Mahwah, NJ: Lawrence Erlbaum.

Proctor, C. P., Carlo, M., August, D., & Snow, C. (2005). Native Spanish-speaking children reading in English: Toward a model of comprehension. *Journal of Educational Psychology, 97*(2), 246–256.

Rasinski, T. V. (1998). How elementary students referred for compensatory reading instruction perform on school-based measures of word recognition, fluency, and comprehension. *Reading Psychology: An International Quarterly, 19,* 185–216.

Rasinski, T. V., & Padak, N. (2000). *Effective reading strategies: Teaching children who find reading difficult* (2nd ed.). Upper Saddle River, NJ: Merrill.

Rea, D. M., & Mercuri, S. P. (2006). *Research-based strategies for English language learners: How to reach goals and meet standards, K–8.* Portsmouth, NH: Heinemann.

Reutzel, D. R., & Cooter, R. B., Jr. (2010). *Strategies for reading assessment and instruction: Helping every child succeed* (4th ed.). Boston: Prentice Hall.

Reutzel, D. R., & Cooter, R. B., Jr. (2012). *The essentials of teaching children to read: The teacher makes the difference* (3rd ed.). Boston: Pearson Education.

Routman, R. (2003). *Reading essentials: The specifics you need to teach reading well.* Portsmouth, NH: Heinemann.

Routman, R. (2005). *Writing essentials: Raising expectations and results while simplifying teaching.* Portsmouth, NH: Heinemann.

Rumelhart, D. E. (1980). Schemata: The building blocks of cognition. In R. J. Spiro, B. C. Bruce, & W. F. Brewer (Eds.), *Theoretical issues in reading comprehension* (pp. 33–58). Mahwah, NJ: Lawrence Erlbaum.

Schickedanz, J. A., & Casbergue, R. M. (2004). *Writing in preschool: Learning to orchestrate meaning and marks.* Newark, DE: International Reading Association.

Scott, J. A., & Nagy, W. E. (1997). Understanding the definitions of unfamiliar words. *Reading Research Quarterly, 32,* 184–200.

Shonkoff, J. P., & Phillips, D. A. (Eds.). (2000). *From neurons to neighborhoods: The science of early childhood development.* Washington, DC: National Academy Press.

Simonsen, S., & Singer, H. (1992). Improving reading instruction in the content areas. In S. J. Samuels & A. E. Farstrup (Eds.), *What research has to say about reading instruction* (pp. 200–219). Newark, DE: International Reading Association.

Smartt, S. M., & Glaser, D. R. (2010). *Next STEPS in literacy instruction: Connecting assessments to effective interventions.* Baltimore: Brookes.

Sousa, D. A. (2006). *How the brain learns* (3rd ed.). Thousand Oaks, CA: Corwin.

Spycher, P. (2009). Learning academic language through science in two linguistically diverse kindergarten classes. *The Elementary School Journal, 109*(4), 359–379.

Stahl, S. A. (1999). *Vocabulary development.* Cambridge, MA: Brookline Books.

Stahl, S. A., & Vancil, S. J. (1986). Discussion is what makes semantic maps work in vocabulary instruction. *The Reading Teacher, 40,* 62–67.

Sulzby, E., & Teale, W. H. (2003). The development of the young child and the emergence of literacy. In J. Flood, D. Lapp, J. R. Squire, & J. M. Jensen (Eds.), *The handbook of research on teaching the English language arts* (3rd ed., pp. 300–313). New York: Longman.

Swan, K. (2003). Learning effectiveness: What the research tells us. In J. Bourne & J. C. Moore (Eds.), *Elements of quality online education: Practice and direction* (pp. 13–45). Needham, MA: Sloan Center for Online Education.

Swinney, R., & Velasco, P. (2006). *Building bridges between language and thinking: Effective scaffolds to help language minority students achieve.* Handout from the Reading and Writing Project, Teachers College, Columbia University. Retrieved from www.ira.org/downloads/we_handouts/WC06_swinney_velasco.ppt

Svinicki, M. (1991). Practical implications of cognitive theories. In R. Menges & M. Svinicki, (Eds.), *College teaching: From theory to practice. New Directions for Teaching and Learning* (Issue 45, pp. 27–37). San Francisco: Jossey-Bass.

Tabors, P. O., Roach, K. A., & Snow, C. E. (2001). Home language and literacy environment final results. In D. K. Dickinson & P. O. Tabors (Eds.), *Beginning literacy with language* (pp. 111–138). Baltimore: Brookes.

Tharp, R. G., & Dalton, S. S. (2007). Orthodoxy, cultural compatibility, and universals in education. *Comparative Education, 43,* 53–70.

Tharp, R. G., Estrada, P., Dalton, S. S., & Yamauchi, L. (2000). *Teaching transformed: Achieving excellence, fairness, inclusion, and harmony.* Boulder, CO: Westview Press.

Thomas, W. P., & Collier, V. P. (1995). Language-minority student achievement and program effectiveness studies support native language development. *NABE News, 18*(8), 5, 12.

Thomas, W. P., & Collier, V. P. (1997). *School effectiveness for language minority students.* (NCBE Resource Collection Series No. 9) Washington, DC: National Clearinghouse for Bilingual Education. (ED436087)

Thomas, W. P., & Collier, V. P. (2002). *A national study of school effectiveness for language minority students' long-term academic achievement.* Santa Cruz, CA: Center for Research on Educa-

tion, Diversity & Excellence. Retrieved November 1, 2012, from http://www.usc.edu/dept/education/CMMR/CollierThomas ExReport.pdf

Tompkins, G. E. (2007). *Teaching writing: Balancing process and product* (5th ed.). Columbus, OH: Merrill.

Tompkins G. E., & Blanchfield, C. L. (Eds.). (2004). *Teaching vocabulary: 50 creative strategies, Grades K–12.* Upper Saddle River, NJ: Pearson Education.

Tovani, C. (2000). *I read it, but I don't get it: Comprehension strategies for adolescent readers.* Portland, ME: Stenhouse.

U.S. Census Bureau. (2000). *American fact finder.* Washington, DC: Author.

U.S. Department of Education. (2002). *The same high standards for migrant students: Holding Title I schools accountable.* Washington, DC: Author. Retrieved November 2, 2012, from http://www.gpo.gov/fdsys/pkg/ERIC-ED467996/pdf/ERIC-ED467996.pdf

Vacca, J. L., Vacca, R. T., & Gove, M. K. (2000). *Reading and learning to read* (4th ed.). White Plains, NY: Longman.

Vail, P. (n.d.). *The role of emotions in learning.* Retrieved November 20, 2012, from http://www.greatschools.org/parenting/teaching-values/751-the-role-of-emotions-in-learning.gs

Vaughn, S., & Linan-Thompson, S. (2004). *Research-based methods of reading instruction.* Alexandria, VA: Association for Supervision and Curriculum Development.

Vélez-Ibáñez, C., & Greenberg, J. (1992). Formation and transformation of funds of knowledge among U.S. Mexican households. *Anthropology and Education Quarterly, 23*(4), 313–335.

Violand-Sanchez, E., Sutton, C., & Ware, H. (1991). *Fostering home school cooperation: Involving language minority families as partners in education.* Washington, DC: National Center for Bilingual Education.

Vygotsky, L. S. (1978). *Mind in society: The development of higher psychological process.* Cambridge, MA: Harvard University Press.

Walqui, A. (2000). Strategies for success: Engaging immigrant students in secondary schools. *ERIC Digest.* (EDO-FL-00-03) Retrieved November 1, 2012, from www.cal.org/resouces/Digest/0003strategies.html

Wessels, S. (2008). *IBA vocabulary framework: **I**gnite, **B**ridge & **A**ssociate vocabulary development for culturally and linguistically diverse students.* Unpublished doctoral dissertation, Kansas State University, Manhattan, KS.

Willis, J. (2006). *Research based strategies to ignite student learning: Insights from a neurologist and classroom teacher.* Alexandria, VA: Association for Supervision and Curriculum Development.

Wolfe, P. (2001). *Brain matters: Translating research into classroom practice.* Alexandria, VA: Association for Supervision and Curriculum Development.

Wolfe, P., & Brandt, R. (1998). Brain science, brain fiction. *Educational Leadership, 56*(3), 14–18.

Wong Fillmore, L. (2000). Loss of family languages: Should educators be concerned? *Theory into Practice, 39*(4), 203–210.

Wong Fillmore, L., & Valadez, C. (1986). Teaching bilingual learners. In M. C. Wittock (Ed.), *Handbook of research on teaching* (3rd ed.). New York: Macmillan.

Wormeli, R. (2005). *Summarization in any subject: 50 techniques to improve student learning.* Alexandria, VA: Association for Supervision and Curriculum Development.

Young, T., & Hadaway, N. (2006). *Supporting the literacy development of English learners.* Newark, DE: International Reading Association.

Zwiers, J. (2004/2005). The third language of academic English. *Educational Leadership, 62*(4), 60–63.

Index

Subjects

academic dimension, 4–5, 7, 171
  in Active Bookmarks strategy, 151, 152, 154
  in DOTS Chart strategy, 74, 75, 77
  in Extension Wheel strategy, 135, 136, 137
  in group configurations, 6
  in Hearts Activity, 143, 144
  in IDEA strategy, 120, 121
  in Linking Language strategy, 17, 18
  in Listen Sketch Label strategy, 54, 56, 57
  in Magic Book strategy, 111, 112, 113
  in Mind Map strategy, 39, 40, 41
  in Mini Novela strategy, 158, 159, 160
  in Pictures and Words strategy, 31, 33
  in Picture This strategy, 23, 24, 25
  in Story Bag strategy, 63, 64, 65
  in Thumb Challenge strategy, 105, 106, 107
  in Tic-Tac-Tell strategy, 89, 91
  in Tri-Fold strategy, 46, 47, 48
  in U-C-ME strategy, 128, 129, 130
  in Vocabulary Foldable strategy, 82, 83, 84
  in Vocabulary Quilt strategy, 98, 99, 101
  in Word Drop strategy, 165, 166, 167
academic language, 69
  DOTS Chart strategy on, 72–80
accountability measures, 1
  in DOTS Chart strategy, 76
  in group configurations, 6
  in Mind Map strategy, 39
  in Thumb Challenge strategy, 107
  in Word Drop strategy, 167
Activation phase, 2, 7–8, 11, 171
  in Active Bookmarks strategy, 151, 155
  in DOTS Chart strategy, 74, 78
  in Extension Wheel strategy, 135, 138
  in Hearts Activity, 142–143, 145, 146
  in IDEA strategy, 119–120, 123
  in Linking Language strategy, 16–17, 19, 20
  in Listen Sketch Label strategy, 54, 57, 59
  in Magic Book strategy, 111, 115
  in Mind Map strategy, 39, 41–42, 43
  in Mini Novela strategy, 158, 161
  in Pictures and Words strategy, 31, 34, 35
  in Picture This strategy, 23, 26, 27

  in Story Bag strategy, 63–64, 66, 67
  teacher dynamics and student outcomes in, 173
  in Thumb Challenge strategy, 105, 108, 174
  in Tic-Tac-Tell strategy, 89, 93
  in Tri-Fold strategy, 46, 49, 50
  in U-C-ME strategy, 128, 131
  in Vocabulary Foldable strategy, 82, 85
  in Vocabulary Quilt strategy, 97–98, 101, 175
  in word-based strategies, 71
  in Word Drop strategy, 165, 168
Active Bookmarks strategy, 150–156
  student academic behavior checklist on, 187
Affirmation phase, 9, 11, 172
  in Active Bookmarks strategy, 153–154, 155
  in DOTS Chart strategy, 76–77, 78
  in Extension Wheel strategy, 137, 139
  in Hearts Activity, 144, 145, 147
  in IDEA strategy, 119, 121, 123
  in Linking Language strategy, 18, 19, 20
  in Listen Sketch Label strategy, 56–57, 58, 59
  in Magic Book strategy, 113, 115
  in Mind Map strategy, 41, 42, 43
  in Mini Novela strategy, 160, 162
  in Pictures and Words strategy, 33, 34, 36
  in Picture This strategy, 25, 26, 27
  in Story Bag strategy, 65, 66, 68
  teacher dynamics and student outcomes in, 173
  in Thumb Challenge strategy, 107, 109, 174
  in Tic-Tac-Tell strategy, 91, 94
  in Tri-Fold strategy, 48, 49, 50
  in U-C-ME strategy, 130, 132
  in Vocabulary Foldable strategy, 84, 86
  in Vocabulary Quilt strategy, 99, 102, 175
  in word-based strategies, 71
  in Word Drop strategy, 166–167, 168
artifacts from strategy implementation, 11
assessment procedures
  authentic, 7, 9
  confirming/disconfirming student learning, 7. *See also* confirm/disconfirm

background knowledge, 2, 4, 172
  activation of, 2, 7–8. *See also* Activation phase
  in Active Bookmarks strategy, 151
  in DOTS Chart strategy, 72, 73, 74
  in Extension Wheel strategy, 135
  in Hearts Activity, 141, 143
  in IDEA strategy, 120
  in image-based strategies, 13–14
  in Linking Language strategy, 15, 16, 17
  in Listen Sketch Label strategy, 54
  in Magic Book strategy, 111
  in Mind Map strategy, 39, 44
  in Mini Novela strategy, 157, 158
  in Pictures and Words strategy, 30, 31
  in Picture This strategy, 22, 23, 25
  in Story Bag strategy, 62, 63
  in Thumb Challenge strategy, 105
  in Tic-Tac-Tell strategy, 89
  in Tri-Fold strategy, 46
  in U-C-ME strategy, 127, 128
  in Vocabulary Foldable strategy, 82
  in Vocabulary Quilt strategy, 96, 98, 175
  in word-based strategies, 70
  in Word Drop strategy, 165
basic interpersonal communication skills (BICS), 166
biography-driven instruction, 2–5, 12, 171, 176
  academic dimension in, 4–5, 6. *See also* academic dimension
  Active Bookmarks strategy in, 154
  cognitive dimension in, 4, 6. *See also* cognitive dimension
  comprehension skills in, 125
  critical concepts in, 172
  DOTS Chart strategy in, 77
  Extension Wheel strategy in, 138
  Hearts Activity in, 141, 146
  IDEA strategy in, 122
  linguistic dimension in, 3–4, 6. *See also* linguistic dimension
  Linking Language strategy in, 19
  Listen Sketch Label strategy in, 58
  Magic Book strategy in, 114
  Mind Map strategy in, 42
  Mini Novela strategy in, 161
  Pictures and Words strategy in, 35

Picture This strategy in, 27
sociocultural dimension in, 3, 6. *See also* sociocultural dimension
Story Bag strategy in, 66
Thumb Challenge strategy in, 108
Tic-Tac-Tell strategy in, 92
Tri-Fold strategy in, 49
U-C-ME strategy in, 131
Vocabulary Foldable strategy in, 85
Vocabulary Quilt strategy in, 100
word-based strategies in, 70–71
Word Drop strategy in, 167
Brain Matters (Wolfe), 14
brainstorming
in DOTS Chart strategy, 74, 76
in Extension Wheel strategy, 139
in Mind Map strategy, 39

Center for Intercultural and Multilingual Advocacy (CIMA), 1, 171
classroom environment
as community of learners, 6
culture of, 5–6
students and teachers as partners in, 5–7
CLD learners. *See* culturally and linguistically diverse (CLD) learners
cognitive academic language proficiency (CALP), 72
in Thumb Challenge strategy, 106
in Word Drop strategy, 166
cognitive dimension, 4, 171
in Active Bookmarks strategy, 151, 152, 154
in DOTS Chart strategy, 74, 75, 77
in Extension Wheel strategy, 135, 136, 137
in group configurations, 6
in Hearts Activity, 143, 144
in IDEA strategy, 120, 121
in Linking Language strategy, 17, 18
in Listen Sketch Label strategy, 54, 56, 57
in Magic Book strategy, 111, 112, 113
in Mind Map strategy, 39, 40, 41
in Mini Novela strategy, 158, 159, 160
in Pictures and Words strategy, 31, 33
in Picture This strategy, 22, 23, 24, 25
in Story Bag strategy, 63, 64, 65
in Thumb Challenge strategy, 105, 106, 107
in Tic-Tac-Tell strategy, 89, 91
in Tri-Fold strategy, 46, 47, 48
in U-C-ME strategy, 128, 129, 130
in Vocabulary Foldable strategy, 82, 83, 84
in Vocabulary Quilt strategy, 98, 99, 101
in Word Drop strategy, 165, 166, 167
collaboration with peers, 5. *See also* peer collaboration and interaction
Common Core State Standards, 1, 2, 172
and Listen Sketch Label strategy, 55
and Magic Book strategy, 113
and Pictures and Words strategy, 32
and Vocabulary Foldable strategy, 84
community, in sociocultural dimension of student biography, 3, 6

comprehensible input, transformative, 5–6
comprehension strategies, 11, 125–170
Active Bookmarks, 150–156
Extension Wheel, 134–140
Hearts Activity, 141–149
Mini Novela, 157–163
U-C-ME, 127–133
Word Drop, 164–170
confirm/disconfirm, 5, 7, 9
in Active Bookmarks strategy, 153
definition of, 172
in IDEA strategy, 120
in Magic Book strategy, 112
in Mini Novela strategy, 160
in Pictures and Words strategy, 32
in U-C-ME strategy, 129
in Word Drop strategy, 165
Connection phase, 7, 8–9, 11, 171
in Active Bookmarks strategy, 152, 155
in DOTS Chart strategy, 75, 78
in Extension Wheel strategy, 136, 139
in Hearts Activity, 143–144, 145, 147
in IDEA strategy, 120, 123
in Linking Language strategy, 17, 19, 20
in Listen Sketch Label strategy, 55–56, 58, 59
in Magic Book strategy, 112, 115
in Mind Map strategy, 40, 42, 43
in Mini Novela strategy, 159, 162
in Pictures and Words strategy, 30, 32–33, 34, 35
in Picture This strategy, 24, 26, 27
in Story Bag strategy, 64, 66, 67
teacher dynamics and student outcomes in, 173
in Thumb Challenge strategy, 106, 108, 174
in Tic-Tac-Tell strategy, 90–91, 93
in Tri-Fold strategy, 47, 49, 50
in U-C-ME strategy, 129, 131
in Vocabulary Foldable strategy, 83, 86
in Vocabulary Quilt strategy, 98, 102, 175
in word-based strategies, 71
in Word Drop strategy, 165–166, 168
consonant–vowel–consonant patterns, in Listen Sketch Label strategy for young CLD students, 57–58
culturally and linguistically diverse (CLD) learners, 1–9
biography of, 2–5
definition of, 172
framework for linguistic and academic development of, 7–9
selection of vocabulary words for, 69–70
teachers as partners of, 5–7
vocabulary development strategies for. *See* vocabulary development strategies
as young students. *See* young CLD students
culture
in classroom environment, 5–6
and linguistic diversity of learners, 1–2, 3–4

and sociocultural dimension of student biography, 3, 6. *See also* sociocultural dimension

disconfirm. *See* confirm/disconfirm
discover phase of IDEA strategy, 119, 120
DOTS Chart strategy, 72–80
student academic behavior checklist on, 181

educator contributors
Abell, Anne, 104
Beursken, David, 53
Blanchard, Lindsay, 110
Bowden, Jennifer, 141
Brenkman, Timothy, 127
Burnham, Shilo, 62
Darby, Reesa, 45
Donahey, Amanda, 118
Fisher, Kristin, 30
Hacker, Sabina, 150
Heathman, Tammie, 164
Hollis, Cathy, 15
Larsen, Jessica, 157
McGee, Miles, 72
Phillips, Anna, 134
Ritter, Kari, 22
Rouse, Mikki, 96
Waite, Marcia, 88
Wasylk, Kerry, 38, 166, 175–176
Werth, Cheryl, 81
English as second language, 3
native language as foundation for learning, 3, 72, 77
existing knowledge. *See* background knowledge
extend phase of IDEA strategy, 119, 121
Extension Wheel strategy, 134–140
student assessment rubric on, 186

family, in sociocultural dimension of student biography, 3, 6
figurative language, Listen Sketch Label strategy on, 53–61
Foldables strategy, 81–87
funds of knowledge, 4, 7. *See also* background knowledge

grammar skills in Extension Wheel strategy, 138
The Great Kapok Tree, as instruction topic, 13, 85–86
group configurations, 6, 7
description of, 172
peer collaboration and interaction in. *See* peer collaboration and interaction in word-based strategies, 71

Hearts Activity, 141–149

i+1 term on process of language learning, 5, 9
in Active Bookmarks strategy, 152
in DOTS Chart strategy, 75

i+1 term on process of language learning (*continued*)
  in Extension Wheel strategy, 136
  in Hearts Activity, 144, 147
  in IDEA strategy, 120
  in Linking Language strategy, 17
  in Listen Sketch Label strategy, 56
  in Magic Book strategy, 112
  in Mind Map strategy, 40
  in Mini Novela strategy, 159
  in Pictures and Words strategy, 33
  in Picture This strategy, 24
  in Story Bag strategy, 64
  in Thumb Challenge strategy, 106
  in Tic-Tac-Tell strategy, 91
  in Tri-Fold strategy, 47
  in U-C-ME strategy, 128, 129
  in Vocabulary Foldable strategy, 83
  in Vocabulary Quilt strategy, 98
  in Word Drop strategy, 166
i+tpsI mnemonic, 6, 7, 11. *See also* peer collaboration and interaction
IDEA strategy, 118–124
idioms, 53
Ignite, Discover, Extend, Affirm (IDEA) strategy, 118–124
image-based strategies, 11, 13–68
  Linking Language, 15–21
  Listen Sketch Label, 53–61
  Mind Map, 38–44
  Pictures and Words, 30–37
  Picture This, 22–29
  Story Bag, 62–68
  Tri-Fold, 45–52
interdependence hypothesis, 72

jigsaw technique in Tri-Fold strategy, 47

knowledge, background, 2, 4, 172. *See also* background knowledge

language
  native. *See* native language
  oral. *See* oral language skills
  and vocabulary development strategies. *See* vocabulary development strategies
learning
  Activation phase in. *See* Activation phase
  Affirmation phase in. *See* Affirmation phase
  comprehensible input required for, 5–6
  confirming/disconfirming of, 7. *See also* confirm/disconfirm
  Connection phase in. *See* Connection phase
  i+1 term on, 5. *See also i*+1 term on process of language learning
  scaffolding for, 2. *See also* scaffolding
  visual cues in, 14
  zone of proximal development in, 2, 4, 5, 9, 134
linguistic dimension, 3–4, 171
  in Active Bookmarks strategy, 151, 152, 154

  in DOTS Chart strategy, 74, 75, 77
  in Extension Wheel strategy, 135, 136, 137
  in group configurations, 6
  in Hearts Activity, 143, 144
  in IDEA strategy, 120, 121
  in Linking Language strategy, 17, 18
  in Listen Sketch Label strategy, 54, 56, 57
  in Magic Book strategy, 111, 112, 113
  in Mind Map strategy, 39, 40, 41
  in Mini Novela strategy, 158, 159, 160
  in Pictures and Words strategy, 31, 33
  in Picture This strategy, 23, 24, 25
  in Story Bag strategy, 63, 64, 65
  in Thumb Challenge strategy, 105, 106, 107
  in Tic-Tac-Tell strategy, 89, 91
  in Tri-Fold strategy, 46, 47, 48
  in U-C-ME strategy, 128, 129, 130
  in Vocabulary Foldable strategy, 82, 83, 84
  in Vocabulary Quilt strategy, 98, 99, 101
  in Word Drop strategy, 165, 166, 167
Linking Language strategy, 15–21
Listen Sketch Label strategy, 53–61
  student academic behavior checklist on, 180
literacy skills. *See also* reading skills; writing skills
  in academic dimension of student biography, 5, 6
  in linguistic dimension of student biography, 4
  in sociocultural dimension of student biography, 3
  of young CLD students, 12. *See also* young CLD students

Magic Book strategy, 110–117
memory
  in Magic Book strategy, 110
  of visual cues, 13, 14
  in Vocabulary Quilt strategy, 96, 97
  in word-based strategies, 70–71
metacognition, 125–126
  in Active Bookmarks strategy, 150
  in DOTS Chart strategy, 73
  in U-C-ME strategy, 128, 129
metaphors, 53
Mind Map strategy, 38–44
  student assessment rubric on, 179
Mini Novela strategy, 157–163
modeling, 9
  in Active Bookmarks strategy, 151, 154
  in Extension Wheel strategy, 138
  in Linking Language strategy, 18, 20
  in Listen Sketch Label strategy, 55
  in Mind Map strategy, 38
  in Pictures and Words strategy, 32, 33
  in Tic-Tac-Tell strategy, 92
  in U-C-ME strategy, 129, 130, 131
  in Vocabulary Quilt strategy, 100
morphology of native and English languages, 4

native language
  diversity of, 1–2
  in DOTS Chart strategy, 72, 76, 77
  as foundation for English language development, 3, 72, 77
  in Hearts Activity, 144, 145
  in IDEA strategy, 121
  in linguistic dimension of student biography, 3–4, 6
  in Linking Language strategy, 16
  in Magic Book strategy, 111, 114
  in Mind Map strategy, 42
  in Pictures and Words strategy, 31, 34
  in Picture This strategy, 26
  and stages of second language acquisition, 25
  in Thumb Challenge strategy, 105
  in Tic-Tac-Tell strategy, 90
  in Vocabulary Foldable strategy, 85
  in Vocabulary Quilt strategy, 96, 99
  in Word Drop strategy, 166
negotiation of learning, 172

observation in DOTS Chart strategy, 72–80
oral language skills
  in DOTS Chart strategy, 77
  in Extension Wheel strategy, 136, 138
  in IDEA strategy, 118, 119, 121
  in Linking Language strategy, 19
  in Pictures and Words strategy, 33, 34
  in Picture This strategy, 26
  in sociocultural dimension, 3
  in Thumb Challenge, 104, 105, 107
  in Tri-Fold strategy, 46
  in U-C-ME strategy, 128
  in Vocabulary Foldable strategy, 81, 84
  in Vocabulary Quilt strategy, 97, 100
  of young CLD students, 12

parents, strategies recommended for
  DOTS Chart, 77
  IDEA, 122
  Mind Map, 41–42
  Mini Novela, 160
  Pictures and Words, 34
  Story Bag, 65–66
  Thumb Challenge, 107
  Vocabulary Foldable, 85
peer collaboration and interaction, 5, 6, 7, 11
  in Active Bookmarks strategy, 151, 152, 153
  benefits of, 126
  in DOTS Chart strategy, 73, 74, 75, 76
  in Extension Wheel strategy, 134, 135, 136, 137, 139
  in Hearts Activity, 142, 143, 145, 146, 147
  in IDEA strategy, 118–119, 120, 121, 123
  in Linking Language strategy, 16, 17, 18
  in Listen Sketch Label strategy, 54, 55, 56, 57

in Magic Book strategy, 111, 112, 113, 115
in Mind Map strategy, 39, 40, 41, 43
in Mini Novela strategy, 158, 159, 160
in Pictures and Words strategy, 31, 32, 33, 34
in Picture This strategy, 22, 23, 24, 25
in Story Bag strategy, 63, 64, 65
in Thumb Challenge strategy, 104, 105, 106, 107, 108, 174
in Tic-Tell-Tell strategy, 89, 90, 91
in Tri-Fold strategy, 46, 47
in U-C-ME strategy, 128, 129, 130
in Vocabulary Foldable strategy, 81, 82, 83, 84
in Vocabulary Quilt strategy, 97, 98, 99, 100, 101, 102, 175
in word-based strategies, 71
in Word Drop strategy, 164, 165, 166
phonics, 125
in Magic Book strategy, 112, 113
phonology of native and English languages, 4
Picture Me a Story version of IDEA strategy, 122
Pictures and Words strategy, 30–37
student academic behavior checklist on, 178
Picture This strategy, 22–29
predictions
in Active Bookmarks strategy, 151
in Story Bag strategy, 62–68
in Thumb Challenge strategy, 105
in Vocabulary Foldable strategy, 82, 85
prior knowledge, 2, 3, 4, 7. *See also* background knowledge
Prism Model, 108, 146

question posing
in Active Bookmarks strategy, 150, 151, 152, 153, 154, 155
in Hearts Activity, 143, 145
in U-C-ME strategy, 127–128, 129, 130

reading skills, 2
in Active Bookmarks strategy, 150–156
in IDEA strategy, 118, 120, 121, 122
in Magic Book strategy, 110
in Vocabulary Foldable strategy, 81, 84
rebus cues in Tic-Tac-Tell strategy, 92
revoicing, 6–7, 9
description of, 172
in Extension Wheel strategy, 136
in Hearts Activity, 142, 144
in Magic Book strategy, 111
in Thumb Challenge strategy, 105
in Vocabulary Quilt strategy, 98

scaffolding, 2
in Active Bookmarks strategy, 151, 153
in IDEA strategy, 118
in image-based strategies, 14
in Listen Sketch Label strategy, 54
in Mini Novela strategy, 157

in Pictures and Words strategy, 32
in revoicing, 6
in Vocabulary Quilt strategy, 101
schemas, 125, 126, 172
in U-C-ME strategy, 127, 131
second language acquisition, stages of, 25
semantics of native and English languages, 4
sentence formation
in DOTS Chart strategy, 76
in Magic Book strategy, 115
in Picture This strategy, 25, 26, 27
in Tic-Tac-Tell strategy, 91, 92, 94
in Vocabulary Quilt strategy, 102
sequencing of information
in Story Bag strategy, 65
in Tri-Fold strategy, 45, 47, 48
show and tell, Magic Book strategy in, 114
similes, 53
sociocultural dimension, 3, 171
in Active Bookmarks strategy, 151, 152, 154
in DOTS Chart strategy, 74, 75, 77
in Extension Wheel strategy, 135, 136, 137
in group configurations, 6
in Hearts Activity, 143, 144
in IDEA strategy, 120, 121
in Linking Language strategy, 17, 18
in Listen Sketch Label strategy, 54, 56, 57
in Magic Book strategy, 111, 112, 113
in Mind Map strategy, 39, 40, 41
in Mini Novela strategy, 158, 159, 160
in Pictures and Words strategy, 31, 33
in Picture This strategy, 23, 24, 25
in Story Bag strategy, 63, 64, 65
in Thumb Challenge strategy, 105, 106, 107, 174
in Tic-Tac-Tell strategy, 89, 91
in Tri-Fold strategy, 46, 47, 48
in U-C-ME strategy, 128, 129, 130
in Vocabulary Foldable strategy, 82, 83, 84
in Vocabulary Quilt strategy, 98, 99, 101
in Word Drop strategy, 165, 166, 167
Spanish language, 1, 13
speaking skills. *See* oral language skills
spelling skills
developmental stages in, 57
in Magic Book strategy, 114
standards-driven outcomes, 172–174
Standards for Effective Pedagogy and Learning, 9
Story Bag strategy, 62–68
strategies for vocabulary development. *See* vocabulary development strategies
strategy artifacts, 11
summarization process
in DOTS Chart strategy, 72–80
in Extension Wheel strategy, 137
in Hearts Activity, 144
in Magic Book strategy, 110, 113

in Mini Novela strategy, 159, 160
in Story Bag strategy, 65
in Thumb Challenge strategy, 104
in Tri-Fold strategy, 45, 48
in U-C-ME strategy, 130
in Vocabulary Quilt strategy, 99
syntax of native and English languages, 4

teachers
as facilitators, 8
joint productive activity of, 9
modeling by, 9. *See also* modeling
as partners, 5–7
revoicing by, 6–7, 9. *See also* revoicing
testimonials on strategies, 11
template examples, 12
for Active Bookmarks strategy, 156
for DOTS Chart strategy, 80
for Extension Wheel strategy, 140
for Hearts Activity, 148–149
for Listen Sketch Label strategy, 61
for Pictures and Words strategy, 37
for Picture This strategy, 29
for Tic-Tac-Tell strategy, 95
for Tri-Fold strategy, 52
for U-C-ME strategy, 133
for Vocabulary Quilt strategy, 103
website resource on, 12
for Word Drop strategy, 170
Thumb Challenge strategy, 104–109, 174, 175
student academic behavior checklist on, 184
Tic-Tac-Tell strategy, 88–95
student assessment rubric on, 182
Tri-Fold strategy, 45–52

U-C-ME in Pictures, 130
U-C-ME strategy, 127–133
student assessment rubric on, 185

visual cues
in image-based strategies. *See* image-based strategies
memory of, 13, 14
in Thumb Challenge strategy, 107
vocabulary development strategies, 2, 5, 11–170
Activation phase in, 7–8. *See also* Activation phase
Active Bookmarks, 150–156
Affirmation phase in, 9. *See also* Affirmation phase
artifacts in, 11
for comprehension skills, 11, 125–170. *See also* comprehension strategies
Connection phase in, 8–9. *See also* Connection phase
DOTS Chart, 72–80
Extension Wheel, 134–140
Hearts Activity, 141–149
IDEA, 118–124
image-based, 11, 13–68. *See also* image-based strategies

vocabulary development strategies
(*continued*)
  Linking Language, 15–21
  Listen Sketch Label, 53–61
  Magic Book, 110–117
  materials needed in, 11
  Mind Map, 38–44
  Mini Novela, 157–163
  Pictures and Words, 30–37
  Picture This, 22–29
  principles of, 70–71
  Story Bag, 62–68
  teacher testimonials on, 11
  Thumb Challenge, 104–109
  Tic-Tac-Tell, 88–95
  tier system of words in, 69–70
  Tri-Fold, 45–52
  U-C-ME, 127–133
  Vocabulary Foldable, 81–87
  Vocabulary Quilt, 96–103
  word-based, 11, 69–124. *See also* word-based strategies
  Word Drop, 164–170
Vocabulary Foldable strategy, 81–87

Vocabulary Quilt strategy, 96–103, 175–176
  and IDEA strategy, 123
  student academic behavior checklist on, 183

website resources
  on rubrics and checklists, 12
  on templates, 12
word-based strategies, 11, 69–124
  DOTS Chart, 72–80
  IDEA, 118–124
  Magic Book, 110–117
  principles of, 70–71
  Thumb Challenge, 104–109
  Tic-Tac-Tell, 88–95
  tier system of words in, 69–70
  Vocabulary Foldable, 81–87
  Vocabulary Quilt, 96–103
Word Drop strategy, 164–170
writing skills
  in Magic Book strategy, 110
  in Mini Novela strategy, 157–163
  in Vocabulary Foldable strategy, 81, 84, 85

young CLD students
  Active Bookmarks strategy for, 154
  DOTS Chart strategy for, 77
  Extension Wheel strategy for, 138
  Hearts Activity for, 146
  IDEA strategy for, 122
  Linking Language strategy for, 19
  Listen Sketch Label strategy for, 57–58
  Magic Book strategy for, 114
  Mind Map strategy for, 41–42
  Mini Novela strategy for, 161
  Pictures and Words strategy for, 34
  Picture This strategy for, 26
  Story Bag strategy for, 65–66
  Thumb Challenge strategy for, 107
  Tic-Tac-Tell strategy for, 92
  Tri-Fold strategy for, 48–49
  U-C-ME strategy for, 130
  Vocabulary Foldable strategy for, 85
  Vocabulary Quilt strategy for, 97, 100
  Word Drop strategy for, 167

zone of proximal development, 2, 4, 5, 9
  in Extension Wheel strategy, 134

Cited Authors

Afflerbach, P., 64
Allen, V., 164
Alvermann, D. E., 73
Anderson, N. J., 5, 126
Anderson, R. C., 125
Anderson, V., 110
August, D., 69, 70, 77, 89, 118

Bailey, K. M., 15, 34
Bean, T. W., 73
Beaty, J. J., 85, 122
Beck, I. L., 69, 70, 88
Birsh, J., 167
Blachowicz, C. L. Z., 22, 38, 69, 73, 127, 134
Blanchfield, C. L., 69
Bortnem, G., 96
Boyd-Batstone, P., 57, 138, 154, 167
Boyle, O. F., 73
Brandt, R., 73, 96
Bransford, J., 119
Bransford, J. D., 5, 96
Bredekamp, S., 15
Bromley, K., 81
Brown, C. A., 6
Burkman, A., 96, 127, 150
Buzan, T., 38, 42
Byers, H., 46
Byers, P., 46

Calderón, M., 5, 69, 70, 88
Carlo, M., 70, 118
Casbergue, R. M., 57
CCSS, 2, 55, 84, 113, 172
Center for Instructional Development and Research, 134
Center for Research on Education, Diversity & Excellence, 9
Chamot, A. U., 73, 157
Coady, M., 110
Collier, V., 2, 3
Collins, M., 89
Cooper, J. D., 73
Cooperstein, S. E., 48
Cooter, K. S., 69
Cooter, R. B., Jr., 69, 70, 125
Copple, C., 15
Council of Chief State School Officers, ix, 2, 55, 84, 113, 172
Coyne, M. B., 70
Crow, J. T., 81
Cummins, J., 3, 72, 85
Cunningham, J. W., 73
Cunningham, P. M., 73
Currie, P., 167
Curtis, A., 15, 34

Dalton, S. S., ix, 141
Darling-Hammond, L., 119

Deffes, R., 137
de Jong, E. J., vii
Dimino, J., 69
Donovan, M. S., 5, 96
Dressler, C., 70
Dubetz, N., vii
Duke, N. K., 62

Echevarría, J., 14, 110, 125
ERIC Clearinghouse on Languages and Linguistics, 4
Escamilla, K., 3
Estrada, P., 141

Feldman, K., 127
Fisher, D., 14
Fisher, P. J., 22, 38, 69, 73, 127, 134
Flavell, J., 125
Flynn, K., 14, 73, 96, 127, 150
Forman, E. A., 6
Freeman, D. E., 77
Freeman, Y. S., 77
Frey, N., 14
Friedlander, B., 151

García, E. E., 15
Gay, G., 62
Gentry, J. R., 57
Gersten, R., 69

Geva, E., 118
Gipe, J. P., 4, 5
Glaser, D. R., 150
Goldenberg, C., 72
Gonzalez, N., 157
Goudvis, A., 13, 14
Gove, M. K., 73
Graham, S., 151
Greenberg, J., 4
Greenberg, J. B., 4
Greenwood, C. R., 73
Gregory, G. H., 45, 96, 127, 150
Gunning, T. G., 30, 70

Hadaway, N., 71
Hakuta, K., 69
Harper, C. A., vii
Harris, K. R., 151
Harvey, S., 13, 14
Herrell, A. L., 164
Herrera, S., ix, 2, 3, 4, 5, 6, 13, 14, 15, 25, 30, 38, 45, 72, 73, 88, 119, 125, 127, 128, 134, 141, 150, 157, 164
Hill, J., 14, 73, 96, 127, 150
Hinchman, K. A., 73
Holmes, M. A., ix, 2
Hoyt, L., 72

Irvine, J. J., 62

Jayanthi, M., 69
Jensen, E., 30, 73, 104, 127
Jordan, M. L., 164
Juel, C., 137

Kapp, S., 70
Kavimandan, S. K., ix, 2
Kim, J., 69
Kinsella, K., 70, 127
Kocevar-Weidinger, E., 48
Konold, T. R., 137
Krashen, S., 5, 72
Kucan, L., 69
Kuzmich, L., 45

Lado, A., 62
Ladson-Billings, G., 62
Langer, J. A., 30, 70
Larreamendy-Joerns, J., 6
Lesaux, N., 137
Linan-Thompson, S., 69
Loftus, S., 70

Maria, K., 5
Marzano, R. J., 14, 69, 70, 73, 81, 104, 130, 141, 167

Mason, L. H., 151
McCoach, D. B., 70
McGee, L., 26
McKeown, M. G., 69
McKinnon, M., 137
Mercuri, S. P., 2, 126
Michaels, S., 6
Miller, S., ix
Moll, L. C., 4, 157
Moore, D. W., 73
Moore, S. A., 73
Morales Cabral, R., 3
Murry, K. G., 3, 5

Nagy, W. E., 70, 73, 81
National Governors Association Center for Best Practices, ix, 2, 55, 84, 113, 172
National Reading Panel, 69
National Research Council, 26
Neitzel, S., 92
Neuman, S., 122
Nieto, S., 15

O'Connor, M. C., 6
O'Malley, J., 73, 157
Osterman, E., 15
Oxford, R.. L., 22

Padak, N., 73
Pearson, P. D., 62, 125
Peregoy, S. F., 73
Perez, D. R., ix, 3
Phillips, D. A., 19
Pickering, D. J., 14, 81
Piper, T., 92
Pollock, J. E., 14
Pratt, L., 85, 122
Pressley, M., 64
Proctor, C. P., 118

Quigley, J. R., 81

Rasinski, T. V., 70, 73
Rea, D. M., 2, 126
Reutzel, D. R., 69, 70, 125
Richgels, D., 26
Roach, K. A., 41
Roit, M., 110
Roskos, K., 122
Routman, R., 30, 157
Rumelhart, D. E., 5, 125

Santoro, L., 69
Schickedanz, J. A., 57
Scott, J. A., 81
Shonkoff, J. P., 19

Short, D. J., 14
Siegel, L., 137
Simonsen, S., 126
Singer, H., 126
Smartt, S. M., 150
Snow, C., 41, 70, 118
Sousa, D. A., 96
Spycher, P., 118
Stahl, S. A., 22, 70, 71, 96
Steenwyk, F. L., 73
Stein, M. K., 6
Sulzby, E., 138
Sutton, C., 41
Svinicki, M., 71
Swan, K., 118
Swinney, R., 70

Tabors, P. O., 41
Teale, W. H., 138
Terrell, T., 72
Tharp, R. G., ix, 141
Thomas, W. P., 2, 3
Tompkins, G. E., 13, 14, 45, 53, 69
Tovani, C., 150

U.S. Census Bureau, 1
U.S. Department of Education, 1

Vacca, J. L., 73
Vacca, R. T., 73
Vail, P., 73
Valadez, C., 110
Vancil, S. J., 22
Vaughn, S., 69
Velasco, P., 70
Vélez-Ibáñez, C., 4
Violand-Sanchez, E., 41
Vogt, M., 14
Vygotsky, L. S., 2, 4, 5

Wadlington, E., 167
Walqui, A., 5
Ware, H., 41
Wessels, S., 70, 71, 96
Willis, J., 96, 110
Wilson-Portuondo, M., 171
Wolfe, P., 14, 73, 96
Wong Fillmore, L., 65, 110, 157
Wormeli, R., 13

Yaghoub Zadeh, Z., 118
Yamauchi, L., 141
Young, T., 71

Zipoli, R., 70
Zwiers, J., 134

About the Authors

SOCORRO G. HERRERA is a keynote speaker, district consultant, and trainer of trainers, as well as a professor in the College of Education and director of the Center for Intercultural and Multilingual Advocacy (CIMA) at Kansas State University. Her K–12 teaching experience includes an emphasis on literacy development, and her research focuses on literacy opportunities with culturally and linguistically diverse students, reading strategies, and teacher preparation for diversity in the classroom. Dr. Herrera has authored several books and numerous articles focusing on issues of instruction and assessment with culturally and linguistically diverse (CLD) students.

DELLA R. PEREZ is an assistant professor and the associate director of undergraduate programming of the Center for Intercultural and Multilingual Advocacy (CIMA) in the College of Education at Kansas State University. Her preK–6 teaching experience emphasized promoting literacy and bi-literacy. Her research focuses on literacy development, comprehension, and bilingualism for CLD students and families.

SHABINA K. KAVIMANDAN is a SIOP mentor and a literacy/ESL coach, as well as a project manager and instructor in the College of Education, Kansas State University. Her K–12 teaching experience includes a focus on literacy development, particularly vocabulary development emphasizing use of students' background knowledge, as well as an emphasis on fluency and comprehension.

STEPHANIE WESSELS is an assistant professor in the Department of Teaching, Learning, and Teacher Education at the University of Nebraska–Lincoln. Her teaching experience includes working with ESL students in the classroom as well as serving as a consultant for a state educational agency. Her research focuses on bilingual family literacy programs. She is particularly interested in vocabulary development that enhances and extends current academic practices in primary grade-level classrooms.